The Trouble with Passion

The Trouble with Passion

HOW SEARCHING FOR FULFILLMENT AT
WORK FOSTERS INEQUALITY

Erin A. Cech

UNIVERSITY OF CALIFORNIA PRESS

University of California Press
Oakland, California

Library of Congress Cataloging-in-Publication Data

Names: Cech, Erin A., 1982– author.
Title: The trouble with passion : how searching for fulfillment at work
    fosters inequality / Erin A. Cech.
Description: Oakland, California : University of California Press, [2021] |
    Includes bibliographical references and index.
Identifiers: LCCN 2021015794 (print) | LCCN 2021015795 (ebook) |
    ISBN 9780520303225 (hardback) | ISBN 9780520303232 (paperback)
    | ISBN 9780520972698 (ebook)
Subjects: LCSH: Job satisfaction. | Self-realization. | Equality.
Classification: LCC HF5549.5.J63 C38 2021 (print) | LCC HF5549.5.J63
    (ebook) | DDC 306.3/60973—dc23
LC record available at https://lccn.loc.gov/2021015794
LC ebook record available at https://lccn.loc.gov/2021015795

Manufactured in the United States of America

30 29 28 27 26 25 24 23 22 21
10 9 8 7 6 5 4 3 2 1

Contents

Illustrations

TABLES

Preface

I was halfway through a student exchange program in Edinburgh, Scotland, and four thousand miles from home when I decided that electrical engineering wasn't my passion. I had been successful during my first three years as an engineering student at Montana State University. I had good grades and a couple of internships under my belt and had finally mastered the art of soldering tiny resistors to circuit boards. Yet something about the sociology classes I was taking to fill out my schedule while in Scotland was speaking to me. I was moved by the course material. I was intrigued by social theory. Sociology gave me tools for questioning the structural and cultural power of the technical systems I was learning to design and the striking lack of racial and gender diversity in engineering that had perplexed me for years. Engineering, it seemed more every day, wasn't for me. And besides, a long string of part-time jobs in the service sector (pizza maker, dishwasher, clothing store cashier, Costco "food sample lady") convinced me that I was done working in unfulfilling jobs.

I remember preparing myself for weeks to tell my parents my plans at the end of my year abroad. I sat them down, took a deep breath, and told them that I would finish my engineering degree, but I wanted to add a sociology major. And I wasn't going to work in engineering as my career. I don't remember much of the rest of that conversation, but I do recall saying to them, "I want to follow my passion." When I applied for graduate school in sociology a couple of months later, I wrote confidently in my personal statement, "I deliberated a great deal about what shape the combination of my degrees would take, but it was my growing and indisputable passion for sociology which ultimately motivated my decision to pursue a PhD."

The irony does not escape me.

I have written a book about the problems entailed in "following your passion" not because I have always been skeptical of passion-seeking. I was a believer, even an evangelist, of the importance of finding fulfilling work. I have written a book about passion-seeking because once I saw it in my research, it became hard to unsee. I began to notice this cultural belief being deployed in the way friends talked to one another about their jobs on my morning bus ride, in how coffee shops advertised for new baristas, in how professors talked to students during office hours, and in how students talked to each other as they stood in line for lunch. Prompted by my engagement in this research, friends and colleagues began to notice it everywhere too. I have written a book about passion because it is an important factor in how many people think about "good work" and deserves our critical attention.

This book takes an unconventional approach. In it, I develop the theoretical concept of the *passion principle*—the belief that self-expression and fulfillment should be the central guiding principle in career decision-making—and examine it using several different types of data. I begin by describing the passion principle, tracking the prominence of this cultural schema among both college-going career aspirants and college-educated workers broadly, and then explain why this schema is so compelling, even as its believers recognize the precarity and uncertainty of the modern labor market. Then I explain how the passion principle, while seemingly beneficial at the individual level, can entrench socioeconomic disadvantage and occupational inequality more broadly. I end the book with a discussion of the implications of the passion principle for scholars, for higher education practitioners and administrators, for career aspirants, and for broader cultural understandings of what constitutes "good work" and "good lives."

I focus primarily on college-going and college-educated workers here because the passion principle is most vivid among and directly consequential for persons with a college degree. But as I show, it is not exclusive to them. There are many alternative empirical avenues I could have explored in this book: How does the passion principle play out among blue-collar workers? Within narratives in K–12 classrooms or vocational training? In other economic, cultural, or national contexts? Readers will inevitably have their own ideas about other social arenas wherein the passion principle might be amplified or challenged and the populations for whom the passion principle might take on greater or lesser salience. Yet this exploration of the passion principle had to start somewhere, and I chose to start with the populations for whom it is most crystalline. I hope it will spark investigation into how the passion principle plays out in many other social arenas.

This book doesn't follow the standard approach of most sociology books (if there is one), yet it is deeply sociological: I use sociology's tools for taking seriously cultural beliefs and practices as legitimate and often powerful social forces and for treating nothing as too sacred for scholarly examination. I ditch disciplinary norms of sticking to one empirical method or one data source. Instead, I walk around the cultural schema of the passion principle with the data sources and analytic procedures most appropriate for the questions I am asking. The chapters in this book are organized thematically, so I often move from interviews to survey data and back again as I make my way through the arguments. Where possible, I triangulate the empirical findings for each argument with more than one data source.

I was compelled to write this book because, as a sociologist interested in subtle cultural processes of inequality reproduction, I know that things widely touted as morally "good" often have a darker side. As a career aspirant who left a path in engineering to pursue my passion in sociology, I have questioned on many occasions what it meant to do so and why following my passion seemed so important at the time. As an educator, I have been uneasy with my instinctual impulse to tell any student showing interest in my discipline to follow their passion and figure out the "employment stuff" later. And as a wary observer of labor force changes over the past two decades, I have increasingly wondered from a sociological and philosophical perspective, what does it mean to say, *I love my work*? The book raises more questions than it answers, but I hope it provides fertile ground for scholars, educators, career aspirants, and workers to think seriously about the individual and societal implications of the cultural ideal of "following your passion."

Introduction

One sunny afternoon in June 2005, Steve Jobs, CEO of Apple Inc., addressed a jovial crowd of newly minted Stanford University graduates and their families. Sharing his thoughts on the meaning of work, Jobs offered the graduates some advice:

> Your work is going to fill a large part of your life, and the only way to be truly satisfied is to do what you believe is great work. And the only way to do great work is to love what you do. If you haven't found it yet, keep looking. Don't settle. As with all matters of the heart, you'll know it when you find it.[1]

Facing this excited and apprehensive audience of career aspirants, Jobs advocated that, above all else, they should seek work that they love. Anything less would be settling.

Jobs's philosophy so resonated with audiences that a dozen newspapers reprinted his speech.[2] But Jobs was hardly the first to make this point. The advice to "do what you love" or, more commonly, to "follow your passion" can be found on dentists' office waiting room posters, throw pillows, coffee mugs, and mobile phone covers.[3] It is shorthand for the idea that people who are making career decisions should prioritize their personal sense of fulfillment and self-expression in those decisions rather than settle for what is available or what will proffer the highest salary.

The refrain of Jobs's advice echoed through many conversations I had with new college graduates. Claire, a graduate from the University of Houston (UH) who worked part-time at a natural history museum, for example, said that loving her work was not just important for her career success; it was key to her quality of life.[4]

> I want[ed] to pursue something that I truly care about and think is very interesting and that I can learn from. I don't want to pick something just because it's a really popular field that has a lot of jobs. Because, yes, finding a job is incredibly important, but it would just hurt me to totally abandon my more social science, more anthropology, liberal studies background, just to find a computer sciences job that was really popular, or go into business school or something . . . just in order to find a job that would make more money. . . . I feel like if I had to pick a job just because it was a job, then it would just be boring to me, and I wouldn't be able to really excel at it because I just wasn't passionate about it. (Middle-class white woman)

As I show in this book, Claire is far from alone among her peers in her endorsement of passion-based career decisions over "abandoning" passion to find a job that might offer more financial security. And I find that many college-educated workers in the United States similarly endorse Jobs's "do what you love" advice.

But if we look more closely at Jobs's comment, we can begin to make out a curious tension. Jobs, who was one of the most successful capitalists of the twentieth century and one of the most demanding of his employees' time and dedication, advised new college-educated career aspirants to follow their hearts rather than seek employment security, professional notoriety, or a decent salary.[5] "Love what you do," he said. "Don't settle."

This tension is not unique to Jobs's philosophy. The tension between capitalist demands for dedicated work and the ubiquitous cultural expectation for individualism and self-fulfillment characterizes many postindustrial societies. On the one hand, modern capitalist economies expect to have workers who are willing to put the needs of their organizations and their employers first. To be an "ideal worker" is to prioritize the desires and interests of one's employer above one's own.[6] White-collar workers are further expected to enact "work devotion"—or single-minded loyalty and allegiance to one's job—even if that devotion is not genuine.[7] This ideal worker expectation prevails in twenty-first-century labor markets even as employers are increasingly less likely to reciprocate such commitments.[8]

On the other hand, cultural expectations for individualistic self-fulfillment are ubiquitous in postindustrial societies.[9] The cultural valuation of individualism and self-expression has grown dramatically since the 1950s and along with it, the expectation that individuals should have as many opportunities as possible to make autonomous choice about the direction and character of their own lives.[10] As a result, demands for self-expressive freedoms have expanded into virtually all social and life realms in places like the United States, including choices of occupations and career paths.[11]

In the midst of these and other tensions and constraints, how do workers and career aspirants actually define good work and good career decision-making? Do they seek to maximize economic stability and security in their career choices? Do they ascribe to Jobs's and Claire's philosophy? How do they balance these considerations in their own career decision-making, and what are they willing to sacrifice to meet their priorities?

Career decisions are serious life decisions. Early occupational pathways can have lasting consequences for wages, mobility, and social status over the course of one's life.[12] Like other major life choices (e.g., whether to relocate to a new city, whether to have children), career decisions are enormously complex, with few formal institutional guidelines. And, like other major life choices, shared cultural meanings about "good" or "right" decisions are important to how people get their bearings and set their priorities, even under the most constrained life circumstances.[13] These cultural meanings, I argue, shape not only how people make decisions about their own career paths but also how they come to understand the labor force overall—whether, for example, they think labor market processes are generally fair and whether they praise or criticize the career decisions of others.

To the limited extent that social scientists have considered these cultural perceptions, most scholars have presumed that people prioritize economic stability, employment security, and/or occupational status in their career decisions. Research on artists and musicians has shown that workers in the culture industry expect to manage tensions between artistic autonomy and employment precariousness as a matter of course and are often willing to sacrifice stable work and robust salaries to pursue their passion.[14] Yet this prioritization of passion is seen as the exception that makes the rule. Career aspirants, scholars often assume, are usually looking for the most well paying, most stable, and/or most prestigious occupational paths they can get given their level of training.[15]

But something is off about that assumption. Casual perusal of best-selling career advice books and popular advice columns reveals titles like *The Power of Being Yourself*[16] and *What's Next? Follow Your Passion and Find Your Dream Job*,[17] which sound more like refrains from Steve Jobs's speech than the sentiments of workers seeking to maximize their economic potential. What do career aspirants (individuals such as college students who are preparing for full-time engagement in the labor force) and workers value in career decisions? What cultural narratives do they use to make sense of career decision-making broadly and to set their priorities, and how are these cultural beliefs reflected in their actual decisions?

In this book, I argue that opportunities for self-expression and personal meaning-making are central to how many workers and aspiring workers— particularly the college-educated—define good work in the context of the contemporary postindustrial labor force. Although most career aspirants and college-educated workers recognize the importance of financial security and are clear-eyed about the challenges of employment in the modern labor force, many prioritize fulfilling work over these considerations. Many even willingly sacrifice a better salary and greater employment stability to pursue work they find fulfilling.

Using a robust, multimethod approach encompassing over 170 interviews with career aspirants and career counselors, four surveys of US workers, and an experiment, I illustrate that a powerful cultural frame of career decision-making is what I term the *passion principle*. The passion principle is a morally laden cultural schema that elevates self-expression and fulfillment—in the form of intellectual, emotional, and personal connections to an occupational field—as the central guiding principle for career decisions, especially but not exclusively among the college-educated. It urges individuals to seek work that is meaningful and to prioritize personal investment in their work. This schema frames decision-making aimed at maximizing one's economic and social status as morally questionable in contrast, in part because it would divert people from paths of self-realization.

WHAT IS PASSION, AND WHO VALUES PASSION-SEEKING?

Passion, as I use it here, refers to a deep personal commitment to an occupational field (e.g., sociology, corporate tax law) or productive task realm (e.g., infant care, computer coding).[18] Although potentially correlated, passion is distinct from individuals' satisfaction with the organizations they work for, the colleagues they work with, and the people who supervise them.[19] It is about individuals' sense of connection to, and sense of fulfillment from, their substantive career fields.

Although passions seem highly individualistic and idiosyncratic, they are fundamentally rooted in the structural positions and environments people inhabit. Our passions are part of our self-conceptions (i.e., our self-understandings), and these self-conceptions do not emerge arbitrarily: who we think we are is partly determined by our social positions and the experiences and environments to which we are exposed.[20] Through a lifetime of socialization within classed, gendered, racialized, and sexualized social institutions, our self-conceptions, and by extension, the tasks we consider interesting, exciting, and meaningful, are patterned by those ascriptive processes.[21] As such, what we are passionate about is neither random nor fully idiosyncratic.[22]

There are several interrelated dimensions to having a sense of passion for one's work: an intellectual connection (finding work interesting or intriguing), an emotional, affective connection (finding excitement, joy, or happiness), and a personal connection (finding the right fit for one's unique sense of personhood). For example, Xavier, a Stanford math major, explained his emotional and intellectual connection to math and its close alignment with his personality.

EAC (AUTHOR): So, you used this word *passionate* before. What does that mean?

XAVIER: Math is just, I love it. When you get something right, and you know it's entirely right because you kind of know the ins and outs. . . . I just get to do a bunch of puzzles, really cool puzzles. It's fun, but it's also something that I feel really challenges me mentally. . . . So, that's, I guess that's the passion. It's just something I see myself doing for the rest of my life. . . . I think that's definitely my personality. (Middle-class white and Latinx man)

Passion for one's work does not come from the notoriety or prestige that work might imbue or from nonwork activities that can be funded by one's income. Nor is passion the same thing as commitment to hard work for its own sake. To be passionate about one's career field means to have a deeply personal and authentic sense of connection to that work.

Hinting at the moral value bestowed on passion-seeking, Will, a business management graduate from Montana State University (MSU), explained why he rejected his friends' path to maximize career opportunities and chose a field he was passionate about instead.

> One of my best friends, he wasted four years on an engineering degree. He hates it. He does not want to do anything with it. Too often people tailor their interests, their hobbies, what they want to do with their lives, around some sort of career or post-grad opportunity. I didn't want to do that because I wasn't gonna spend four or five years of my money and my time educating myself on something I didn't give a damn about. . . . There was no way I was gonna just go to college and waste four years on an engineering degree. I know that [engineering] might secure me a better job, but I didn't want to do math anymore. [*Laughs*] I wanted to do something I was passionate about and I wanted to learn about. (Middle-class white man)

I asked students and college-educated workers what they thought should be the most important factor when people make career decisions. Among the one hundred students I interviewed across three universities, over three quarters explained that passion should be a central factor in career decision-making, while only 9% and 21% said income and employment security, respectively, should be top priorities. These college-going career aspirants were not alone in their valuation of passion-seeking: over 75% of US college-educated workers I surveyed rated passion-seeking as important in good career decision-making in the abstract, and over two-thirds rated the importance of passion-based considerations *more* highly than they rated the importance of salary and employment security in their conceptualizations of good career decisions.

Career aspirants and workers were more pragmatic when it came to decisions about their own careers. Yet striking numbers of college students and college-educated workers prioritized fulfilling, self-expressive work in their *own* career decisions over fields that offered greater security and/or high salaries. Many were willing to make financial sacrifices to secure meaningful work.

These career aspirants and workers found the passion principle a compelling approach to career decision-making because they believed that it promised to insulate them from the drudgery that might await them in the workforce. Isaiah, a UH graduate enrolled in a pharmacy program, explained the stakes he saw in having a job he can "really love." Unless he loves his work, he feared he will live an unhappy *life*.

> I never really liked the idea [of] a time-is-money type of diagram where it's, like, okay, the only way I'm going to make money is to go to work, and if I go to work and actually do this service for eight hours, and then come home, and then have a certain amount of time to enjoy with my family, and then I have to do the whole process all over again. I kept thinkin' about that long term. Unless I really love my job, I won't feel like I'm actually happy. (Upper-class Black man)

Although passion-seeking sometimes meant risking financial instability, career aspirants often believed it worth the sacrifice. UH student Brianna, for example, switched from accounting to journalism to follow her passion into broadcast journalism.

> [Being a reporter] is something I've always wanted to do. When I was a kid, I used to dress up in my mom's blazers and pretend to give the news. I went to school initially for accounting just because I thought, well, I could make this much money if I wanna be an accountant. . . . When I was going to school, I was like, okay, this is not what I wanna do. I can't see myself doing [accounting] for the rest of my life. I said, you know what, forget all this. I'm gonna do what I wanna do. Forget being an accountant; go for being a reporter. (Upper-class Black woman)

After graduating, Brianna earned a master's degree in broadcast journalism and got her foot in the door at a small news station in the Midwest. As I show, other career aspirants who shifted their career paths to pursue their passion weren't always so lucky.

The passion principle often appears agentic and positive to the individuals who believe in it: it promises opportunities for prolonged self-expression and fulfillment while providing relief from the potential drudgery of a life of participation in the paid labor force. And yet, as I argue below, it can also have a darker side.

FOUNDATIONS OF THE PASSION PRINCIPLE

Although this book shows that the value placed on passion-seeking is widespread, its popularity is relatively recent in the long history of industrial and postindustrial capitalist employment. From the late nineteenth century through the postwar era, stability and economic security were the most highly valued considerations in career decision-making.[23] For those who could attain white-collar jobs (typically, white middle-class men), the cultural notion of ideal work was that which offered long-term employment stability, comfortable working conditions, decent pay, and maybe even a pension.[24]

This ideal is reflected in career advice books from the mid-twentieth century.[25] For example, a 1958 book, *Personal Adjustment to Business*, written by James Gates and Harold Miller, advised career aspirants to thoughtfully balance their skills and physical and economic needs when making career decisions: "Decisions should be based on a study of as many facts and circumstances as are available to the careerist. . . . Decisions must be based on logic, avoiding emotional, biased, or entrenched thinking."[26] For Gates and Miller, financial security was the fundamental basis of good career decision-making because "security of employment fulfils a vital psychological need."[27] One need not be intrinsically interested in the work before starting a job: interest can be "cultivated for virtually any job if we use our curiosity enough to probe into the potentialities of the job."[28] Gates and Miller cautioned those who might dream too far outside the bounds of pragmatism: "Our society looks with special favor on the man who decides on a legitimate and attainable career for himself, and then plunges forward boldly and strongly into the required preparation."[29] Although work that was "engrossing as well as profitable" would be a bonus, Gates and Miller underscored that it was far better to have a dull job than no job at all.[30]

This perspective stands in stark contrast to the decision-making advice that has come to dominate career advice books in more recent decades.

For example, Auren Uris's 1974 *Thank God It's Monday* noted, "The perfect job is one that makes it possible for you to wake up after a great weekend and nevertheless say happily, 'Thank God it's Monday.'"[31] He contrasts his ideal of a "self-actualizing man" to one he called the "Horatio Alger Man (1860–1945)," who achieved material success for himself alone, and the "Organization Man (1945–1965)," who was caught up in the rat race and loyal to their company above all else. Uris spelled out his credo for the self-actualizing person:

> I intend to find fulfillment in my work.
>
> I will not sell my soul for a mess of pesos; no amount of money can offset frustration, stagnation, or boredom.
>
> I will not remain in a job from which I get insufficient pleasure and job satisfaction.
>
> I will not sacrifice personal values or convenience to job demands.[32]

Uris's recommendation to leave a job one does not find fulfilling is in sharp contrast to Gates and Miller's advice twenty years earlier.

By the 2010s, the emphasis on self-fulfillment and self-actualization was standard fare in career advice books.[33] For example, in his 2013 book, *What You're Really Meant to Do,* Robert Steven Kaplan proposed that "the key to achieving your aspirations lies not in 'being a success' but rather in working to reach your unique potential."[34] He argued that one must begin by considering one's passion independently of practical considerations like salary or security. Only later is it appropriate to worry about pragmatic concerns.

> Getting in touch with your passions may require you to give your fears and insecurities a rest and focus more on your hopes and dreams. You don't need to immediately decide what action to take or assess whether your dream is realistic. . . . Again, allow yourself to focus on the *what* before you worry about the *how.*[35] . . . If you're true to your convictions and principles, I know you're far more likely to *feel* like a big success. In the end, that feeling will make all the difference.[36]

It generally goes unacknowledged in Kaplan's book, and others like it, that the people who can even entertain the idea of taking such risks typically already enjoy the greatest economic, racial, and gender privileges.[37]

What might have fostered such a growth in the emphasis on self-expression and fulfillment in career decision-making? Although a full examination of the historical emergence of the passion principle is outside the scope of this book, as I discuss in Chapter 2 and review below, there are key economic and cultural processes that collided in the 1970s through the 1990s that provided fertile ground for the expansion of the passion principle as a career decision-making guide.

The first change was a major shift in the structure of work in the United States. The institution of work has become more precarious in the past four decades, with owners shirking more of the risks of business ownership and profit-making to workers. In decades past, the "capital-labor accord," or the mutual commitment and loyalty built between organizations and their long-term (white-collar) workers, was the norm: workers were expected to commit to the organization they worked for and, in turn, the organization would commit to retain and even advance those workers if they proved skilled and reliable.[38]

Today, such voluntary dedication to workers among organizations is a rarity, as is workers' decades-long dedication to a single company.[39] Aggressive deregulation, sweeping technological change, globalization, and shifts in corporate governance have reduced worker power and eroded the loyalty that organizations once showed to workers who were loyal to them.[40] As a result, twenty-first-century work is marked by "equality of uncertainty."[41] For workers without a college degree or access to decent-paying trade jobs, work stability was never taken for granted. Now, even the most privileged, well-educated white-collar professionals face the possibility of job instability and financial insecurity.[42] And recognition of this instability is widespread: workers take for granted what Allison Pugh calls a "one-way honor system," in which employees expect—and are expected to—enact moral obligations to work hard for their employer. Little beyond a paycheck is expected from employers in return.[43]

Along with the rise in worker precarity over the past four decades, powerful cultural shifts have taken place. The political sphere saw the rise of *neoliberalism*, a political and economic ideology that advocates for radical free market capitalism under the presumption that economic and social well-being is best achieved by scaling back governmental regulations and resisting redistributive processes that might restrict the free market.[44] Neoliberalism promotes the idea that individuals are solely responsible for their own economic and social success or failure and that government assistance and social welfare programs are demotivating and unnecessary.[45] Neoliberal beliefs about personal responsibility for one's livelihood and career outcomes bled out of the political realm in the 1980s and 1990s and into nearly every US institution.

This surge in neoliberal policies and perspectives ran alongside a sharp uptick in cultural expectations for individualism and self-expression in the United States and other postindustrial nations. Individualism has long been a core American value, but after World War II, and especially in the 1980s and 1990s, demands for self-expressive choice-making expanded into virtually every realm of life.[46] This is reflected, and likely amplified, by the massification and curricular expansion of higher education over the past half century.[47] Not only should our shoes and cars and dishware express our sense of individuality, so too should our choice of religion, neighborhood, college major, and occupation. Self-expression is now a *moral* expectation of oneself and others: it shapes people's expectations of others' behaviors and serves as a "feeling rule" that directs what people want to feel about themselves and their circumstances.[48]

Social theorists have argued that these and other late twentieth-century structural and cultural changes introduced a deep sense of existential uncertainty to many people's lives—uncertainty about who we should be, how we should live our lives, and where we are to find meaning. In contrast to finding meaning in one's community as in centuries past, postindustrial citizens tend to find meaning in a "reflexive project of the self"— an ever-evolving personal narrative about who we are as individuals and where we are headed that we continuously work on and reflect on over the course of our lives.[49] For many, but especially the most sociodemographically advantaged, this self-reflexive project becomes a central goal of lives lived within postindustrial societies.

So we have the cultural valuation of individualized, self-expressive action on the one hand and an increasingly uncertain labor market that nonetheless demands an unwavering work ethic on the other. How do modern career aspirants and workers orient their decisions when individualism reigns, work is increasingly precarious, and professional workers are expected to work longer hours than ever? As I argue, the historical, economic, and cultural context of the past several decades means that the passion principle is an especially alluring approach to career decision-making for those privileged enough to consider it.

THE CUTTING EDGE OF THE PASSION PRINCIPLE

In this book, I explain what the passion principle is, who believes in it, what it means for individual career aspirants and workers to follow it, and what sort of work it does for existential meaning-making about good lives. But the consequences of the passion principle reach far beyond its implications for individual career decision-makers. I argue that this cultural schema has a more nefarious side. While the passion principle may seem beneficial to individual workers by encouraging them to search for fulfilling corners of the labor force, it may, in the aggregate, actually help reproduce processes of socioeconomic inequality and occupational segregation. Not everyone has the financial, educational, or social resources to parlay their passion into gainful employment. I find that socioeconomically privileged passion-seekers are more likely to end up in stable, well-paid work related to their passion, while college-educated passion-seekers from lower-class families are more likely to end up in precarious employment far afield of their passion. In addition, the passion principle helps frame patterns of occupational segregation and inequality as the benign result of individual passion-seeking while scaffolding beliefs (like the meritocratic ideology and the personal responsibility trope) that dismiss occupational inequality and resist structural solutions that could help address that inequality.[50] Finally, the demand-side manifestation of the passion principle means that it feeds into the culture of overwork, encouraging passionate professionals to tolerate contingent or underpaid employment and allowing employers to exploit workers' passion in the name of their bottom line. Broadly, this book seeks not only to examine the passion principle as a schema informing individual career decision-making, but also how the passion principle contributes to structural and cultural processes of social inequality.

THE CULTURAL SCHEMA OF THE PASSION PRINCIPLE

This is a book about a cultural schema. Cultural schemas are shared cultural frameworks for "viewing, filtering, and evaluating what we know as reality."[51] We learn schemas through lifelong experiences of socialization and come to understand ourselves, our experiences, and broader social and institutional processes through them.[52] Schemas are not only *cognitive* frameworks for understanding reality; they also have *moral* and *emotional* dimensions. Schemas, in short, help us make sense of a complex social world and orient our actions within it.[53]

The first half of this book establishes the passion principle as a cultural schema and illustrates its ubiquity among career aspirants and workers. The second half examines how prioritizing passion-seeking affects individual career aspirants and interfaces with aggregate structural and cultural processes. How might the passion principle—when utilized as a guiding principle by individual career aspirants and as a broader cultural prescription for how workers ought to make decisions—help perpetuate processes of sociodemographic inequality? While cultural valuation of passion-seeking seems to be ubiquitous, this concept has not yet been systematically examined in social science scholarship as a site of social reproduction.

Some scholars suggest that schemas are too flimsy, too weak, to do any real work in the social world. After all, they are only beliefs. Traditional structuralist approaches in social science tend to downplay cultural beliefs and practices as inconsequential, particularly in comparison to laws, institutions, and concrete resources.[54] Individuals may value passion-seeking, but they are ultimately at the mercy of the structural forces in which they are embedded. Some cultural scholars argue further that cultural beliefs are too fleeting in individuals' minds to make much of a difference in their lives, and, besides, people hold contradictory meanings about the same things.[55] So why write a book about a cultural schema?

Individual agency is indeed constrained; one cannot study career decision-making without acknowledging the tremendous structural constraints people face as they move through school and the labor force.[56] And individuals indeed hold and deploy contradictory meanings about the labor market and their place within it. Yet cultural schemas about good careers and good career decision-making likely wield power nonetheless.[57]

In instances where action is less habitual, such as lengthy and highly deliberative career decisions, cultural meanings are likely to impact behavior by shaping the strategies of action people believe are available and desirable.[58] Decision-makers often act as though their narrative accounts of the world are true; cultural meanings can help shape behaviors as people seek to enact their visions of their future selves and future lives.[59]

Within well-documented structural and cultural constraints, I argue, cultural schemas of good careers and good career decision-making are consequential for the lives of individual career aspirants and workers. They influence what opportunities career decision-makers pursue or may foreclose for themselves, the risks they are willing to entertain, the economic and cultural resources they require for advancement, and the benchmarks against which they judge their success or failure. Beyond these individual-level outcomes, dominant schemas of career decision-making can entrench aggregate processes of socioeconomic inequality. These schemas may presume economic, cultural, and social capital that is unevenly distributed, such that career decisions made on the basis of these schemas perpetuate the advantages of some career aspirants and the disadvantages of others. Moralized beliefs about good career decision-making may also lend cultural legitimacy to patterns of labor market inequality, influencing what career aspirants and workers expect of their peers, their employers, and the labor force broadly.

Although I focus here on the United States, the passion principle may be salient in other places (especially Anglophone and western European countries) that similarly venerate individualistic self-expression, that have seen an expansion of higher education, and where neoliberal ideals of labor force participation hold sway.[60] In these contexts, the passion principle may find a sturdy foothold among college-educated young adults and help shape broader cultural narratives about career decision-making.

PASSION AMONG THE COLLEGE-GOING AND COLLEGE-EDUCATED

The passion principle may be present—with varying levels of salience—at many life stages. It is perhaps at its most crystalline among young adults finishing their formal education and moving into the workforce, but these cultural considerations of good jobs and good career decision-making may stretch across the life course. Notions of passion-seeking likely arise in primary and secondary school classroom discussions about occupations and in high school counselors' advice about what paths are available and desirable after high school. It is likely parroted in students' admissions essays and mulled over throughout college. Once people are in the workforce, the passion principle may become especially salient again when changing jobs or industries (whether of their own volition or not). It is probably most evident among white-collar workers but may exist in some sectors of blue-collar work (e.g., "cultural tastemaker" bartenders, baristas, and barbers) as well.[61] It is also present in narratives of "encore careers," or the ideal of finding fulfilling work after retirement.[62]

Because "following your passion" is a culturally valued *life* goal as well as a career goal, it is likely central to individuals' self-reflexive projects long before and long after career launch. The salience and consequences of the passion principle may be built into our assumptions about what we are asking when we inquire what a child wants to be when they grow up and is even evident in notions of the "post-retirement career," when individuals can "finally" do what they have always wanted to do.[63]

Out of the need to bound my inquiry, this book focuses most intently on the passion principle during an important part of a normative life course for US college-educated young adults: finishing college and entering the labor market. I also attend to broader patterns and implications across the college-educated workforce. As I argue in the conclusion, one of the reasons that the passion principle is such a resonant cultural schema is because it dovetails so nicely with normative ideals of individualistic, self-reflexive projects. Therefore, I could have easily looked at high school students' beliefs about decision-making or the meaning-making and identity work of people preparing for retirement. All, I suspect, would have provided insights into the passion principle.

Importantly, though, only a minority of young adults have the privilege to pursue a college education. At present, only about a third of the US workforce has a college degree. College tuition and fees have spiked over the past thirty years, and student loan debt has ballooned to keep pace.[64] The passion principle is not exclusive to the college-educated. As I show, seeking fulfilling work that aligns with one's sense of self is highly valued across the labor force. Yet the current structural realities of the US labor market and the increasing instability of blue-collar and service sector jobs mean that fewer non-college-educated workers have structural positions that would allow them to prioritize self-expression and fulfillment over stability and salary.[65]

College-going career aspirants are better positioned than most to bring the nuances of the passion principle's role in career decision-making to light. They have arguably the most cultural resources, structural opportunities, and time to conceptualize good work in diverse ways, as well as the greatest flexibility to make career decisions based on those conceptualizations. This freedom and flexibility is buttressed by higher education's institutionalized expectations that students' career deliberations will unfold gradually over months or years.[66] Although blue-collar and service sector workers may share similar schemas of career decision-making, they typically have less freedom to align their cultural priorities with their employment decisions.[67] In addition, college students are grappling with their career decisions long before they jump into postgraduate jobs or workplaces. This helps isolate their assessment of career decision-making schemas from their assessments of specific jobs or employers.

While my analysis is mostly restricted to the college educated, the consequences of the cultural schema I discuss are not limited to them. As I argue, the passion principle, when used toward prescriptive and explanatory ends, may downplay the structural challenges blue-collar and service sector workers face and cast occupational inequalities as the result of individual failings within an otherwise fair labor market. Further, the prominence of the passion principle among college-educated workers—many of whom supervise blue-collar and service sector workers—may mean that expectations for expressing passion for one's job may be imposed on wait staff, security guards, janitors, and bus drivers, as well as one's white-collar coworkers. The passion principle is a normative and even *moral* imperative, in that it weighs on other workers as a standard they know they are not able to live up to.[68] I leave it to other scholars to explore the manifestations of the passion principle among workers in these other sectors, but I suspect it has some salience there too.

Casting a critical eye on the passion principle, especially among those privileged enough to have followed their passion and found fulfilling work (or have enthusiastically encouraged others to do so), may be unsettling. It can feel so *right* to nudge a young person to "go for it" and pursue their passion. Storytelling tropes of mavericks who risk it all to follow their passions are popular if not clichéd. What could be so bad about prioritizing meaning in one's work? Interrogating a cultural schema that is widely valued (particularly in academia) is bound to challenge perspectives that some readers may take for granted. My goal is not provocation for its own sake. Rather, I am interested in pulling back the curtain from a beloved cultural schema to reveal what it means, how it might work only to the advantage of some, and how it may mask and help reproduce the disadvantages of others.

DATA SOURCES

My exploration of the passion principle draws on a number of sources. The data for this study came together gradually, and each data collection effort inspired the next. As a methodological pragmatist, my overarching empirical goal was to gather as much useful information as possible for understanding specific dimensions and consequences of the passion principle within the scope of the book.

Interviews with Career Aspirants

The initial spark for this project came from interviews I conducted with Stanford undergraduate students. I was piloting a project on career decision-making and was immediately struck by the centrality of self-expression and fulfillment in students' discussions of good decision-making in the abstract and their more specific discussions of their own career choices. From these pilot interviews, I designed a three-site interview study with a diverse sample of one hundred college students enrolled at three comprehensive, four-year institutions: Stanford University, Montana State University, and the University of Houston. These institutions usefully vary by region, competitiveness, and demographic composition. The student interview sample was composed of 35 respondents from Stanford, 30 from UH, and 35 from MSU. The sample overrepresented students of color (14% Latinx, 25% Black, 14% Asian or Asian American, 11% another race/ethnicity, 53% white); 52% identify as women, and 48% identify as men. Half of the students majored in a science, technology, engineering, and math (STEM) field. Nineteen percent of students were from working-class backgrounds, 50% were from middle-class backgrounds, and 31% were from upper-class backgrounds.[69] To get a better handle on the passion principle among college students across a wider array of four-year institutions, I conducted a supplemental survey of 522 students through the MTurk task platform. These survey results are summarized in Chapters 1 and 2 and reported in Appendix B.

As my analysis unfolded, it became clear that I needed to track what happened to these career aspirants after they left college. Did they ultimately follow their passion? What happened when they tried? I followed up with 35 of the original student interviewees two to five years after they left college, seeking to understand the rest of their experiences in college, their transitions after college, and their early labor market experiences.

I conducted four additional empirical investigations: interviews with career counselors and coaches, a survey of US college-educated workers, an experimental survey, and secondary analysis of existing nationally representative surveys. More detailed information about sampling and analysis for each data source can be found in Appendix A.

Interviews with Career Counselors and Coaches

Career counselors and coaches are part of a category of professionals that claims jurisdiction over career advising.[70] Their advice, and the cultural frames they mobilize when giving it, may deeply impact their clients' decision-making. To understand how career-advising professionals' perspectives and approaches might amplify or provide alternatives to the passion principle, I draw on interviews with 24 career advisers across a variety of contexts: 7 career counselors serving students at Stanford, MSU, and UH; 7 working for other academic institutions (University of Michigan, Rice University, and Houston Community College); and 10 private career coaches who work with students and employed clients outside of formal university contexts.

Survey Data of US Workers

While the students I interviewed typically espoused the benefits of passion-based career decisions, and the career-advising professionals were often singing from the same song sheet, it is an open question whether the passion principle is salient among college-educated workers generally. Therefore, I conducted a survey of a proportionally representative sample of US college-educated workers. I fielded the Passion Principle Survey (PPS) to a sample of 1,750 respondents (including 665 hiring managers) via the survey platform Qualtrics. The sample is proportionally representative of the US college-educated workforce by gender, race/ethnicity, age cohort, and a 14-category occupation measure. The PPS included tailor-made questions about workers' attitudes about career decision-making and the labor force, which allowed me to conduct statistical analyses that triangulate the patterns identified in the interview data. With these survey data, I was able to understand not only the prevalence of the passion principle among US college-educated workers but also the extent to which it varies across demographic groups.

I fielded the PPS in October 2020, during a period of economic and political uncertainty in the context of the coronavirus (COVID-19) pandemic. At the time of the survey, the economy had partly recovered from its freefall earlier that year, yet millions of Americans still felt economic strain.[71] I had previously fielded the PPS in 2018, during much different economic and social circumstances. My decision to redeploy the PPS during a time of economic uncertainty was purposeful: if the passion principle was salient among college-educated workers even in such a time of uncertainty, I suspect it will continue to be salient during more "settled" times. Figure A.1 in Appendix A compares 2020 and 2018 versions of the survey on focal measures I use throughout the book. The salience of the passion principle changed little since 2018. The consistency of results across these two time periods underscores the stickiness of this cultural schema.

One drawback of the PPS is that, because of its sampling strategy, it is not fully representative of college-educated workers in the United States. In order to explore the prevalence of passion-related factors among and outside college-educated populations, I analyzed data from several existing nationally representative surveys: the 2008 National Survey of the Changing Workforce (NSCW), the 2016 Merit Principles Survey (MPS), and the 1989–2006 waves of the General Social Survey (GSS). Detailed information about these surveys can be found in Appendix A.

Survey Experiment

Finally, I drew on data from a 2018 survey experiment that explores the possible demand side of the passion principle. Respondents in the Passion Principle Experiment (PPE) were randomly assigned to review one of four fictitious job applications to either an accounting job at an IT firm or a youth program manager job at a community nonprofit (a 4x2 design). The applicants' cover letters varied slightly, with one cover letter expressing passion for the work and the other three expressing interest in the city, the organization, or the salary. This design allowed me to test whether passionate applicants are preferred over applicants motivated by other factors and whether evaluators' preferences are related to their assessment of the applicants' willingness to work especially hard.

This combination of data allowed me to interrogate the passion principle from multiple points of view: students in the process of making important career-relevant decisions, career counselors and coaches who advise young people during that process, college-educated workers already in the workforce, and potential employers. The interview data helped paint a detailed portrait of this cultural narrative and how people explain passion-seeking and utilize the passion principle in their own decision-making. The survey data allowed for systematic examination of the prevalence of the passion principle across sociodemographic variation and among working populations. And the experimental data allowed for controlled examination of a particular set of arguments about the demand side of the passion principle.

SUMMARY OF CHAPTERS

Chapter 1 describes the concept of the passion principle in detail and explores its salience among college students and US college-educated workers. Drawing on interviews with students and surveys of US college-educated workers, I investigate the cultural schemas respondents use to understand good career decision-making. I find that most students (like Claire, Xavier, and Brianna), and the majority of college-educated workers, prioritized passion-based considerations in their abstract sense of good careers and good career decisions. They recognized that salary and job security are important considerations, but most believed those factors should not be prioritized at the expense of interesting, fulfilling, and meaningful work.

Adherence to the passion principle also was generally high across demographic groups. Over 70% of students from each gender, racial/ethnic, and class category believed passion should be a central factor in career decision-making. In the quantitative PPS data, I find that college-educated workers from wealthier backgrounds were more likely to emphasize passion-seeking than those from working-class backgrounds. Asian and Black workers were also slightly less likely than white respondents to see passion as important in career decisions.[72] However, there are no systematic differences in the valuation of passion-seeking by class background, highest degree, or whether respondents were born in the United States. Among these college-educated workers, there is also little variation in adherence to the passion principle across occupational category. Only a minority of college-educated workers (22%) rated more practical considerations like money and employment security as more important than passion-related factors in their conceptualizations of good career decision-making in the abstract. Overall, while the passion principle is one of many schemas that are culturally available to respondents, it was highly salient in their cultural conceptions of good career decisions.

These results captured respondents' abstract cultural schemas about good career decisions. What about when it comes to how they prioritize considerations in their *own* career paths? Contrary to the expectations of some social science literatures, the passion principle is at the heart of many students' decisions. Passion-related factors were central to the majority of students' choices of college major and their postcollege planning. While around a third of students prioritized well-paying and/or stable work over passion when choosing their major and planning their path after graduation, the remaining two-thirds elevated finding meaningful, fulfilling work to their top priority, often above maximizing salary or job security. Many students believed a college degree would provide an economic *floor* above which they would be able to have access to a salary they could live comfortably on regardless of the major they chose or the career field they pursued and below which they would be unlikely to fall. And, as a later chapter shows, many of these career aspirants continued to prioritize passion-seeking after college as they sought out a place in the labor force.

Seeking fulfillment and meaning was also important to how college-educated workers thought about their own career paths. Nearly half of the PPS respondents (46%) ranked passion-related factors as their top priority when considering whether they would take a new job (compared to 21% and 13% who ranked salary and job security, respectively, as their top priority). And among college-educated workers who had voluntarily switched career paths at some point in their lives, nearly half reported doing so for reasons related to seeking greater meaning or fulfillment in their work.

Further, my analysis of NSCW data, which represents the entire US workforce, revealed that those without a college degree were just as likely as those with a college degree to value passion-related considerations (in this case, "meaningful work") in whether they would take a new job. However, workers without a college degree (who are often blocked from the most well paying and secure jobs in the labor market) typically rated salary and employment security of higher importance than passion-related concerns in their considerations of whether they would take a new job.

Chapter 1, in short, details the prominence of the passion principle among an interview sample of college-goers and national survey samples of workers. But where does this schema come from, and why do its adherents find it so compelling? Chapter 2 provides historical context for the passion principle, particularly in the tensions between employer demands in a postindustrial economy and the ubiquitous cultural expectations for individualism and self-expression.[73] It then documents the reasons adherents are so enticed by the passion principle.

Drawing on the interview data with college students and the PPS survey data, I describe two reasons respondents found this schema so persuasive. First, most adherents saw passion as an important driver of occupational success. Unlike money and job security, passion was presumed to provide intrinsic motivation for investing the long hours and hard work required for success in the white-collar labor force. Respondents contrasted the motivation provided by passion with the inadequacy of money to furnish the same drive. For example, a UH student majoring in biology and English said:

> If you don't have any other incentive except for a monetary one, [then] . . . it doesn't give you the passion or the motivation that you really need to succeed at something. You have to really feel it, you have to really want it, and just wanting money . . . can't drive you enough to get you to do your best, to be the best. (Upper-class West Asian woman)

Even more, career aspirants maintained that passion-seeking leads not only to better work, but to a *better life*. They expressed existential anxiety about the labor market and believed that having work they were passionate about was a way to inoculate themselves against the drudgery people risk encountering when they participate in the labor force. For example, a chemical engineering student at MSU explained the health problems she believed might emerge if one "dreaded" one's work.

> If you dread something, then that's a sign that you shouldn't be doing it for twenty-five years, 'cause you're probably gonna give yourself a heart attack, so health, I guess. I mean, yeah. I'd say just go for it [follow your passion] if you're dreading something. Change your life. Do it right then instead of ten years later. (Working-class white woman)

This reasoning was not limited to career aspirants: the PPS data suggest that college-educated workers attributed similar benefits to following one's passion.

As a guiding principle, passion-seeking was seen as allowing career aspirants and workers to comport with ideal worker expectations while reducing the risk of self-estrangement that they believed is endemic in the labor force. Thus for individual career aspirants, the passion principle seems to offer a resolution to the tensions between the ideal worker demands of the capitalist labor force and the cultural expectations for self-expression.

For the small group of respondents who were critical of passion-seeking, they critiqued the potential sacrifice of money, employment security, and family time that people might endure if they put their passion first. There were only whispers of critiques of the intense individualism that the passion principle promotes. Even the most ardent critics of the passion principle left unquestioned the premise that paid work should be a core part of one's self-reflexive project.

Chapter 2 also attends to several institutional and structural factors that might amplify or challenge the passion principle. Although a number of factors likely affect the extent to which career aspirants adopt the underlying assumptions of the passion principle, the interviews revealed three contextual factors that were particularly important to the salience of the passion principle in students' decision-making: pressure from family, interactions with peers, and the guidance of career counselors and coaches.

Wealthy and working-class students were more likely than their middle-class peers to report that their parents encouraged them to prioritize stability in their career seeking. Wealthy students' parents pressured them to follow paths that would maintain their standard of living, and many working-class and first-generation students felt pressure from their families to pursue careers that would be stable, well paid, or prestigious. It is worth noting, however, that many students rejected these family pressures on principle, arguing that it was their life to live. In contrast to these family pressures, students' classmates roundly encouraged their passion-based deliberations.

While only a minority of college students sought advice from career counselors and coaches, the career-advising professionals I interviewed more often reiterated the passion principle than offered viable alternatives to it. Some even questioned clients who prioritized salary and employability, encouraging them to ask themselves how much money they "really need to live." On balance, among career aspirants' peers and within their institutions, the passion principle was more likely to be amplified than challenged by their social milieu.

These first two empirical chapters articulate the passion principle as a cultural schema and explain what cultural and institutional factors draw college-educated career aspirants and workers to it as a career decision-making priority. In the second part of the book, I explore the darker side of the passion principle—the ways the pursuit of passion and the cultural valuation of the passion principle may help perpetuate processes of socio-demographic inequality.

Chapter 3 catches up with 35 of the original students I interviewed to understand what role passion-seeking played in their career paths after college and whether such passion-seeking disproportionately disadvantaged some graduates. Consistent with the results from previous chapters, I found that passion-seeking organized many respondents' career decision-making after leaving college: over 75% prioritized passion-based considerations on par with or above job security and/or salary considerations in searching out early jobs or advanced degree programs, and 60% reported that they were in jobs or degree programs that aligned with their passion. For example, Katelyn, an upper-class MSU graduate, followed her passion into high school teaching; Devon, a middle-class marketing graduate from MSU, followed his into the air force; and Lupita, a working-class sociology graduate from UH, followed hers into a part-time social work job.

This passion-seeking often entailed sacrifices of time, money, and stability. Some spent months or even years searching for employment that matched their passion; some took underpaid, temporary, or contract positions trying to gain access to their desired path; and some left or turned down higher-paying options in favor of work they found more fulfilling.

I found important class differences in who was able to successfully launch into career paths that were both meaningful and economically secure. Respondents from more socioeconomically privileged families tended to have stronger financial *safety nets* that allowed them to navigate the employment precarity that passion-seeking often entailed. They were also more likely to have access to *springboards*—cultural, educational, and social capital—that helped them connect with stable work in their passion. The ability of these college graduates to gain entry to secure jobs or promising advanced degree programs in line with their passion was neither randomly nor equitably distributed.

These results also reveal another connection between passion-seeking and socioeconomic privilege. Not only were first-generation and working-class students less likely on average to secure gainful employment in their passion, passion-seeking was also more likely to lead these respondents into unstable employment, even as many juggled tens of thousands of dollars in student loan debt. Seeking paths in their passion after college was particularly risky for working-class and first-generation college graduates, especially when following their passion involved a shift in their career trajectories. For example, Kiara, a Stanford graduate from a working-class family, left a pre-med fellowship program to follow her passion into online video creation. Despite having completed a coveted six-month internship with a large online media company, Kiara could only manage to secure occasional contract work with the company. In contrast, Jasmine, a Stanford classmate from an upper-middle-class family, was similarly unsure about her passion after graduation but was able to take three years to travel, volunteer, and work odd jobs (supported financially by her parents) while she figured it out. With guidance from her family, Jasmine eventually applied to and enrolled in a prestigious master's program in public health.

More privileged graduates who tried to follow their passion but fell short of securing work in their passion often still ended up in fairly well paid, stable positions. Working-class passion-seekers who struggled to find work in their passion, by contrast, more frequently ended up underemployed or precariously employed in work far outside their passion.

These trends are echoed in the nationally representative NSCW data on US workers: college-educated workers from upper-class backgrounds are more likely than their college-educated peers from working-class backgrounds to be employed in stable work that strongly aligned with their passion. In contrast, college-educated workers from working-class backgrounds were twice as likely as those from upper-class backgrounds to be working in precarious jobs outside their passion.

Although safety nets and springboards were valuable for career aspirants regardless of what they prioritized in their employment searches, these resources were especially consequential for passion-seekers. Compared to those who prioritized financial security or job stability and who were willing to grab economically viable employment opportunities even if they weren't particularly fulfilling, those committed to passion-seeking often endured months or even years of unemployment or temporary work before finding secure work that aligned with their interests. As working-class respondents had less access to the springboards and safety nets that could help them through this rough patch, passion-seeking was especially risky for them.

Chapter 3 thus illustrates that not everyone benefits in the same way from the pursuit of their passion, in part because not everyone has the same safety nets and springboards to secure work that is both fulfilling and stable. Although this chapter focuses mainly on socioeconomic differentiation, it also has implications for racial/ethnic and gender inequality. Because women-dominated fields tend to be less well paid and less stable than fields traditionally dominated by men, passion-seeking may incur even greater financial risks for women than men.[74] Further, because students of color are more likely than their white counterparts to be from disadvantaged socioeconomic backgrounds, these patterns may aggravate racial/ethnic disparities in postcollege career outcomes.[75]

These patterns raise important questions about the potential devaluation within higher education of career aspirants who prioritize monetary and job security concerns. Not only does such devaluation potentially hamper the mobility prospects of many low-income and first-generation students; it undermines the moral legitimacy of the mobility goals of higher education, which is heralded as one of the most powerful social equalizers in the United States. Beyond that, this chapter suggests that higher education's promotion of passion-seeking, without adequate financial support or affordable tuition for students from working-class backgrounds, actually helps perpetuate class inequalities among students and graduates.

Chapter 4 pivots from considering the passion principle as something that guides the career decisions of individuals to thinking about the passion principle as a broader sense-making narrative. Here I explore ways that the passion principle may scaffold justificatory narratives that explain away wider patterns of occupational inequality as the benign result of individual choices.

Specifically, I ask, might the passion principle, beyond being a guide for individuals' own decision-making, serve as a *prescription* for how people believe the workforce should operate (i.e., individuals should follow their passion regardless of the sacrifices it might entail) and as an *explanation* of why occupational segregation and inequality exist in the first place? Drawing on the PPS data and the follow-up interviews with career aspirants, I explore how the passion principle is entwined with broader beliefs about the labor market—specifically, the meritocratic ideology and neoliberalism's personal responsibility trope—that deny the existence of structural disadvantages and instead blame individuals for their labor market shortfalls.[76] I find that those who are strongly committed to the passion principle are more likely to believe that the labor market operates fairly and tend to see one's position in society as one's personal responsibility alone. Adherents of the passion principle are also more likely to believe that structural gender, racial/ethnic, and class obstacles in the workforce can be overcome if one simply puts in enough passion-oriented effort.

From these empirical patterns, I argue that the passion principle may help *choicewash* societal patterns of occupational inequality, that is, explain them as simply the benign outcome of individual choices within an equitably functioning and opportunity-rich social context. By portraying occupational decision-making as the result of idiosyncratic passion-seeking rather than as structurally and culturally derived, and by individualizing success and failure as the outcome of personal hard work alone, the passion principle may help choicewash these enduring patterns of occupational inequality as the legitimate, fair outcomes of passion-seeking. These patterns, I argue, have important consequences for public discourse about the need for, and the legitimacy of, policies and programs aimed at mitigating occupational inequalities.

In the final empirical chapter, Chapter 5, I ask whether there might be a *demand side* to the passion principle. Many interview respondents across socioeconomic backgrounds expressed willingness to sacrifice pay or stability for work they found meaningful. Several student interviewees, for example, articulated expectations and even willingness to work long hours, "eat ramen noodles" for dinner, and be "a really poor twenty-something" if it meant that they could do work they were passionate about. Further, in survey data, I found that college-educated employees who are passionate about their work are more likely to report that they give more to their employing organizations than their jobs require and are less likely to want to leave those jobs.

This raises a question: Might employers benefit from, prefer, and even exploit the passion of employees? I conducted a survey experiment to explore this possibility. Respondents were randomly assigned to review one of four applications to one of two fictitious jobs, an accounting position in an IT firm and a youth program manager position in a nonprofit organization. The applications for each position were the same except for a single line in the cover letter explaining why they were interested in the job. In one version, the applicant expressed passion for the work. In the other three versions, the applicant expressed interest in the organization, interest in the city where the job is located, or interest in the salary range of the position. And indeed, respondents were more likely to believe that the passionate applicant would work harder and take on extra responsibilities than those who rated applicants motivated by salary or commitment to the organization. And yet the raters—including those who had hiring authority in their own workplaces—did not offer passionate applicants higher salaries. This finding was mirrored in two very different kinds of jobs: the youth program manager job (where we might expect passion to be a factor in hiring) and the accounting job (where passion might seem less central to the decisions of hiring managers).

These patterns are echoed in representative NSCW data on US workers as well. Holding demographics and job characteristics constant, employees who are passionate about their work do *not* enjoy higher salaries than their less passionate peers, even though passionate employees are significantly more engaged and are more likely to report that they put more effort into their work than what is required of their job.

In sum, the passion principle may have a demand-side edge: employers prefer passionate workers over workers who show commitment to the organization or interest in the job's compensation. This preference derives in part from potential employers' expectation that passionate workers will work harder for the same salary. I explain how this points to the passion principle's role as a mechanism of workforce exploitation in its own right.

The conclusion discusses the implications of the findings in previous chapters for social science theories about work and labor markets; for the actions of college educators, administrators, and policy makers; and for career decision-makers themselves.

This book offers several sociological insights. It advances understanding of a central but understudied factor in career processes: a dominant cultural schema about career decision-making that is located at the nexus of capitalism's demand for obedient workers and ubiquitous cultural expectations for self-expression. It argues that the passion principle allows individual workers to resolve this tension—while binding workers more closely to capitalist modes of production. In addition, to the extent that it is a salient schema among career aspirants generally, the passion principle may help perpetuate overwork and ideal worker expectations. By framing the pursuit of fulfilling work as a salve for overwork and precarity and by encouraging personal investment in one's paid work, the passion principle may foreclose career aspirants' consideration of alternative perspectives on labor force participation, such as prioritizing work that supports self-expressive hobbies, work that allows one to maximize time with family and friends, or work that is driven by the needs of one's community rather than one's personal interests.

From a policy perspective, the passion principle may help perpetuate socioeconomic and other disadvantages among college-going and college-educated workers. I call for policies and resources in higher education that provide working-class and first-generation students with the same opportunities and tools for securing employment as their more privileged peers (whether or not they seek passion). In addition, educational institutions and career-advising professionals need to carefully reflect on the ways their messaging may devalue career aspirants who prioritize money or mobility goals over passion or may represent passion-seeking as the only morally valid approach to career decision-making.

Passion-seeking is particularly risky for career aspirants in the US labor market because of the meager support structures available to workers therein. Cuts to welfare programs, the lack of universal healthcare, and yawning gaps between the minimum wage and a livable wage mean that those who sacrifice for work in their passion are at greater risk in the United States than they might be in other postindustrial nations with more robust welfare states.[77] Passion-seeking is so risky, in other words, in part because there are fewer stable, well-paying jobs and fewer social protections for those who seek passion without the assistance of safety nets and springboards.[78]

More broadly, the passion principle is an example of how a taken-for-granted, seemingly benign cultural belief might in fact bolster capitalist processes. Touted as an individual-level solution to the potential for drudgery and overwork in the labor force, passion-seeking seems to prop up the very system from which individual career aspirants seek refuge. Passion-seeking, as a way to find meaning amid potentially self-estranging work, serves employers too. Many passionate career aspirants seemed comfortable with the idea of long hours or salary sacrifices if it meant finding work they love. And passionate workers work harder for their organizations but aren't paid more. Passion-seeking is not a collective solution that may address the labor force problems faced by many; it is an individualistic one—and one consistent with neoliberal tropes of individual responsibility.

Finally, questioning the passion principle challenges a refrain in popular discourse that is echoed in op-eds, magazine articles, motivational seminars, and self-help books. By providing a critical perspective on that refrain, this book raises the possibility of more complex narratives about good career decision-making. Fleshing out those narratives requires reconsidering whether passion should be the yardstick by which we measure good work. Other kinds of work can also allow individuals to manage the potential drudgery and self-estrangement of the labor force: work that is contained neatly within predictable hours with stable benefits, work that provides free time and resources to explore creative activities or volunteering, and work that provides ample time to invest with family and friends. The postindustrial capitalist labor force demands obedient, dedicated, overworking workers; passion, however, is not the only way for workers to confront those demands.

In the epilogue, in lieu of offering an alternative ethos of career decision-making, I provide a number of guiding questions to help career aspirants—and the families, educators, and institutions that support them—loosen the grip of the passion principle on their imaginings of a good career and consider a more holistic set of decision-making points. In particular, I urge career aspirants and workers to: recognize and reflect on the sociodemographic privilege that the passion principle both presumes and perpetuates; seek diversity in their meaning-making portfolios beyond paid employment and find other ways to further their self-reflexive projects; and champion collective rather than individualistic solutions to the problems of the paid workforce.

By investigating what good work means and how people orient their lives to access that work, this book bumps up against thorny moral and existential questions. At bedrock, this book raises the question of whether seeking passion in paid work is indeed a universally desirable path to good jobs and good lives. Over half a century ago, Herbert Marcuse wrote that Americans often expect to "find themselves" in their consumption of automobiles and kitchen appliances.[79] But adherents of the passion principle also expect to find themselves in the *production* of these commodities—in the marketing of automobiles or the designing of kitchen appliances. Labor force participants may believe that loving their occupation will mean that work won't feel so much like work, but they are still workers, still contributors to a capitalist economy—along with those who labor in jobs that hold little option for the expression of passion—that benefits off of their work. Instead of encouraging career aspirants to follow their passion as a way to tolerate the difficulties of the white-collar labor force, we might advocate instead for their investment in more structural and collective solutions—those that hold more potential for restructuring the institution of work.

But the passion principle is not just a cultural schema that impacts occupational decision-making. It is also bound up in deeper cultural meaning-making of a life worth living. Having passion for our work can both provide direction for how we should spend our time and be an extension of our self-identity. For individuals, "following your passion" provides one highly culturally valued answer to the enduring question Weber raised, citing Tolstoy, "What shall we do and how shall we live?"[80] The passion principle not only can serve as a vector along which the reflexive project of the self progresses; it also suggests an answer to the question of who we should *be*.

I do not attempt to weigh in on such questions. All I can do in good conscience is to note that it is worth taking a step back to understand the passion principle as one possible ideal of good career decisions that arises out of particular socioeconomic circumstances and helps entrench those same circumstances. By understanding this cultural schema, we can be better equipped to envision alternatives to it—for our organizations, for our institutions, and for ourselves.

1 What Is the Passion Principle?

> Thinking about a new career . . . should speak to your
> heart. It should say something like this: Use this opportu-
> nity. Make this not only a hunt for a job, but a hunt for a
> life. A deeper life, a victorious life, a life you're prouder of.
> The world currently is filled with workers whose weeklong
> cry is, "When is the weekend going to be here?" . . . Their
> work puts bread on the table but . . . they are bored out of
> their minds. . . . The world doesn't need any more bored
> workers. Dream a little. Dream a lot. One of the saddest
> pieces of advice in the world is, "Oh come now—be realis-
> tic." The best parts of this world were not fashioned by
> those who were "realistic."
>
> Richard N. Bolles, *What Color Is Your Parachute?*

The advice above comes from the most popular career advice book ever
published. *What Color Is Your Parachute?* has sold over 10 million copies
worldwide, and the author, Richard Bolles, has released an updated edi-
tion yearly since 1972. *Parachute* has been a pillar of the career-related
self-help genre that started in the 1970s,[1] and it still sells over twenty
thousand copies a month.

The labor market is of course far more complex than the picture Bolles
paints. Workers—even those with college degrees—face increasing precarity, diminished employer loyalty, and deskilling in many industries.[2] They
experience greater income inequality, are expected to work longer hours,
and have fewer protective programs such as robust unemployment
benefits to lean on than in decades past.[3] In this chapter, I ask whether
Bolles's perspective is shared among the college-going career aspirants

and college-educated workers who actually confront these labor market complexities. When deciding how to navigate the labor force, do career aspirants and workers really prioritize what speaks to their heart? Do they pursue the most "realistic," economically viable, or financially stable career paths available to them? Or do they prioritize other considerations like free time or family?

To examine these questions, I draw on in-depth interviews with college students and quantitative data on US workers from the Passion Principle Survey (PPS) and the National Survey of the Changing Workforce (NSCW). I explore how career aspirants and college-educated workers think about good career decision-making in the abstract and what factors they prioritize when making career decisions in their own lives.

As it turns out, many people give the color of their parachute top billing. Some career aspirants approached career decision-making with a desire to maximize their potential for economic security and financial success. But a more common guiding belief was the passion principle. Many career aspirants centered personal fulfillment and self-expression in their abstract sense of good career decision-making and put passion-related factors at the top of their priority list when considering their own majors and post-college careers. Some, like Bolles, downplayed financial considerations like salary and security as undesirable or even morally problematic. This high value of passion-seeking is also evident among college-educated workers' abstract assessments of good career decisions and even in the decisions many have made in their own career paths along the way.[4]

I argue at the end of the chapter that beyond helping to inform individuals' career decision-making, the passion principle serves a broader role in sociodemographic differentiation in the labor market. The cultural value vested in passion-seeking may not only help perpetuate occupational segregation by gender and race/ethnicity; it may also serve as a conduit for the reproduction of class privilege and disadvantage.

HOW DO CAREER ASPIRANTS MAKE CAREER DECISIONS?

Documenting the dynamic forces at play in the capitalist labor market, and the divergent benefits and burdens faced by workers therein, has been central to sociology from its beginnings as a discipline. However, comparatively little scholarship has directly investigated career aspirants' *cultural meaning-making* regarding their occupational decisions, as I do here. Instead, much social science literature has relied on scholars' presumptions about how people make decisions, distilling the motivations of individuals from societal-level economic patterns or from institutional-level theories about how labor markets work.

Classic literature in sociology and economics, for example, typically assumes that workers in capitalist economies unilaterally prioritize the most monetarily advantageous employment opportunities available to them.[5] For Marx, workers are motivated to find work that best maximizes economic returns on their labor.[6] For Weber, workers' interest in economic advancement typically structures their career decisions.[7] This search for economic advancement is tied to Weber's conceptualization of a "calling" embedded in the Protestant ethic, the belief among early American Protestants that worldly financial success was a sign of spiritual salvation.[8] Although the term "calling" is used in common parlance today as a synonym for passion, Weber's conceptualization captured individuals' commitment to hard work for its own sake and their sense of moral duty to use their talent to contribute to the good of their community.[9]

Rational actor and neoclassical economic theorists, particularly human capital theorists,[10] argue that people make career decisions on the basis of rational cost-benefit calculations about which investments in education and training will net the greatest economic gain.[11] These scholars presume that career aspirants have a clear sense of what career paths are available to them at a given skill level and make career decisions by prioritizing the paths that will translate their skills into the best possible financial position.

Social mobility scholarship in sociology, further, theorizes that opportunity for economic advancement, alongside monetary considerations, is a primary factor motivating career decision-makers. This research is particularly concerned with workers' ability to improve their standard of living compared to that of their parents.[12] Social mobility research typically assumes that career aspirants seek to climb as far up the socioeconomic ladder as they possibly can given their training and skill level.[13] Studies of students' selection of college majors by socioeconomic class, for example, have found that students from working-class backgrounds and those who are first in their family to attend college (i.e., "first-generation" students) are more likely than their peers to be concerned about their ability to get a job immediately after college and are thus more likely to enroll in professional degree programs like engineering or nursing than more esoteric fields like philosophy.[14]

Other scholars have argued that career aspirants may prioritize a job's prestige in order to sustain or improve their social status. For example, many of the Ivy League students recruited by the elite professional service firms that Lauren Rivera studied were lured by visions of the "good life" these high-flying firms seemed to offer.[15] Some of the college-educated young adults Ellen Lamont interviewed were similarly motivated to find prestigious, well-paying jobs in the San Francisco area.[16] And some of the women Elizabeth Armstrong and Laura Hamilton encountered in their residence hall ethnography were aiming for glamorous jobs in fashion, media, and sports.[17] For such career aspirants, ideal career paths were those that would allow them to climb the social as well as the economic ladder.

Yet as Eli Wilson notes, "The draw of a particular line of work is only partially encapsulated in its material benefits."[18] Beyond economic, mobility, and status considerations, social scientists have argued that career aspirants may intentionally incorporate considerations of their salient social identities into their career decisions. Some scholars have posited that gendered family plans may lead women and men to shape their career decisions in gender-traditional ways. Future fathers, they argue, seek economically viable "provider" jobs, while future mothers seek "flexible" work they believe will facilitate their caregiving activities.[19] More recent research has raised doubts that family plans and other overtly gender-oriented considerations drive career decision-making among contemporary career aspirants, especially early on in careers.[20] Young heterosexual women increasingly expect their partners to value and encourage their professional aspirations and share childrearing responsibilities, while men are increasingly distancing themselves from traditional breadwinner expectations.[21] Yet gender is commonly an *implicit* factor in career decision-making. Once in the workforce, women with children face structural and cultural challenges integrating gendered work and family demands. Mothers, even those who work full-time, shoulder the majority of caregiving responsibilities in heterosexual families and are culturally expected to prioritize childrearing over their careers.[22] As such, gendered work-life balance issues can take center stage in career decision-making once career aspirants are in the labor force, even if those constraints are not part of decision-making at career launch.

Career decision-making may also explicitly incorporate aspirants' racial and ethnic identities. For example, African American and Native American students are more likely than their white peers to value and prioritize career paths that specifically advance opportunities and collective well-being in structurally oppressed and underserved racial/ethnic minority communities.[23] These career aspirants may take cues from community and social movement leaders about what skills are most needed to advance community well-being (e.g., legal credentials, healthcare training) and direct their career paths accordingly.[24] In contrast, white career aspirants' more frequent denial of structural racism may lead them to avoid occupational pathways (e.g., social work) that expect nuanced recognition of sociodemographic oppression or challenge color-blind racial ideologies.

Beyond explicit or implicit accounting of social identities in career aspirants' decisions, recent sociological research has explored ways that gendered, racialized, and class-differentiated priorities are implicitly woven into decision-making through career aspirants' seemingly *idiosyncratic* interests and values.[25] Scholars in this vein argue that because selves are social constructs that are shaped by the social institutions in which those selves develop, when career aspirants seek congruence between their sense of self and their career path, they end up unwittingly reproducing sociodemographic differentiation such as gender segregation. This also dovetails with work in vocational psychology that examines the role of "person-vocation fit" in people's career choices, or the extent to which a person's interests align with the day-to-day requisite tasks of an occupation.[26] This research highlights the importance of individual values and interests as motivators in career decision-making and argues that we cannot ignore self-expressive goals as possible factors in career decisions. Yet there is little consensus on the factors that career aspirants and workers prioritize in their career decision-making. It is unclear how these decision-makers rank self-expression next to economic, mobility, or sociodemographic considerations, or even what such self-expressive decision-making might look like in action. This chapter investigates the factors that career aspirants and college-educated workers prioritize in their understanding of "good" careers in the abstract and how they draw on those priorities when making decisions about their own career paths.

To understand these processes among career aspirants, I examine in-depth interviews with one hundred college students at three geographically and sociodemographically diverse four-year comprehensive institutions: Stanford University, the University of Houston, and Montana State University. Appendix A provides information about sampling design and data analysis.

I then draw on quantitative data from the PPS to investigate whether the priorities articulated by these students are mirrored among the college-educated workforce more broadly. And I use NSCW data to see whether those priorities are mirrored among non-college-educated workers who do not enjoy the same privileged access to white-collar jobs. Detailed information about the PPS and NSCW can be found in Appendix A.

To be sure, career aspirants' and workers' cultural schemas of good career decision-making are not the only factors that determine how their career paths will ultimately play out. Not everyone is equally likely to be able to put their career priorities into action. Access to stable and well-paying career paths is partly determined by personal and family networks,[27] cultural and social capital,[28] and economic resources.[29] Systemic discrimination by gender, race, class, sexual identity, and other axes also still affects who gets what jobs and how they fare once there.[30] Nonetheless, it is important to investigate the cultural schemas that career aspirants and workers use to understand and prioritize their career decision-making. Cultural schemas like the passion principle may shape the paths along which career aspirants and workers search for opportunities and the opportunities they may voluntarily close off for themselves. As I argue at the end of this chapter, these schemas also have implications for factors such as occupational segregation and the perpetuation of the economic privilege of well-off career aspirants.

CULTURAL PRIORITIES OF GOOD
CAREER DECISION-MAKING

To understand what college-going career aspirants value in their abstract conceptions of good career decision-making, I asked the students I interviewed a series of purposefully broad and open-ended questions, such as "What are good reasons for choosing an academic major?," "What are not good considerations?," and "What do you think are the most important and least important considerations when making career decisions?" I didn't stipulate what they could or could not say, allowing them to define "good" in whatever way they wished. Their answers were often complex and multifaceted, as well as careful and thoughtful. Here I was interested in their assessments of decisions about career fields, not about the best industries or companies to work for or the best kinds of people to have as colleagues.

The interviews revealed that a salient factor in students' understanding of good career decision-making was a personal, self-expressive connection to their career fields—what I came to call the passion principle. Formally stated, the passion principle is a cultural schema that elevates self-expression and fulfillment of one's idiosyncratic interests and unique sense of personhood as the most valuable and morally legitimate consideration in career decision-making.[31] For the majority of students I interviewed, passion was a prerequisite factor in how they conceptualized good career decisions. As I discuss below, financial and employment security considerations were neither absent nor ignored in students' responses; they just didn't receive top billing as often.

An MSU anthropology student explained that passion-based work means "you enjoy it, you love it, it's intriguing to you, it's always making your mind think and want to educate yourself and learn more and contemplate." She pitied those who had not found their passion, as though their lives were incomplete.

> [Choose an occupational field] because you love it. [*Laughs*] That's the short and the long of it. And I think that some people have this different idea in their heads and it's probably because they haven't found what they love. They haven't found their passion. And it's very sad to me. (Upper-class Native American and white woman)

WHAT IS "PASSION"?

Passion has many meanings in popular and academic lexicons. Here I define it as a person's deep personal commitment to an occupational field (like architecture or counseling) or a productive task realm (like sculpting or project logistics). I use the term "passion" to capture this idea because it is shorthand in popular culture for one's personal connection to an occupation or task field and because it was used over and over by career aspirants I interviewed. The personal connection can be cognitive, emotional, or moral or a combination of these. But to be a passion, that connection must be genuinely and individualistically felt.

When I asked students to explain what they meant when they referred to "passion," they typically responded like this MSU architecture student.

> That's a good question. . . . My definition of passion, I guess, would be feeling that fulfillment in something every day, and maybe it's not every day that you go to work and you're fulfilled, but over time you feel a curiosity and a desire to progress in whatever you're studying or working towards. (Upperclass white man)

Similarly, Xavier, the Stanford math major mentioned in the introduction, explained his passion for math as its close alignment with his interests and personality.

> It's fun, but it's also something that I feel really challenges me mentally. . . . That's the passion. It's just something I see myself doing for the rest of my life. . . . I think that's definitely my personality. (Middle-class white and Latinx man)

Respondents described passion as an authentic and idiosyncratic extension and expression of their unique sense of personhood.

Passion is, then, a *self-expressive characteristic* rooted in and reflecting one's self-conceptions.[32] Such self-conceptions are at the heart of our individuality: they are the theories we develop about ourselves as unique individuals within a deeply individualistic culture.[33] Our self-conceptions form over the course of our lives and shift and adapt as we encounter new cultural and institutional circumstances. Self-expressive behaviors like passion-seeking are how we *enact* individualism.

Although self-conceptions seem fundamentally idiosyncratic, they are profoundly shaped by our social environments and biographies. Our very sense of self—who we think we are—is socially constructed. It is partly construed by the ascriptive categories like gender, race, and class that we are born and socialized into and by the constraints and resources that are available to us as a result of our social position.[34] Through a lifetime of socialization and gendered, classed, and racialized social expectations, we tend to develop self-conceptions that are patterned by, and inflected with, these ascriptive categories.[35]

In addition, the activities we consider interesting and exciting are highly dependent on our structural and cultural circumstances. We typically develop interest in topics only when we have prolonged exposure to them and when our interest is encouraged and validated by those around us.[36] If someone is curious about ballet, for example, but has neither the opportunity nor the encouragement to investigate it, ballet is unlikely to become their passion. Thus what we come to be passionate about is neither arbitrary nor fully idiosyncratic.

Among the students I interviewed, passion encompassed three interrelated self-expressive ties to an occupation or field. The first was a connection to the field's knowledge content, finding it "interesting," "intriguing," or "intellectually engaging." A mechanical engineering student at MSU explained, "I think the best reasons for choosing a subject would be curiosity and play, just whatever makes you want to think about things, poke and prod what you know" (middle-class white man).

The second component was an emotional connection, whereby one's occupational tasks evoke positive affective responses like "excitement," "happiness," and "joy." As a Stanford computer science student explained it, "You have to enjoy the subject. It's like a gateway condition. . . . It's a necessary prerequisite" (upper-class Asian man). Several respondents used metaphors of romantic love, like the business student at MSU who noted, "You just want to pick a job that will make you happy . . . like, doing what you love. I think you should take as many classes as you can to find out what you do love, kind of like dating" (upper-class white man).

The third component passion entailed was a "match" between an occupational field and one's idiosyncratic experiences and biographically curated tastes and values. An English education major at MSU explained,

"If you feel [your occupational choice] to be a good match for you and you feel that in your head and your heart, then it's the right path for you" (middle-class white woman). Echoing her classmate, an anthropology student suggested that the "right fit" would have a sense of destiny: "You believe within yourself that it is what you're supposed to be doing, . . . this is what will fulfill your highest potential" (working-class white woman).

These three components were interwoven and mutually reinforcing in students' responses. Most students mentioned at least two of the three when articulating their idea of passion.

Importantly, passion for one's occupation is distinct from satisfaction with one's particular job or employer. For example, a neonatal nurse may be passionate about neonatal care but dislike his colleagues and be frustrated with the hospital where he works. He may switch to a new hospital with new colleagues, but he would still be working in his passion.[37] Passion is also distinct from one's commitment to hard work as a moral virtue or one's commitment to a career field for the notoriety, prestige, or salary it provides.[38]

In addition, respondents typically understood passion as a dichotomy: either a person was passionate about a career field or they weren't. Career aspirants presumed that individuals just "know" that something is their passion the same way one is presumed to just "know" that one is in love, much like Steve Jobs's statement, "You'll know it when you find it."[39] (But as I show in later chapters, the development of passion is not really a dichotomous process at all.)

Students expressed little judgment about which fields were most deserving of passion. Pursuing passion did not necessarily mean choosing fields like creative writing or music in which personal experiences and perspectives could be explicitly incorporated into the substantive work. A highly formalized field like mathematics could still be considered self-expressive if an aspiring mathematician (like Xavier) found fulfillment in the elegance and logic involved in mathematical computation.[40]

Students' notions of passion also allowed room for the subject of one's passion to change over time. Their narratives not only included discussions of "finding" one's passion, but also tales of realizing when their passion had "changed" or "shifted" to something else. Following one's passion, then, does not necessarily mean pursuing the same occupation for one's lifetime. As a cultural schema, the passion principle is generally agnostic about the subject of that passion. To follow one's passion means to *elevate the pursuit of a self-expressive, fulfilling career path as the central guiding principle of career decision-making,* regardless of what that passion is or whether the subject of one's passion shifts over time.

Tellingly, students who did not know what their passion was found the absence quite distressing. They often reported feeling "stressed," "overwhelmed," and anxious about their career decisions. Yan, for example, entered Stanford as a pre-pharmacy major but wasn't sure if that was really her passion.

> So I came in and was like, "Oh, maybe I want to do pre-pharm," but then I heard about CS [computer science], and I was like, "Oh, maybe that'll be cool." So I tried CS this quarter and I was like, "Eh, it was fun but I don't know if that's something I could do for the rest of my life." So okay, I guess I'll stick with pharmacy for now, but even then I'm not sure how set I am in it. I know I like sciences. I'm just not sure exactly what I want to do. . . . So I'm kind of freaking out about that right now. (Middle-class Asian woman)

Yan's quickened and strained tone revealed her anxiety about not knowing what she wanted to do in the future.[41]

These anxieties speak to the cultural salience of passion as both a *reflection* and an *expression* of one's self-conceptions. To be without a definitive passion, even if someone does not ultimately prioritize it in their career decision-making, means to not be in touch with a core part of one's sense of self.

THE PROMINENCE OF PASSION

To assess the prevalence of passion-related factors vis-à-vis other career considerations, I examined the guiding principles that career aspirants emphasized in response to interview questions about what they thought people should prioritize when choosing academic majors, as well as what they thought people should prioritize when making career choices more broadly. I found that passion was the most commonly articulated priority: 89% of respondents said passion-related considerations should be a central consideration when students are selecting college majors, and 84% said passion should be a central guiding principle when students are choosing career

Table 1.1 Proportion of college student interview respondents who said passion, financial considerations, and employment opportunities should be top priorities when choosing a major and a career path (N = 100)

	N	Passion-Related Considerations	Financial Considerations	Employment Opportunities
TOP PRIORITY WHEN SELECTING A MAJOR				
All	100	89%	9%	21%
Women	56	92%	8%	26%
Men	44	88%	10%	17%
Stanford	35	100%	3%	21%
MSU	35	79%	14%	22%
UH	30	86%	10%	21%
White	53	85%	15%	21%
Racial/ethnic minority	47	93%	2%	20%
Black	25	91%	0%	17%
Asian	14	93%	14%	21%
Hispanic/Latinx	14	85%	14%	14%
Lower SES	19	89%	11%	33%
Middle SES	50	89%	6%	11%
Upper SES	31	88%	12%	27%
TOP PRIORITY WHEN SELECTING A CAREER PATH				
All	100	84%	20%	11%
Women	56	85%	16%	11%
Men	44	84%	26%	11%
Stanford	35	94%	11%	06%
MSU	35	79%	18%	18%
UH	30	83%	33%	06%
White	53	82%	21%	10%
Racial/ethnic minority	47	88%	20%	12%

Table 1.1   (continued)

	N	Passion-Related Considerations	Financial Considerations	Employment Opportunities
Black	25	91%	7%	9%
Asian	14	71%	29%	14%
Hispanic/Latinx	14	78%	14%	11%
Lower SES	19	75%	25%	16%
Middle SES	50	84%	16%	7%
Upper SES	31	94%	24%	16%

NOTE: Respondents were allowed to give more than one top priority if they thought two or more were equally important (only 26% did so). Respondents could identify as more than one racial/ethnic category. To protect confidentiality, racial/ethnic categories with fewer than 10 respondents are not listed separately in the table. SES = socioeconomic status.

fields. A quarter of respondents said financial security and job opportunities should be equally or more important than passion-related considerations. But more than half spoke of both good major selection *and* career decision-making in ways that elevated passion-related considerations above all else.

The salience of the passion principle was surprisingly consistent across demographic subgroups in the sample. Table 1.1 presents the proportion of students who gave passion-related factors as the top priority in their understanding of good major selection and good career choices, broken down by school and demographic categories. (Students were allowed to give more than one top priority, but only 26% did so.) Although there is some variation by demographic category in the proportion of people giving passion-related responses, nearly 80% of respondents in each category referred to passion-related considerations as a top priority in good decisions about majors and career paths.

FINANCIAL- AND EMPLOYMENT-RELATED GUIDING PRINCIPLES

The students I interviewed discussed two other central guiding principles for career decision-making: financial considerations and employment opportunities. About one in five students (21 of 100) believed employment considerations such as the job opportunities and security a field could provide should be the priority in career decision-making.[42] An MSU engineering student explained that employment stability and access to benefits should be at the top of the list in making career decisions: "I would say security and benefits. You want to look for some kind of job that offers you some kind of long-term ability to stay and play. And since we tie access to medical care or reasonably priced medical care to employment, you want to look for that" (working-class white man).

Several other respondents (9 of 100) explained that salary should be the top consideration when choosing a career field. For example, a UH communications major said, "Unfortunately, money, you know, you have to consider money into it, consider what position in your life you're at. You know, . . . the general population, they value money whether they like it or not" (middle-class West Asian man). Similarly, an accounting student at UH noted the importance of a salary capable of supporting oneself and, in the future, one's family.

> I mean, I guess, one of the prime reasons . . . is money. Like you have to be able to support yourself. You have to be able to support the family you want. Like the things that you do, they have a dollar sign on them. I guess the more, like, genuine answer, especially for me, I just want to be able to experience life in different ways. (Middle-class Asian and white woman)

Consistent with previous research, there was some demographic variability in students' prioritization of economic considerations. Echoing literature on the parental pressures Asian students face more often than their peers to pursue economically viable degrees,[43] a higher proportion of Asian students (29%) centered financial considerations in their notions of good career decision-making compared to their white, Black, and Latinx peers. Yet, as Table 1.1 shows, the passion principle was articulated by at least 70% of students in each demographic category as centrally important in their abstract notions of good major choices and good career decisions.

In contrast to the literature reviewed above speculating that career aspirants prioritize opportunities for economic gain above all else, a higher proportion of students explicitly *dismissed* financial and employment considerations as good guiding principles than the proportion of students who prioritized them. When I asked outright what role financial considerations should play in people's career decision-making, 61% of students stated that money was a bad guiding principle, largely because it did not guarantee the sort of opportunities for self-fulfillment that are central to the passion principle. A Stanford economics major explained how pursuing a career for money would risk the fulfillment that the passion principle promises to foster.

> I think money is not a good reason to pursue a career. . . . You might find yourself questioning your existence or don't know yourself later in life; and, really, I'd like to be able to go home every day and know I did something that I enjoy. . . . I think money is kind of a really bad reason to pursue a career. (Middle-class white man)

Other students questioned the rationality of basing one's career decisions on employment opportunities. A UH biology student argued that choosing a field on the basis of employment opportunities did not make sense because job security is never guaranteed: "If you aren't really passionate about it and you're dreading going to work and you're dreading staying late and you're driven by just money, then if you get laid off or the company goes under, then you are left with nothing because you never pursued what you wanted" (middle-class white woman). To this student, even if a passionate worker was laid off, at least that person was still left with their passion intact.

Students who were critical of prioritizing financial or employment considerations recognized, as one said, that "we obviously live in a capitalist society so you have to make money" but argued that these considerations should not be the central motivator for career decision-making. A UH anthropology student explained that "money isn't enough of a reason" for career selection.

> I guess money is important . . . I mean, you know, without money you're not gonna get by, . . . but I also think that if you love something sometimes you have to sacrifice, you know, money for what you love. (Middle-class Native American and white woman)

I discuss below and in later chapters whether students were actually willing to make such sacrifices themselves when they left school and entered the labor force.

This interview sample is relatively large and includes students enrolled in three demographically and regionally divergent universities. But what about college students beyond this sample? As I discuss in Appendix B, I conducted a supplemental survey of 522 college students enrolled in different types of four-year institutions across the US. In these data, I found very similar patterns of prioritization: 78% of students agreed that passion-seeking should be central to major selection, and 77% agreed that it should be central to career choice. Sixty-five percent rated passion as more important on average than they rated financial and employment concerns in their abstract notions of good career decision-making. Like the interview respondents, Asian students and working-class students were less likely than their peers to prioritize passion-seeking in their assessment of good career decision-making. Yet there were no other significant demographic differences or differences across students enrolled in different types of schools.

THE PASSION PRINCIPLE BEYOND COLLEGE STUDENTS

A majority of students in the interview sample identified self-expression and fulfillment as the most important guiding principle in their ideas of good career decisions in the abstract. Do college-educated workers across age groups, class background, and occupations express similar enthusiasm for passion-seeking? Perhaps the students' cultural commitments were anchored in their particular institutional location (higher education), their particular stage in the life course (career launch), or their particular cohort (millennials). The pervasiveness of passion-related narratives about career decision-making in popular media,[44] self-help books like *What Color Is Your Parachute?*,[45] and career counseling and coaching practices[46] suggests that this valorization of passion-related career decisions may not be restricted to college students at all.

To understand the salience of the passion principle more broadly, I turn to the sample of US college-educated workers from the Passion Principle Survey.[47] I asked PPS respondents two sets of questions designed to tap into their abstract cultural beliefs on good decision-making about college majors and career paths. The first set of questions asked them to give advice to a hypothetical first-year college student who was trying to choose a major: How important is it that a major be "interesting," "personally meaningful," or something they are "passionate about"? A second set of questions asked PPS respondents how important those same factors should be when someone is choosing a career field. Means on these measures can be found in the darker bars in Figure 1.1.[48] Together, these six measures capture multiple facets of a sense of personal connection to work as well as a more direct notion of "passion." I averaged the six items together to create a robust scale of adherence to the passion principle.[49] This scale is represented by the penultimate bar in Figure 1.1.

Like the students, these college-educated workers generally subscribed to the idea that people *should* prioritize passion-related considerations in their choice of college majors and in their choice of career paths. Respondents rated passion-related factors halfway between "somewhat" and "very" important on average (mean on the passion principle scale: 4.46 of 5).

Figure 1.2 disaggregates the averages on the passion principle scale by demographic groups. Here the most obvious pattern is the consistency in adherence to the passion principle across groups.[50] All demographic groups have an average that lies between "somewhat" and "very important" (4 and 5), and all averages sit within about a quarter of a point of one another on a 5-point scale.[51] Supplemental regression models confirm these similarities. In models predicting respondents' score on the passion principle scale by their gender, age, race/ethnicity, socioeconomic background, level of education, and whether they were born in the United States, I found no difference by gender in adherence to the passion principle.[52] I also found that older college-educated respondents were just as likely as younger college-educated respondents to adhere to the passion principle, contrary to assumptions that the passion principle is only relevant to millennial-generation career aspirants or is the purview of only the youngest or most inexperienced workers.

Yet, as with the student data, there were notable differences by class background. Likely because of their privileged access to well-paying and stable jobs (see Chapter 3), college-educated workers raised in wealthier families were significantly more likely to adhere to the passion principle than those from working-class families.[53]

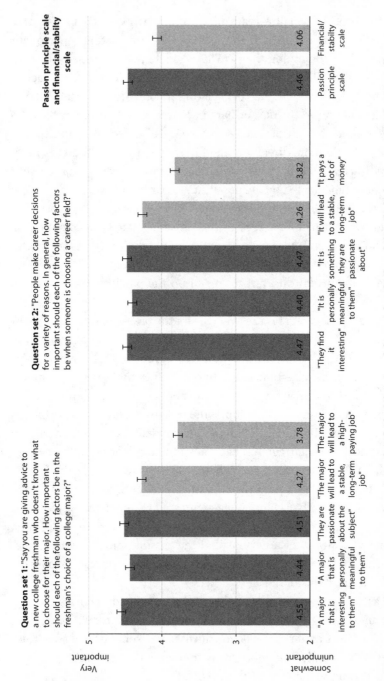

Question set 1: "Say you are giving advice to a new college freshman who doesn't know what to choose for their major. How important should each of the following factors be in the freshman's choice of a college major?"

Question set 2: "People make career decisions for a variety of reasons. In general, how important should each of the following factors be when someone is choosing a career field?"

Passion principle scale and financial/stability scale

"A major that is interesting personally to them" — 4.55
"A major that is personally meaningful to them" — 4.44
"They are passionate about the subject" — 4.51
"The major will lead to a stable, long-term job" — 4.27
"The major will lead to a high-paying job" — 3.78
"They find it interesting" — 4.47
"It is personally meaningful to them" — 4.40
"It is something they are passionate about" — 4.47
"It will lead to a stable, long-term job" — 4.26
"It pays a lot of money" — 3.82
Passion principle scale — 4.46
Financial/stability scale — 4.06

Very important — 5
Somewhat unimportant — 2

Figure 1.1 Average importance of passion-related (dark bars) and financial and job stability (light bars) considerations in college-educated workers' beliefs about good college major and career decision-making (PPS data).

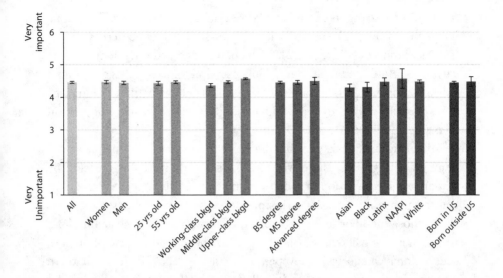

Figure 1.2 Importance of passion in college-educated workers' beliefs about good career decision-making, by demographic category (PPS data).

There were also notable points of racial/ethnic variation. First, Asian respondents adhered to the passion principle less strongly than their white peers.[54] Although little research has attended directly to racial differences in how individuals conceptualize good career decisions, some research speculates that college-going and college-educated Asian career aspirants are more likely than their white peers to prioritize social mobility over other career-related concerns because of the mobility pressures many first-generation Asian students experience from immigrant parents.[55] Black college-educated workers also adhered to the passion principle slightly less than their white peers.[56] This is consistent with work suggesting that Black career aspirants may be more likely than their white peers to prioritize employment trajectories that would help their families and communities financially, as well as with research showing the considerable disadvantages Black workers face securing well-paid jobs compared to white peers with the same levels of education and experience.[57] Holding race/ethnicity constant, whether respondents were born in the United States was not a significant predictor of adherence to the passion principle.

Despite these points of statistical variation, there is remarkable similarity in the average agreement with the passion principle across demographic groups (see Figure 1.2). As such, when considering demographic variation in adherence to the passion principle among college-educated workers, it is more useful to ask which groups believe in the passion principle most strongly than to ask which groups tend to adhere to the passion principle and which do not.

Mirroring the consistency in adherence to the passion principle across demographic groups, there was also little variation in this measure by respondents' occupation or employment sector. Although the strength of commitment to the passion principle varied by about 7% across occupations whose members adhered most and least strongly, once again, there was striking consistency in adherence to the passion principle across occupational categories (see Appendix C, Figure C.1).[58] In addition, there was no significant difference in adherence to the passion principle by whether respondents were employed in the for-profit, nonprofit, government, or education sector.

The college students described earlier frequently valued passion-related concerns *above* financial and job security concerns in their cultural conceptualizations of good career decisions. Yet few of those career aspirants were in the labor force full-time. What about college-educated workers with extensive labor force experience? Even if they value passion-seeking, are they more inclined to value job security and salary considerations over passion in their cultural understandings of good career decision-making?

The PPS data suggest that is not really the case. When college-educated respondents were asked to assess the importance of selecting a college major that would lead to "a stable, long-term job" or "a high-paying job," the average rating of these factors was significantly lower than respondents' average rating of the importance of passion-related factors (see Figure 1.1). When asked a related question about choice of career field in general, college-educated workers' rating of the importance of passion-related considerations was again higher on average than their rating of the importance of job security or salary considerations.

Furthermore, looking within PPS respondents' own rankings, a large majority of these college-educated workers (67%) rated passion-related factors of *higher* average importance than they rated economic considerations

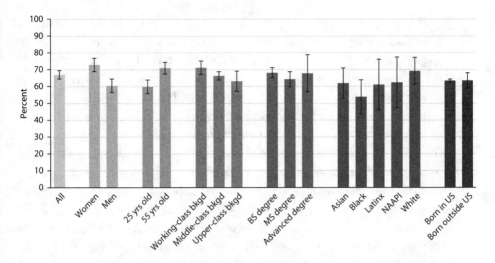

Figure 1.3 Proportion of college-educated workers who rated passion *more important* than they rated salary and job security considerations in good career decision-making, by demographic category (PPS data).

of job security and salary. Figure 1.3 presents the proportion of respondents in each demographic category who personally rated passion-related considerations higher than they rated the importance of economic considerations in their assessments of good career decision-making.[59] Again, there are a few points of demographic variation. Black college-educated workers are less likely than white respondents to rate passion higher than economic concerns, consistent with the patterns in Figure 1.2. Men were significantly less likely than women to rate passion higher than economic concerns, possibly as a result of the policing of men's masculinity, which may discourage their prioritization of emotional connections to work over financial considerations.[60]

There is also interesting age variation: although younger and older workers were equally likely to adhere to the passion principle (see Figure 1.2), older workers were more likely than younger cohorts to elevate passion considerations above economic concerns. It may be that younger respondents are more concerned with economic stability relative to their older peers as they launch their careers and start families, while older workers are reflecting on decades of experience in the labor force.[61] This variation by age is substantively small, however: the average adherence to the passion principle varied by only about 5% across age cohorts.

Beyond these points of variation, I find no difference by socioeconomic status, education level, or immigrant status in respondents' likelihood of rating passion considerations over economic concerns. Across the board, over half of respondents in each demographic category rated passion more highly than economic factors in their ideas about good career decision-making.

Broadly, these PPS results echoed many college students' valuation of passion-related decision-making criteria. The belief that passion should be central to career choice was not endorsed only by members of certain sociodemographic groups, by certain age cohorts, or even by workers only in certain occupations. The majority of workers across the college-educated workforce prized passion-based considerations in their cultural conceptualizations of good career decision-making.

DOES THE PASSION PRINCIPLE INFORM INDIVIDUALS' PERSONAL CAREER DECISION-MAKING?

Is "follow your passion" just an empty platitude—one that sounds good in the abstract but gets overshadowed by practical or financial considerations as career aspirants and workers make decisions about their *own* career paths in a precarious labor market? To examine this question, I first return to the student interviews. Did they make decisions about their majors and plan their career priorities after college consistent with the passion principle? This cohort of career aspirants was not naive about the labor force; they were generally aware of the precariousness and instability of employment and the wide variance in salaries across occupational fields.[62] Most of the students I interviewed were in high school during the Great Recession, and many saw family members and neighbors struggle with unemployment or home foreclosure.[63]

Yet in spite of the precarity in which students were grappling with their future careers, the passion principle not only dominated how most students conceptualized good career decision-making in the abstract, but it was also typically a priority in their decision-making about their own career paths. Most respondents (80%) explained that intellectual fascination, enjoyment, and/or personal connections to an occupational field were central factors in their personal choice of academic major. For example, a Stanford student explained that she sought out a major in line with her passion: "I think I wanted to really enjoy it and really find myself actually, like, interested in it as opposed to just something that I have to do. I think I found that with pysch[ology]. I really like it" (working-class Latinx woman). A UH student noted that he struggled to decide between math and political science but settled on the latter because it "fulfilled" him.

> Well, coming in, I didn't really know exactly what I was supposed to major in. . . . Political science was the only thing that engaged me, that and math. But then I had to choose and I got more—I felt more fulfilled doing political science, though, so I chose political science. (Working-class Black man)

Another UH student explained the role passion played in deciding on her major.

> Not being honest with yourself about who you are [is a problem]. . . . Everything's not for everybody, like . . . everybody's not meant to be, you know, find a cure for breast cancer. So I think your job should be, this is what I wanna do. . . . I feel like a lot of people . . . don't like their careers because they aren't happy—they're doing it because they need money, I need this, I need that, I need—no, you don't need anything, you will be fine. You just have to follow your instincts, your gut. . . . [That's] the lesson I'm taking now and running with it trying to find a new major. (Middle-class Black woman)

Some students, like Yana, privileged employment security in their choice of major.

EAC: So tell me, what's most important to you in your major?

YANA: I think it would have to be if I can get a job after college because it's—if I'm—you know, I'm gonna put in all this hard work and effort into getting my major I need to make sure that there's some sort of, I don't want to say guarantee, but . . . that my degree will help me actually get somewhere and to do something rather than just the uncertainty that I don't really know what it's gonna do. So that's why I also have biology, because with English . . . like, the opportunities [are] just so different, you know, and I think with my biology major . . . I always knew that if I did that, then I would have a job at the end and I would . . . [know] that I have a path goal. (Upper-class West Asian woman)

Even though Yana was passionate about English, she decided to major in biology as well to increase her chances for stable employment after college.

Figure 1.4 presents the proportion of interview respondents by gender, school, racial/ethnic minority (REM) status, and socioeconomic status (SES) who prioritized passion-related and financial- and employment-related factors in their choice of major. Respondents were free to name multiple priorities if they weighed two or more factors equally in their choice of major, and about a quarter did so. Respondents in every demographic category gave passion-related explanations for why they chose their major (Figure 1.4, Panel A) more frequently than factors related to financial considerations (Figure 1.4, Panel B) or employment opportunities (Figure 1.4, Panel C). The proportion of students who prioritized passion was generally similar across demographic category (around 80%).[64]

I also asked students what factors were most important as they considered what they would do after graduation. Once again, nearly three quarters of respondents explained that passion-related factors were top considerations in their postgraduation career planning. An engineering student at Stanford explained it this way:

> I want to be excited about what I do every day. . . . I understand that there are things that go on in a job that are a little annoying or tedious, but if overall I'm getting to do something that just feels like this is really *me* . . . and it's all coming naturally, then that's what I'd really like to do. (Upper-class Black woman)

Similarly, an MSU business major didn't know another way to answer the question than to reference passion.

EAC: What is most important in your thoughts about what you will do after graduation?

INTERVIEWEE: Like other than just being passionate about what you have? Like, you just kind of [have to] like what you do, I guess. I don't really know how else to answer that. (Middle-class white man)

As with the question about choice of major, far more students (72%) prioritized passion-related factors in their postgraduation career planning than salary considerations (15%) or employment opportunities (21%). See Figure 1.5, Panels A, B, and C. These relative prioritization patterns

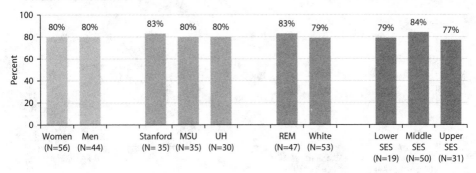

A. Passion-related factors

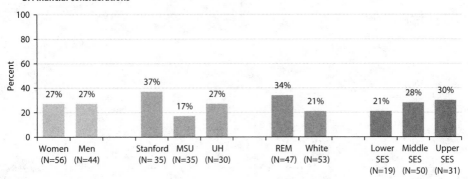

B. Financial considerations

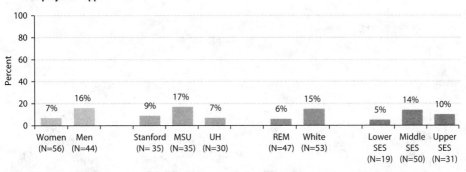

C. Employment opportunities

Figure 1.4 College students' top priority when choosing their major (interview data, N = 100). Numbers represent the frequencies of students in each demographic category who gave each factor as the most important reason for their choice of major. Students were allowed to name multiple reasons if more than one was centrally important in their decision-making. A few students mentioned answers (e.g., family planning) not included here. As such, proportions across the three panels for each demographic group may add up to more or less than 100%. REM = racial/ethnic minority; SES = socioeconomic status.

A. Passion-related factors

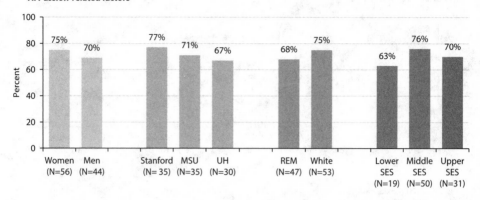

B. Financial considerations

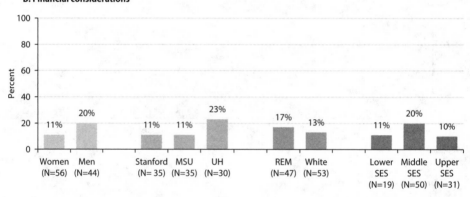

C. Employment opportunities

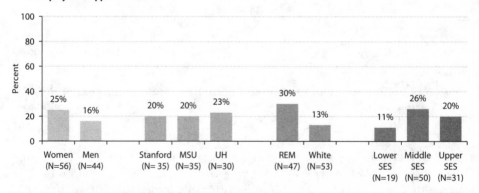

Figure 1.5 College students' top priority in planning for their postgraduation career path (interview data, N = 100). Numbers represent the frequencies of students in each demographic category who gave each factor as the most important consideration in their postgraduation career planning. Students were allowed to name more than one factor, and a few students mentioned factors (e.g., location) not included here. As such, proportions for each demographic group may add up to more or less than 100%. REM = racial/ethnic minority; SES = socioeconomic status.

were generally similar across gender, school, racial/ethnic minoirity status, and class background.

Reflecting their preparation to enter the labor force, students were more likely to prioritize financial and employment concerns when talking about their postgraduation plans than they did when discussing their major selection.[65] For example, an MSU student explained, "After graduation, I think that it's important that I have a stable job, so that income is steady and whatnot" (middle-class white and Asian woman). Steven, a bioengineering major at Stanford, was also looking for job security first and foremost after he graduates.

> I think at least immediately after graduation I'd want some sort of plan where in the future I'd have job security where I can—I wouldn't have to worry about getting laid off or positions running low. So I would prefer, like if I have the chance to go back and get my master's, I feel that would really make me more valuable to the company so I'd be able to stay there for as long as I would like. (Middle-class Asian man)

A handful of students were enticed by the lure of fancy cars and nice vacations and sought out lines of work that promised such luxuries.[66] But the rest of the students who prioritized financial considerations did so with more modest financial goals in mind—being able to support themselves or pay off student loans.

A few respondents noted that salary range and employment security were especially important to them because they wanted to support a family at some time in the future. Adam, a sociology major at UH, explained:

> I'm always going to have my family in mind. I want to be a dad and a husband, and there's a few things that, if you're going to be those roles, that you have to take care of. . . . I don't want to have a family that worries about money ever, just because it shouldn't be about that. I lived a happy life and never had to worry about money issues because my parents just always took care of it, and I want to do the same for my kids. . . . So, yeah, family is always the biggest thing in mind because I have all these goals for myself and things that I think I can do, but it's all for my family. (Middle-class white man)

Adam planned to apply for a position as a forensic analyst at the FBI, where he believed he could "make a good $70,000 a year."[67]

Other students gave economic and stability considerations equal weight alongside passion considerations. This tended to sound like a statement from Yvette, an MSU nursing major.

EAC: So tell me, what's most important in your thoughts about what you'll do after graduation?

YVETTE: Probably doing something that will build up my career, so not necessarily jumping into my absolute dream job but something that I think could get me there, maybe. So, I mean, I'm not obviously expecting to find an entry-level nursing position where I'm like, this is what I want to do forever, but maybe sort of heading in that direction of the field that I want to eventually be in. So that's kind of the most important thing to me. (Middle-class white woman)

Yvette saw her more immediate goal of secure employment in the nursing field as a step toward her longer-term goal of landing her "dream job" as an intensive care nurse. In response to the same question, her peer at Stanford said that his top priority in his career path after graduation was "something that strikes a balance between my interests and stability in the future."

Five students described a multistep process for choosing a major, whereby they first identified fields they thought would provide the greatest economic security and then decided which field most interested them. More often, though, the sequential consideration of economic concerns and passion happened in the opposite order—deciding what fields interested them and then choosing from among them the most economically secure path. For example, a kinesiology student at UH was passionate about sports but shifted her career goals from coaching to sports administration because of the higher salary potential she believed the latter offered.

I wanted to be a coach . . . because I love sports and everything. So when I came here, I was going to do the health option or sports and fitness or whatever it was to be a coach. But then I started thinking—because, like now, teachers and coaches, they don't really make a lot, so I decided I wanted to do sports administration. (Working-class Black woman)

It is important to distinguish between students' considerations of career fields and their preferences for particular organizations or jobs within those fields. Considerations of salary and security were more common when students discussed particular jobs in specific firms or sectors. The majority of students I spoke with believed passion-based factors should drive career paths, and economic and employment concerns should be considered later on as one was considering the specific jobs or organizations *within* a particular field.

In the end, half of respondents gave *only* passion-related reasons for why they chose their major and as factors that were centrally important as they planned their career paths, saying nothing unprompted about employment or income considerations.[68]

These patterns of prioritization were echoed in the supplemental survey of college students described in Appendix B. In that sample, over 70% of students somewhat or strongly agreed that "pursuing my personal interest or passion was the most important factor to me in choosing my college major." As with the interviews, working-class students were more likely than their wealthier peers to prioritize salary and job security. And Asian students were less likely than their white peers to prioritize passion in their career decision-making. I found no other significant differences in passion principle adherence by demographic category (gender, race/ethnicity, class background, type of major).

The supplemental survey also asked students who had changed majors at some point during college (about a third of the sample) why they had done so. Forty-two percent changed majors to "a subject I was more interested in or passionate about," compared to 22% and 17% who changed majors to subjects they presumed would have more job opportunities or greater salary potential, respectively.

A COLLEGE DEGREE AS AN ECONOMIC FLOOR

Why did money and job security considerations not dominate more students' major choices and postgraduation career planning? Students were not naive about the structural realities of the labor market. They understood that employment was not guaranteed and that some fields have greater salary potential than others. However, most saw a college degree as providing an economic *floor* below which they would be unlikely to fall—

providing access to a range of jobs that would provide enough money and job security for a middle-class life, regardless of what degree or career path they pursued. Many explained that "any major could be lucrative" in theory and could lead to jobs that would provide the foundation for a comfortable standard of living. A UH political science major elaborated: "I hear a lot of people telling me, well, you shoulda chose something . . . you could get a job [in] afterwards, but it's like, they make jobs for anything, so you might as well get what [degree] you want and then you figure the rest out later."

Claire, mentioned in the introduction, was clear-eyed about the limited opportunities for wealth accumulation that her desired career path would offer (a point her parents frequently reminded her of) but said that was fine as long as she loved her work.

EAC: So where does money fit in, do you think?

CLAIRE: Money is important. My parents are always telling me I need a high-paying job, but I would rather have a job that I love without being paid as much. I worked for the Houston Zoo for a while as a volunteer with the zookeepers, and they love their jobs. They love the animals they take care of. We started talking because they were like, . . . "We don't get paid a lot. We get paid enough to pay our bills and buy food and go out," and I was like, "That's fine for me." I'm not used to grandeur. I'm used to having enough, and that would be absolutely fine for me. People want to get these degrees so that they can make millions of dollars, but then you end up selling your soul and being empty. (Middle-class white woman)

Trevor, a kinesiology student at UH, was also asked to directly compare the importance of meaningfulness of a career and "good money." Trevor explained that a high salary and the ability to buy "expensive things" was not as important to him as liking his work.

TREVOR: I wanted to do something meaningful, something that I would enjoy, but I also wanted to make good money.

EAC: Which of those is more important than the other, do you think?

TREVOR: Hm. Something that I'd enjoy.

EAC: Why is that important?

TREVOR: Because I'm going to be doing it for a long time. I don't—I don't like— well, I like expensive things, but it's just not that important to me. I just want to be comfortable. I don't want to have a bunch of luxurious possessions, I just want to be able to take good care of myself and part of that is doing what you like to do. I've had a lot of jobs in the past, and the ones that I enjoyed really stand out. I know it's important to enjoy what you do because I've had jobs that I really hated and I've had jobs that I've really loved. (Middle-class white man)

AJ, a civil engineering student at MSU used a similar rationale to explain that he would gladly sacrifice a higher annual salary to be satisfied with his career field.

I think it's probably not so good of a reason to choose [a career field] for the money, and, I guess, good reason to choose it, if you're interested in it or it's kind of what you want to do. . . . Because, I mean, overall in your life, money doesn't—the amount of money you make matters little and kind of how happy you are, like satisfaction with your career, is probably more important than you know, a $5,000 or $10,000 difference in careers. (Middle-class white man)

Echoing these interview responses, two-thirds (67%) of the supplemental survey sample of college students agreed that "any [college] major can lead to jobs that pay enough for a comfortable life" (see Appendix B).

Of course, a college degree does not provide a guarantee of financial stability or security, and plenty of college graduates work in precarious jobs, are unemployed or underemployed, or flounder in contract or gig work without benefits.[69] The students most likely to endorse this "economic floor" understanding of a college degree were those from working- and middle-class families; students from more privileged families tended to have a more informed grasp of the white-collar labor market. I discuss these class differences in access to cultural capital in Chapter 3.

There were certainly career aspirants in this sample who prioritized status and wealth accumulation and others who believed that only certain career fields would lead to a sustainable salary or steady employment.[70] These interviews showed, however, that such economic and employment considerations, which have dominated theoretical and empirical scholarship on career aspirants' decision-making, are by no means the only, or even the most popular, guiding principles career aspirants use to make career decisions.[71]

TRANSLATING PASSION INTO THE WORKFORCE

Does passion continue to be relevant as these career aspirants leave college? Chapter 3 draws on follow-up interviews with these career aspirants to describe their transition from college to the labor force. It shows that many of the college-educated respondents remain enticed by the idea of passion-seeking after they leave college. Here, it suffices to provide a few examples of what adherence to the passion principle looks like after college. Amber, an MSU chemical engineering graduate, vividly described what having passion for her work means to her.

> I feel really passionate about everything I talk about at work. . . . I think that I feel like I do something good every day. . . . I feel like it was almost a hobby. I enjoyed solving the chemical engineering problems. . . . Today, I actually enjoy talking about my job and the things that we're doing. I'm sure I annoy the crap out of my fiancé when I come home. . . . I mean, it's definitely challenging, but I think that . . . I found something good to want to be passionate about. (Working-class white woman)

Many career aspirants were willing to make big changes to their career paths and potential sacrifices of long-term financial security as they turned their abstract commitments to passion-seeking into action. Aliyah, a dance teacher who was a math major at UH when I first met her, explained five years later how following her passion meant "letting go" of concerns she had about her future financial stability.

> I was always told if you're an artist that you shouldn't major in art because you become a starving artist. . . . So that was something that I had to kind of settle with when I made the decision. . . . I was like, "Now I know I'm a dancer. That's who I am." I'm much more happy about it. . . . Futuristic worries, I would say, about how am I going to make a living, . . . I kind of had to just let go of that. . . . I think if you don't have that fulfillment in what you do, you don't really know the lengths that you can go, especially if you're in your calling and you're doing what you're supposed to be doing. . . . I don't think I could ever go into another job where I'm not happy doing it. It's just pointless. (Middle-class Black woman)

Ultimately, Aliyah said she "got tired of chasing" the promise of financial stability and made the switch from math to dance.

IS THE PASSION PRINCIPLE SIMPLY A
JUSTIFICATORY NARRATIVE?

If the passion principle is such a valued cultural schema for career decision-making, might respondents who privately prioritized financial or stability considerations have framed their interview responses in passion-based terms to conform to social expectations or to avoid embarrassment? If the passion principle is widely understood as a morally legitimate way to explain one's decision-making, perhaps interviewees felt compelled to downplay the extent to which they did, in fact, prioritize financial or employment security in their decision-making. Although this certainly could have played a role in students' interview answers, I used two tactics to minimize this possibility. First, I used as neutral language as possible when asking about their career decision-making. Instead of asking, "How did you *choose* your major?," for example, I asked, "How did you *end up in* your major?" Second, I explicitly asked respondents about financial and employment security concerns if they had not raised these issues on their own. (This is evident in several of the interview excerpts above.) In other words, I opened the door for them to express alternatives or counterpriorities to passion. But few walked through that door. In all, half of the college students I interviewed did not mention financial considerations or job security at all when discussing their career decision-making priorities before I prompted them.[72] Further, the high level of adherence to the passion principle among the college-educated respondents in the anonymous online student survey (Appendix B) and the PPS data suggests that the strong prevalence of the passion principle among interviewees is not solely driven by their desire to give the "right" answer to my questions in face-to-face interviews.

But this raises another question: Even if career aspirants were honest about their prioritization of passion-seeking in their current and future career plans, could their casting of their decisions in passion-based terms be a justificatory narrative for less culturally exalted decision-making criteria? Although there are likely some career aspirants who used the passion principle to justify to others and to themselves the legitimacy of pathways they may have originally chosen for other reasons (e.g., because of economic concerns or academic underperformance), I do not suspect that this is driving the broader patterns I documented above. First, there are numerous examples throughout this book of career aspirants making passion-based decisions about their college majors and careers while turning away from paths that would have provided them with higher salaries and more secure employment. Recall Brianna, for example, who originally sought to be an accountant "just so I could make more money" but then decided, "I can't see myself doing this for the rest of my life," and pursued broadcast journalism instead. In such instances, career aspirants knowingly sacrificed financial stability to prioritize passion.

Second, even if career aspirants had originally changed course for non-passion-related reasons but came to see their current path as their passion "all along" (e.g., they didn't have the grades to get into medical school and decided they were actually passionate about nursing instead), that would still speak to the allure of the passion principle as a way to interpret their lived experiences. Whether the content of one's passion is derived in part from opportunities lost or not encouraged in the first place is less consequential to the argument here as long as respondents now understand their new field as their passion and act in ways that privilege that passion. Although I cannot fully rule out the possible effects of social desirability and justificatory framing on the patterns in these interviews, if respondents see passion as such a socially desirable frame that they would be motivated to explain their decision-making to a stranger through it, that would suggest that the passion principle may be even more ubiquitous than I argue it is.

DO COLLEGE-EDUCATED WORKERS PRIORITIZE PASSION?

The PPS results discussed above suggest that college-educated workers, like the college students I interviewed, prioritized passion-related considerations in their abstract cultural conceptualizations of good career choices. But what about when it comes to making career decisions in their own lives?

I examined a set of measures in the PPS data that asked college-educated workers how important a variety of factors would be if they personally were

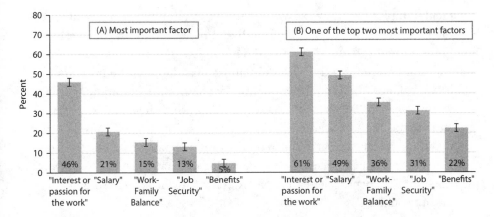

Figure 1.6 Proportion of college-educated workers who ranked each of five considerations as (a) the most important factor and (b) among the top two most important factors in deciding whether they would take a new job in the future (PPS data).

deciding to take a new job. Survey respondents were asked to rank the importance of five factors—salary, job security, benefits, work-life balance, and passion for the work—from most to least important in their decision to take a new job. (See Figure 1.6.)[73] I find that nearly half (46%) of these college-educated workers ranked passion for the work as their number one priority in a new job, compared to just 21% and 13% who ranked salary and job security, respectively, as their top priority.[74] As the second set of bars in Figure 1.6 illustrates, 61% of respondents ranked passion as one of their top two priorities in a new job, compared to 49% who listed salary and 36% who listed work-life balance in their top two priorities. While this measure taps respondents' speculative assessment of what they *would* prioritize when taking a new job, the results are telling because they ask workers about their *own* career paths as opposed to the more abstract questions about what they value in career decision-making generally.

What about workers who have actually made career shifts? What drove those shifts? Half (50.2%) of the college-educated respondents in the PPS data reported changing career paths at some point in their work lives. An open-ended follow-up question asked these respondents why they switched careers.[75] Twenty-one percent left their original careers involuntarily after being laid off, after their industry closed, or as the result of physical or mental impairment. For example: "I was in warehouse management, but the business went under"; "Medical-based retirement from engineering; [I] chose to do physical labor that did not require the mental abilities that had diminished." Another 16% explained that they switched careers to better balance work and life demands. For example: "to spend more time w/ my family"; "Parent took ill, and I needed a job with more flexible time and responsibilities to care for her." Just over one-fourth (26.5%) explained that they changed career paths to pursue greater financial stability or economic opportunity: "Needed a higher paying job that was more steady for the future"; "My previous career path did not provide enough stability for me or my family."

In contrast, 42% reported that they left their prior career paths in order to pursue more meaningful or fulfilling work: "My previous job wasn't meaningful, and I wanted to find a job I enjoy"; "Saw an opening to become a Park Ranger, my dream career, so I took it." In other words, college-educated workers who voluntarily changed career paths were just as likely to do so to pursue more meaningful work as they were to pursue higher salaries, greater economic stability, or work-family balance. Although these are retrospective accounts of people's actions that are subject to their current meaning-making desires, many of these college-educated workers reported uprooting already established career paths in search of more fulfilling work.

The PPS data are beneficial in that they include measures that ask about the passion principle directly. However, they are not strictly representative of the US workforce overall. I thus turn to the nationally representative National Survey of the Changing Workforce data to examine the relative salience of passion-related and economic concerns among college-educated and non-college-educated workers across the labor force.

The NSCW asked a sample of US workers the importance of several factors in whether they would "decide to take a new job in the future." The NSCW results corroborate the findings among the college-educated workers in the PPS: in both surveys, college-educated workers on average rated "meaningful work" more highly than "job stability" and being "well paid" in their considerations of whether they would take a new job.[76] College-educated NSCW respondents also rated meaningful work more highly than "work-life balance." See the leftmost cluster of bars in Figure 1.7.

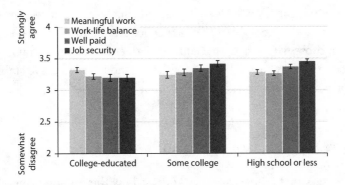

Figure 1.7 Predicted means by education level of the importance of four factors on whether US workers would consider taking a new job (NSCW data, N = 2,286).

Importantly, the NSCW data show variation on these items by level of education. Workers with a high school degree or less (the rightmost cluster of bars in Figure 1.7) rated salary and job security as more important on average than they rated meaningful work in whether they would take a new job. Among those with some college (the middle cluster of bars), job security was also significantly more important on average than meaningful work. This is likely a reflection of the structural difficulties of securing stable work with a livable wage for workers without a college degree.[77] Weak social provisions like employer-contingent health insurance and declining collective bargaining opportunities mean that workers in the United States without a college degree are at greater risk of falling below the poverty line, even when they work full-time.[78] As such, non-college-educated workers start off at a structural disadvantage in being able to access jobs with a decent wage and reasonable employment security in the first place.

Respondents without a college degree still see work meaningfulness as important, however. The average for the importance of meaningful work among those with some college or no college lies between "somewhat important" and "very important" and is statistically indistinguishable from the level of importance college-educated workers give to meaningful work.[79] While job security and salary are rated significantly higher among those without a college degree than among those with a degree, there is no significant variation in the importance to workers of having meaningful work by education level.[80] Overall, then, having meaningful work is highly valued across the labor force—among college students, college graduates, and even those with less than a college degree. But the importance of job security and salary varies inversely with the amount of access to stable and well-paying jobs that workers' education level provides.

PASSION OF/FOR THE PRIVILEGED?

The chapters that follow explicitly address how the passion principle—as a guiding principle and as a prescriptive narrative—help perpetuate structural and cultural processes of inequality. In the rest of this chapter, I consider how the ubiquity of the cultural valuation of passion-seeking itself might perpetuate socioeconomic differences among career aspirants.

Among the college students I interviewed, adherents to the passion principle generally devalued their peers who prioritized employment opportunities and salary in career decision-making. Beyond the assessment that "money can't buy happiness," respondents often saw selecting career paths on the basis of economic concerns as "shallow," "greedy," or "selfish." A Stanford human biology student explained that ignoring passion for the sake of security is akin to "betraying ourselves."

> I just think that society would be a lot happier if people were just doing what they really want to do. I think that, you know, every time we lie to ourselves and say, "I'm going to do this because this is good for me or because it will get me a good job later on," you know, we're betraying ourselves, and we're just, like, adding to the sad factor everywhere. (Middle-class white woman)

Accordingly, respondents were often dismissive of classmates from working-class backgrounds who prioritized economic mobility. A Stanford economics major explained:

> If [students] come from . . . a very poor background, then maybe there is this hunger . . . to go for majors that will yield the big bucks. . . . But in the process you're kind of exhausting yourself to death. What's the whole point? School is supposed to be enjoyable. (Middle-class Black man)

A UH history major echoed this disapproval.

I think society is so tied into finances and they miss out on, like, the important things. Like, do you really need to make more than $100,000 to be happy? Like, honestly? I don't think so. But people will [choose lucrative fields] just because they want that kind of money and they want this amazing lifestyle that they didn't have before, I guess. I mean, I'm just saying this because I know people like that right now. So I don't think it's good because . . . they just do it for money . . . it's just not gonna make them happy in the end. (Upper-class Latinx woman)

In the face of this devaluation, working-class students with the explicit goal to use their degrees to advance their socioeconomic standing sometimes felt caught between their mobility projects and the dominant expectations to pursue their passion. A UH student discussed earlier, for example, struggled to decide between majoring in accounting or political science. He originally chose accounting because he thought it would provide financial security. But he felt pressured by his classmates and professors, and by his own adherence to the passion principle, to switch to political science—his passion—even though he wasn't sure how he would find employment with a political science degree. Similarly, a working-class MSU student explained that she entered college interested in making money, but as a result of engagement with her peers, monetary concerns were now "at the bottom" of her list of priorities.

I've only been in college six weeks, but already I'm, like, . . . my financial expectations for the future have dropped so much. . . . When I went [to college] I was, like, I'm going to make tons of money, but now I'm, like, it doesn't matter anymore. . . . I don't need a ton of money to be happy. (Working-class white woman)

Encouraging first-generation and working-class students to deprioritize economic mobility and job security in lieu of passion-seeking may divert their mobility projects and help perpetuate patterns of disadvantage among career aspirants after they leave college.

Although preference for passion-based careers was generally similar by socioeconomic background among the career aspirants I interviewed, working-class students who prioritized passion anticipated financial difficulties in the labor force that their more privileged peers did not. Working-class students were more likely than their classmates to expect to encounter obstacles to following their passion. Some students who wanted to continue with their passion after graduation but lacked adequate resources to do so anticipated disappointment about what their future might hold. For example, a first-generation UH sociology student expected that she would need to find a job that would help her pay off student loans before continuing a career in social work, her passion.

> The thing that's always running through me is student loans. . . . It sucks because, you know, I just want to be happy in a job, but it's like I know I have all these things that I have to pay and pay back and, you know, it's kind of scary. So hopefully I just get a good job that I like for a while and I could stick to while . . . I pay off my debt. (Working-class Latinx woman)

Similarly, a Stanford student in psychology explained that he will probably need to put the pursuit of his passion—elementary school teaching—on hold to help support his siblings through college.

> Well, for a year or two I might get some sort of job [because] . . . I have some little brothers who still need some money to get through college so I might have to help out . . . it would be nice to do. . . . teaching abroad or something like that, . . . [but] I guess wherever I can find short-term work. (Working-class white and Latinx man)

Students intended these jobs outside their passion to help them get on their feet financially as temporary detours on their path to meaningful work. Of course, these detours may not be temporary at all. Particularly for working-class students, temporary jobs as administrative assistants or consulting firm temps may default to long-term paths as they find it difficult or untenable to change course. Chapter 3 follows up with career aspirants after they leave college to assess the extent to which such class-based differences indeed emerged.

WHO IS PASSIONATE ABOUT WHAT? PASSION-SEEKING AND OCCUPATIONAL SEGREGATION

As I noted at the beginning of the chapter, the broader self-conceptions on which passion is based are partially construed by one's cultural and structural environments. Thus, when people make career decisions by identifying what seems to match their sense of self, they often select occupational paths that follow well-worn grooves of occupational segregation by gender, race/ethnicity, and class background. This is especially evident in the context of gender. Over the past half century, there have been enormous gains in public approval of women's participation in professional and leadership positions.[81] More than ever, women's parents and partners are encouraging them to pursue their chosen professions with gusto.[82] Yet what women and men tend to find fulfilling and self-expressive is still highly gender differentiated, as the self-conceptions on which that expression is based are partly the outcome of lifelong gender socialization. In previous research, I found that women and men college students with more gender-traditional self-conceptions (e.g., women who see themselves as emotional, men who see themselves as logical) were more likely to end up on more gender-typical (women-dominated and men-dominated) career paths.[83] Passion-seeking, in other words, helps reproduce the gender imbalance of these gender-typed occupations, even when self-expressive passion-seeking *seems* fundamentally gender-neutral.[84]

Other research has shown that young adults' self-expressive interests are shaped in similar ways by racial structures.[85] For example, Maya Beasley's research on African American college students found that many students sought paths that aligned with personal commitments to advancing racial justice.[86] This tended to draw students toward social science and policy-oriented majors and away from STEM fields. Yet the fields students were drawn away from were precisely those with the highest average income and the greatest opportunities for stable employment.

In terms of class segregation, young adults' exposure to different career paths depends in part on what is available in their class milieu: the jobs of their parents, neighbors, relatives, and community members.[87] Developing passion for an occupational field requires exposure to at least some of the knowledge content and characteristic tasks of that field.[88] Yingyi Ma, for example, showed that working-class and first-generation students are less likely to pursue fields like philosophy and art history in part because they have limited exposure to them in their K–12 education and thus have fewer opportunities to develop interest in those arenas.[89] Class inequality in exposure to various cultural and social domains likely perpetuates class differences in what types of occupations people feel "fit" their personal interests and values.[90] While fields of study that demand the most cultural capital (e.g., art history, international relations) are not necessarily the most highly paid, such occupations may feed into processes of cultural distinction that help wealthy students reproduce their class-based standing.[91]

Thus, when career aspirants choose majors or pursue career paths that align with their self-expressive passions, they often follow paths that reflect, and, in turn, reinscribe, gender, racial/ethnic, and class patterns of occupational segregation.[92]

LOOKING AHEAD

This chapter asked how college-going career aspirants conceptualize good work and good career decision-making in the abstract and marshal these conceptualizations in their own career decisions[93] and whether these conceptualizations are echoed within the college-educated workforce generally. I found that the dominant guiding principle that career aspirants used to understand good career decision-making—the passion principle—elevates the expression of individualistic identities, values, and interests over explicitly economic considerations like maximizing employment or salary potential. Through survey data of workers, I found that the passion principle is a popular cultural schema of good career choices in the US workforce broadly, particularly among the college-educated. The popularity of this schema was generally consistent across class, gender, race/ethnicity, and occupation.[94]

The findings in this chapter have several broader theoretical implications. First, the cultural valuation of passion, and the devaluation of the maximization of salary and job security, contradicts economic theories on career decision-making that assert that career aspirants privilege human capital investments that advance their lifetime earning potential or employment security.[95] It also diverges from mobility and status attainment literatures that presume career aspirants typically prioritize financial and status concerns in their career decision-making.[96] Not only did most career aspirants seem to deemphasize such concerns above the economic floor they presumed a college degree would provide, but many questioned the moral legitimacy of such brazenly practical decision-making.

Second, I argue that the popularity of the passion principle contributes to inequality in two important ways. First, the moral devaluation of college students' privileging of money and job security considerations marginalizes and devalues working-class and first-generation students with mobility projects and may nudge students away from the mobility goals they entered college with. In addition, because passion-seeking entails the enrollment of one's self-conceptions in career decision-making, and those self-conceptions are inflected by one's gender, race/ethnicity, class, and other social characteristics, following one's passion often entrenches these patterns of occupational segregation in the aggregate. Yet because passion is conceptualized as inherently idiosyncratic, it does not *seem* classed, gendered, or racialized. As such, the passion principle may cloak enduring patterns of occupational segregation as the benign outcome of individual passion-seeking.

The rest of the book illustrates several other ways that the passion principle, while appearing at first glance to be beneficial at the individual level by offering career aspirants inoculation from the potential self-estrangement of a life in the paid workforce, may serve as a cultural mechanism of inequality reproduction in the aggregate.

2 Why Is the Passion Principle Compelling?

I just think you have to love it and [be] passionate about
what you do [for work] in order to do it for the rest of your
life. . . . I think that's important because like I said, you're
doing it for the rest of your life and you don't wanna be
stuck at a job that you don't like or that you feel, like,
hesitant to go to work every day. . . . When you're passionate
about something, you love going to work, it's not even work
to you.

Alejandra, working-class Latinx woman

Alejandra, a sociology major at the University of Houston, thoughtfully
explained the value she saw in having a job that aligns with her passion.
Like many of her peers, Alejandra was not naive about the complexities of
the labor market and was anxious about her ability to get a job in social
work after graduation. Nevertheless, she underscored the importance of
passion-based considerations in her career decisions.

In this chapter, I explore the reasons career aspirants and college-
educated workers were so enticed by the idea of passion-seeking, even as
they faced a precarious labor market. I begin by situating the passion
principle in a broader cultural and historical context, arguing that economic and social changes starting in the 1970s produced conditions ripe
for the expansion of the passion principle. Then, using interviews with
career aspirants and results from the Passion Principle Survey (PPS),
I illustrate the specific ways that the passion principle resonates with
college-educated career aspirants and workers. Pursuing passion seems to
resolve one of the central tensions of white-collar employment in the

postindustrial capitalist economy: the structural requirements that employees put in long hours and hard work in a competitive professional environment and the cultural expectations to live individualistic, self-expressive lives. Passion principle adherents presumed that passion would motivate the hard work necessary for success in the labor market while also being a source of meaning in what might otherwise be decades of estranging, boring, or unfulfilling paid work.

Among the career aspirants, I find that the passion principle's salience is amplified by the curricular structures of academic institutions and students' peer interactions, as well as by the professional career advisers who serve both students and college-educated clients. Some career aspirants recounted pressures they felt from their families to prioritize economic or employment factors in their decisions, but many pushed back on such pressures as affronts to their individualism.

Finally, this chapter examines the perspectives of those who are skeptical of the passion principle as a career decision-making guide. Such skepticism was relatively rare among career aspirants. It also did not cohere into salient counternarratives beyond calls to prioritize financial considerations. Part of the passion principle's salience, then, is the lack of culturally exalted alternatives to this schema that similarly promise to motivate hard work and protect workers from drudgery-filled work.

I argue that while the passion principle may help individual career aspirants and college-educated workers resolve some of the challenges of modern labor force participation, this approach to decision-making may legitimize demands for overwork among professional employees and exacerbate the exploitation of white-collar workers in the long run.

HISTORICAL FOUNDATIONS OF THE PASSION PRINCIPLE

Capitalist labor markets, as a matter of course, generally demand that employees direct their work efforts toward their employers' interests and needs, regardless of what employees themselves find interesting or meaningful. Although this core expectation of paid employment has remained unchanged over the past half century, economic, political, and cultural shifts since the 1970s have collided to transform the structures and expectations of the paid workforce.[1] Jobs have become more precarious over time, and worker power—the ability of workers to negotiate with their employers for better working conditions and pay—has diminished over the past four decades. Factors like technological change, reduced governmental regulation, and declining union strength have radically shifted the relationship between organizations and the workers they employ.[2] Further, the risks of doing business in a global, postindustrial economy have increasingly been shifted from the owners of organizations to their employees. US workers have consequentially experienced a sharp increase in contract work, part-time work without benefits, and other forms of contingent work (e.g., "gig economy" jobs like rideshare services).[3]

At the same time, the welfare state that has protected unemployed, underemployed, and low-wage workers since the New Deal has receded. Neoliberal policies like limited government and the privatization of once-public goods and services have become the norm, and workers are expected to fend for themselves in the unpredictable seas of business boom and bust cycles, outsourcing, and corporate consolidation.[4]

These economic and legislative changes have dramatically altered how organizations hire and manage workers and what workers can hope to get from their employers. Companies' loyalty to their employees has declined since the 1970s and, in turn, so has the expectation that workers will stay in one organization or even one occupation over the course of their careers.[5] Today, even among college-educated workers, employment precarity and uncertainty is more the rule than the exception.[6] The expansion of higher education has meant that a growing proportion of the workforce in postindustrial nations has a college degree, but a college degree does not guarantee access to white-collar jobs.[7] Exacerbating this trend, the economic recoveries after the Great Recession and the COVID-19 pandemic were not evenly distributed; instead, rising incomes for executives and high-level managers further cleaved the top 1% of earners from everyone else.[8] Workers across the employment spectrum are acutely aware of this precarity and have struggled to manage it in their day-to-day lives.[9]

Although the topography of the employment landscape has shifted under the feet of workers over the past half century, cultural norms defining what it means to be an "ideal worker" have not.[10] Workers in all sectors of the labor force are expected to enact devotion to their employers and jobs, whether on the clock or not and whether they have caregiving responsibilities or not. Many blue-collar and service workers must be on call, ready to pick up a shift with only a few days' (or a few hours') notice.[11] White-collar workers are routinely expected to overwork—to work more than what is legally considered a full-time workweek and to be available on evenings and weekends via email or text message.[12] This "one-way honor system" demands hard work from employees as a moral obligation, while the cultural norms of the market economy, and even among workers themselves, rarely expect employers to reciprocate such dedication.[13] Professional and nonprofessional work has thus come to require longer hours and offer less security but has become no less rife with demands on workers to give their all to their paid work, regardless of burnout, over-work, uncertainty, or a lack of livable wage.[14]

These structural realities create a complex decision-making landscape for today's career aspirants and workers. As noted in the previous chapter, most social science research has assumed that earnings potential and employability are the central—if not sole—priorities in career decision-making. Many scholars assume that workers and career aspirants respond in more or less economically rational ways to the employment structures in front of them, seeking opportunities to maximize their salaries and financial security whenever possible.[15]

Yet widely shared cultural schemas may direct people away from such economically rational decision-making as they seek meaningful directions for their lives. People regularly eschew economically rational decisions on the basis of cultural values and moral expectations.[16] What may appear irrational or nonsensical to theorists and scholars may be perfectly sensi-ble to individual decision-makers given the cultural and moral landscapes they inhabit.

One of the most deeply rooted cultural beliefs in the United States, and one particularly relevant to the context of career decision-making, is the "cult of the individual."[17] Over the past century, the "individual" has become the master human identity.[18] Economic growth after World War II expanded the structural capabilities to provide existential security to more people than ever before and shifted the broad cultural focus from life goals of physical and psychological stability (food, shelter, education) toward life goals of sustained individualistic fulfillment.[19] The cultural valuation of self-expression has grown dramatically since the 1950s, and along with it, the expectation of institutionalized opportunities for individuals to have their own bit of space to make autonomous choices about the direction and character of their own lives.[20] As a result, demands for greater self-expressive freedom and personal choice have expanded into virtually all social and life realms.[21] Individualistic self-expression is, for many, what Anthony Giddens called a "reflexive project"—an evolving narrative that one nurtures, refines, and enacts over the course of their life.[22] Many Americans, in turn, take advantage of this freedom to seek out social circumstances and consumption practices that affirm and advance their self-reflexive projects.[23]

One especially relevant dimension of the institutional expansion of self-expressive opportunities is the proliferation of curricular options that accompanied the growth of higher education in the last half of the twentieth century. The massification of postsecondary education gave those outside elite populations access to advanced career training for the first time. As colleges and universities sought to recruit new students, they expanded the number of academic specialties offered and encouraged highly individualized choices among those specialties (instead of structuring them as test-in models popular in other countries).[24]

Paralleling the expansion of higher education, and helping to seed it, was the advancement of women's rights in the educational and work spheres in the last third of the twentieth century. After Title IX and the Equal Rights Act, women flooded into previously male-dominated professions like law, business, medicine, and some sciences.[25] The past forty years have seen increased workforce participation of women and cultural shifts that encourage women's investment and engagement in full-time work.[26] At the same time, birthrates have declined, and women and men are partnering and having children later in life. For many college-educated young adults, college-then-career-then-family is an expected and normatively desirable life event sequence.[27] Unlike generations past, the widespread expectation that women will make career decisions in anticipation of their future childcare responsibilities or that men will choose fields on the basis of opportunities for breadwinning has eroded.[28] Women are still burdened with the lion's share of caregiving responsibilities, even when they work full-time, but young adults with college degrees typically expect and desire that women will have opportunities to reach the same professional heights as men. Career aspirants are now commonly encouraged to prioritize their own career decisions on the basis of their personal preferences, not traditional expectations of gendered professional roles.

Alongside the increased value of self-expressive action and the institutional changes that enable it, the expansion of neoliberal norms of self-sufficiency has led to an increased emphasis on life trajectories driven by personal choice rather than collective or communal priorities.[29] These neoliberal norms have promoted choice-based structures in educational and labor market institutions, and with them the belief that career aspirants are best able to live up to their potential if they are given as much freedom as possible to determine their own life trajectories.[30]

These expanding structural opportunities and cultural desires for individualistic, self-expressive decision-making seem to be in tension with the enduring expectations for dedicated workers in a precarious labor market. How can workers meet both the demand that they be ideal workers and the expectation that they live highly individualized, self-expressive lives? Unlike the goals of employability or wealth maximization, the passion principle may appear to career aspirants as a way of resolving these conflicting expectations. If one finds self-fulfillment in one's occupation, then expectations to live up to ideal worker norms may seem less self-estranging.[31] Some degree of precarity may even feel like a necessary sacrifice for work that advances one's sense of self. As such, pursuing passion may seem quite rational to those who prioritize it: it promotes rolling paid work into the self-reflexive project rather than spending a lifetime doing work tangential or even threatening to one's sense of self. Below, I explain that respondents are drawn to the passion principle for precisely these reasons: most believe that being passionate about their work will promote their success in the labor market by motivating their alignment with ideal worker norms while simultaneously fostering a fulfilling, meaningful life.

HOW NEW IS THE PASSION PRINCIPLE?

The previous chapter demonstrated that the passion principle is popular among college-educated cohorts generally, not just the cohort of students

I interviewed. In fact, the cultural valuation of dedicating oneself to a vocation goes back hundreds of years.[32] The modern iteration of this idea, and its intensity and democratization, likely emerged in the wake of the economic changes and the rise of neoliberal political and economic policies in the 1970s and the acceleration of cultural expectations for self-expression and individualism in the 1980s and 1990s.[33] Although a robust accounting of the historical emergence of the passion principle is outside the scope of this book, the confluence of the cultural, institutional, and economic changes reviewed above likely seeded the rise of this approach to career decision-making. The inability to rely on one's employer for stable work, the expectation for longer hours and dedication, and the occupational individualization and specialization brought about by growth in college enrollment, alongside the expanding cultural and social valuation of free expression and individualism and the existential drive for meaning in a postmodern world, may have created a perfect storm for the popularization of passion-based considerations in career decision-making.

To represent the growth of emphasis on passion-seeking over this period, I used Google Ngrams to track the mentions of phrases referring to passion-seeking printed in books published since 1950. Figure 2.1 presents an Ngram of mentions of the term "follow your passion" in books published between 1950 and 2008.[34] Mentions of this phrase were comparatively rare before 1980; afterward, mentions grew exponentially through the 1980s, 1990s, and early 2000s. In contrast, mentions of economic priorities like "earn more money" remained relatively stable over the same period.

Data from representative samples of Americans in the General Social Survey (GSS) similarly suggest that passion-related considerations have been a popular part of cultural understandings of good work since at least the late 1980s. Although the GSS asked about job-level rather than career field–level considerations and captures only one element of passion, these data provide a useful glimpse into the stability of these beliefs over time. Specifically, the importance that Americans attached to having "interesting work" was consistently strong from 1989 (when the question was first asked) through 2016 (the solid lines in Figure 2.2). There was a slight increase (about 5%) in the average importance of interesting work over this twenty-seven-year period. The importance of interesting work became more similar by education level over this period as well: by 2006, there

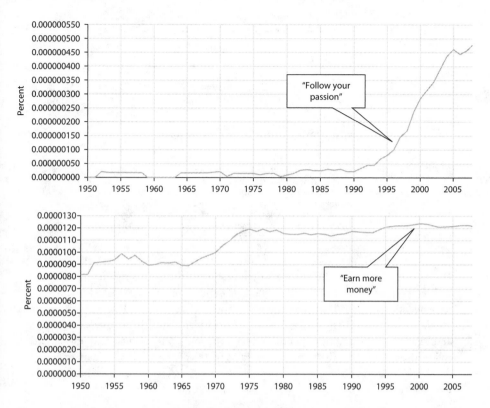

Figure 2.1 Google Ngrams representing the frequency of the phrases "follow your passion" and "earn more money" in books published between 1950 and 2008.

was no longer a statistical difference in the importance of having interesting work between respondents with a college degree and those with less education (the light solid line vs. the dark solid lines in Figure 2.2). During this same period, respondents across education levels rated salary considerations of lower importance on average than they rated having interesting work. Similar to the patterns by education level in the NSCW data discussed in Chapter 1 (see Figure 1.7), the ratings for the importance of salary in 2016 sat just below "somewhat important" for college-educated workers but were significantly higher for those without a college education compared to those with a college degree. While the GSS item on the importance to respondents of "interesting work" captured only part of the passion principle, it suggests that being personally interested in one's

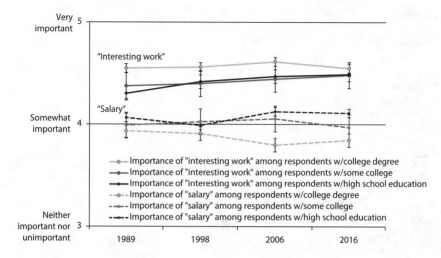

Figure 2.2 Importance to US workers of "interesting work" and "salary" in their jobs, by education level (GSS data 1989, 1998, 2006, and 2016). The GSS asked respondents, "On the following list there are various aspects of jobs. Please circle one number to show how important you personally consider it in a job: 'An interesting job' and 'salary' (1 = very unimportant to 5 = very important)." Educational categories: college degree or higher (light gray lines), some postsecondary education (dark gray lines), and high school education or less (darkest lines). Dots represent weighted means. Error bars represent 95% confidence intervals.

work has been a popular factor in ideas about good career decisions across the college-educated and non-college-educated US workforce for at least the past three decades.[35]

The next section draws on qualitative interview and quantitative PPS data to understand why so many career aspirants and workers— particularly college-educated workers—value passion-related considerations in job-related decisions.

THE ATTRACTION OF PASSION-SEEKING

The interview data suggest two central reasons that career aspirants found the passion principle a compelling cultural schema for career decision-making: (1) they believed that passion motivates the hard work needed to be successful in the labor force; and (2) they believed that having work one loves is a key feature of a good life. The PPS results suggest that these beliefs resonate among college-educated workers as well.

Reason 1: Passion Motivates Hard Work

The first reason that respondents were invested in the passion principle was the connection they made between being passionate about work and being an effective labor market participant. Many respondents assumed that passionate workers would be more motivated than those driven by money, prestige, or promotion. Intellectual, emotional, and/or personal connections to one's occupational field, they felt, will drive the intensive investment of time and energy needed for survival in the modern professional workforce. The students I interviewed expected to work long hours as a matter of course and saw passion as providing the stamina needed to persist. As a UH sociology major said:

> I think interest is always the most important [consideration in choosing a career] because if you want to do something, then you'll be intrinsically motivated to be good at it. . . . If you're not interested in something, then you're not going to want to take the initiative to be good at it. (Middle-class white man)

A business major at MSU noted that enjoying work motivates people to do good work.

> You have to enjoy what you do, and that's—that's what makes you get up in the morning, and that makes you better at your job too if you're doing something you like. You're going to pursue it more rather than if . . . you're doing something boring every single day, it's just going to suck. (Middle-class white man)

Students frequently contrasted the motivation they saw originating in passion to the inability of a desire for a high salary to furnish the same drive. A biology student at UH explained it this way.

> If you don't have any other incentive except for a monetary one, [then] . . . it doesn't give you the passion or the motivation that you really need to succeed at something. You have to really feel it, you have to really want it, and

just wanting money, . . . it can't drive you enough to get you to do your best, to be the best, which is what you need to do if you want to be successful in anything. (Upper-class West Asian woman)

If students did not address the issue of financial stability directly, I asked them whether economic considerations or passion is more important when making career decisions. Reflecting the typical responses of her classmates, a UH student who had not yet decided on her major explained that if someone has passion for their work, the money will follow: "I think it should be more interest than economic stability. If you're interested, then the money will come to you" (upper-class Asian woman).

The college-educated respondents in the PPS generally agreed with this sentiment. When asked whether "money is a better motivator for hard work than personal interest," over half of respondents disagreed. To explore variation in responses to this question, I compared the results of those who strongly adhered to the passion principle (i.e., passion principle believers) and those who were less enticed by it (i.e., passion principle skeptics). As explained in Chapter 1, I measured adherence to the passion principle with a scale capturing respondents' belief in the importance of passion when one is choosing a college major and career field (see Figure 1.1).[36]

The first pair of columns in Figure 2.3 presents the means for passion principle believers and passion principle skeptics for the money-as-motivation question.[37] Holding variation by gender, race/ethnicity, class, education level, and job characteristics constant, passion principle believers were significantly less likely than passion principle skeptics to agree that someone motivated by money would work harder at their job than someone motivated by personal interest.[38]

Is respondents' assessment of the motivating power of passion accurate? To a certain extent, it is. As Chapter 5 shows, employees who are passionate about their work are indeed more likely to report that they put more effort into that work than is required. This is consistent with social psychological literature on motivation that shows that people are more invested in tasks when they are motivated intrinsically by their own interests than when they are motivated extrinsically by pay or status.[39] However, as I show in Chapter 5, the corollary—that passion-driven hard

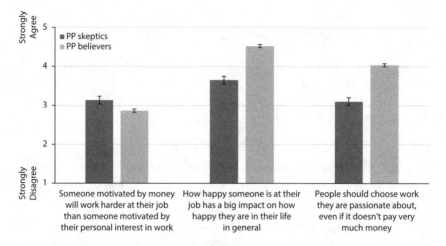

Figure 2.3 College-educated workers' beliefs about career decision-making by passion principle adherence (PPS data).

work leads to financial success—is less certain, as passionate workers are not necessarily better rewarded for their extra effort.

The belief that passion drives hard work seems, for many respondents, to ease one of the major challenges of white-collar work: living up to expectations to be dedicated, ideal workers.[40] Passion principle believers tended to see passion as a *source* of hard work and sustained commitment, as something that flows naturally out of one's personal investment in their career field. Respondents recognized that the professional labor force often demands long hours and loyalty to one's employer, even though organizations rarely reciprocate such dedication.[41] Most saw passion as an effective motivator to sustain such effort.

Reason 2: Passion-Seeking Leads to a Good Life

Adherents to the passion principle found this cultural schema compelling because they saw it not only as key to a good job but also as key to a good *life*. In the interviews, students expressed deep ambivalence about the decades of work awaiting them, fearing they would be stuck in a job that they hate. They saw having passion for work as a way to avoid or at least mitigate this potential for self-estrangement.[42] Brianna, the UH journalism major described in the introduction, explained:

> You don't wanna waste time because you don't wanna be forty years old going to work every day hating what you do. You wanna have a career . . . where you get up every day and you're looking forward to going to work and doing your job. (Upper-class Black woman)

Many students believed that long-term participation in the paid labor force could result in self-estrangement if one was not personally committed to the subject of their work.[43] Providing an especially poignant articulation of what he envisioned as a life lived doing self-estranging work, an MSU mechanical engineering student noted:

> I guess the shortest answer is I get one life on this planet. And so far most of it's been spent in classrooms . . . preparing me for a job. I'm going to go work, . . . to this cubicle or some meeting or boardroom or production floor. I'm going to go there for the rest of my life. And then maybe if I've been careful and lucky I'll be able to retire for the last four years with bad hips and bad heart and no hearing before I die. I mean that's life. And if I'm going to play that game I at least want something that isn't too dreadful for the next fifty years. (Working-class white man)

The existential underpinnings of respondents' understanding of the role of work in their lives is striking. They drew a clear line from having a career without passion to unhappiness in life in general. Not only is such work potentially "dreadful" on a day-to-day basis, but it threatens to betray one's very sense of self.

Thus students typically perceived choosing a career for self-expressive reasons as *rational* because it promised them some inoculation from the potential drudgery and self-estrangement of paid work. For example, a music composition major at UH explained that choosing a career path by other considerations risks one's long-term happiness and health.

> [A bad career field is] something that you don't like at all but you think there's a good job for you. You're going to be miserable the rest of your life. You're going to be miserable in college, and you're going to be miserable in your field . . . I can't imagine working sixty, and nowadays it is sixty, hours per week doing something, "Eh" [Scrunches up her face, shrugs one shoul-

der, and frowns.] I hope you have enough alcohol to see you through your life.... Being happy [is the most important factor]: waking up in the day and doing exactly what you want to do. Maybe not exactly, all day long, but I'm not going to spend eight hours miserable and having to rely on gaming or alcohol. You should be happy at your job. We only live on earth so long. Why on earth would you do work you're not happy at? (Middle-class Latinx woman)

Two UH classmates, one in kinesiology and the other in sociology, noted that if everyone has to make money one way or another, it should at least be in a field that that brings them joy.

You've just got to make sure that it's what you want to do because when you graduate, you're out of college, it's the real world and you're going to be doing that for a long time and then if it's not what you want to do you're going to be sad and depressed. So then you're going to have to do it because you've got to make money. (Working-class Black woman)

You should love what you do, or you should find something that you enjoy doing every day because how horrible would it be to live a life where you're working all day in something that you don't like. To me, it just doesn't seem like the way that you would want to live. So being able to enjoy the material of your major, like I enjoy reading about sociological experiments and soci- ologists and what they discover. That's interesting to me. I think it should be interesting to the person. (Upper-class white man)

Because they saw so much at stake in prioritizing fulfilling work, career aspirants were willing to sacrifice pay and financial stability for work that gave opportunities for long-term self-fulfillment—even as they recognized the potential for precarity that passion-seeking could entail.[44]

Importantly, the subject of one's passion did not need to be white-collar work. Respondents did not draw a moral line between career paths that did or did not require a college degree. In his ethnographic research on cultural tastemakers in bartending, butchery, hairstyling, and distilling, for example, Richard Ocejo found that many had college degrees and knowingly abandoned their training in white-collar fields to find fulfill- ment in their work: "For them, getting one of those blue collar tastemaker jobs is a search for meaning in work . . . and for an occupation to anchor their lives and provide them with purpose."[45]

My interviewees, and the tastemakers Ocejo studied, weren't alone in this prioritization. Among the college-educated PPS respondents, the great majority of adherents to the passion principle (86%) agreed "that people should choose work they are passionate about, even if it doesn't pay very much money" (see Figure 2.3). In contrast, only 42% of passion principle skeptics agreed that people should be ready to sacrifice salary for passion-based work.

Although most working-class students were just as invested in pursuing work they found meaningful as their more privileged peers (see Chapter 1), many justified their commitment to passion-seeking as a direct attempt to avoid the draining and unfulfilling labor that characterized their parents' work lives. For example, a UH sociology student explained that watching her parents go to work each week in a South Texas strawberry field underscored for her the importance of pursuing work she loves.

> [My parents] were in their careers out of necessity. . . . They immigrated from Mexico and they worked in the fields. . . . That's the only job they could get. It's not as fulfilling as doing something that you really enjoy. . . . I just realized that if you're not doing something that you are interested in, that you fully enjoy, then your quality of life tends to come down. . . . I think that if I've sacrificed so much to go to school and they've sacrificed so much for me to go to school, I think I owe it not only to me but to them also to love what I do. (Working-class Latinx woman)

Similarly, an MSU math major explained that watching his father endure the boredom of a manual labor factory job instilled in him the importance of finding meaningful work in his own life: "[He] worked at Nabisco for, like, thirty years just working out of an oven. . . . I don't think it was exactly what he wanted out of life" (working-class white man).

In short, most interviewees believed that the work that awaited them in the labor force would occupy a majority of their waking hours for the foreseeable future. For example, a physics student at MSU said, "You go to work from eight to five, Monday through Friday, for a really long time for most people" and most adults "spend at least half [their] life" in paid employment (upper-class white man). To avoid a future of waking up as a "miserable" middle-aged person who hates their work, many career aspirants valued and sought out occupational paths they found meaningful.[46]

This connection between fulfilling work and a good life was made by college-educated workers in the PPS as well. I asked the survey respondents the extent to which they agreed that "how happy someone is at their job has a big impact on how happy they are in life in general." Passion principle believers were much more likely than passion principle skeptics to agree that people's lives are better with jobs they are passionate about (see Figure 2.3).

Does being passionate about one's work actually lead to a better life? On the one hand, research suggests that people who are passionate about their work have better health and wellness outcomes than people who are not and who work the same number of hours in the same type of jobs.[47] In examining the National Survey of the Changing Workforce (NSCW) data, I found similarly that workers who reported that "my work is meaningful to me" had lower self-reported stress, lower likelihood of depressive symptoms, and fewer sleeping problems than their peers.[48] However, these empirical connections between passion-based work and wellness do not address the underlying issue of who is able to get such jobs in the first place or the more existential question of whether working sixty or seventy hours a week in a job one is passionate about is really preferable to, or healthier than, for example, working forty hours in a job that isn't one's passion but supports one's endeavors and interests outside of work. I address these considerations in the conclusion.

WHAT SHOULD JOE DO?

To understand college-educated workers' decision-making logic using a more concrete example, I asked the PPS respondents to assess a case in which a white-collar worker was at a critical career juncture. Respondents read the following vignette about their "friend Joe" and were asked to advise Joe what to do.

> Your friend Joe currently works as an Information Technology (IT) professional. He is skilled at his job and makes good money. Joe doesn't like his IT job—he finds it boring and unfulfilling and dreads going into work most days. Joe's friend is opening a new restaurant in town and has offered Joe a job as the restaurant manager. Joe has always wanted to manage a

restaurant—it seems interesting and exciting to him. The new restaurant manager job would pay about 20% less than Joe's current IT job, and there's no guarantee that the restaurant would succeed past the first year.
Based on this information, what would you advise Joe to do?

- Stay in his current IT job.
- Leave his IT job and become the restaurant manager.

This question asked respondents to adjudicate between two paths—one (staying in IT) that is stable and known but unfulfilling and another (leaving IT for the restaurant management position) that requires sacrifices of stability and salary but offers opportunity for fulfillment.[49] The majority of the college-educated PPS respondents (66%) advised Joe to leave his IT job and take the opportunity to be a restaurant manager. Even the majority (59%) of respondents who had hiring authority in their own jobs advised Joe to leave IT. Consistent with the passion principle schema, the proportion of respondents who would advise Joe to leave IT varied dramatically between passion principle believers and skeptics. Over two-thirds (70.1%) of passion principle believers said they would advise Joe to leave his IT job, compared to only half (48.7%) of passion principle skeptics. There were no differences in the likelihood that respondents would advise Joe to leave his IT job by gender, race/ethnicity, class background, education level, occupation, or other demographic characteristics.[50]

I asked respondents to explain their advice to Joe in an open-ended follow-up question. Table 2.1 summarizes the main themes given by respondents who advised Joe to leave his IT job for the restaurant manager job (left column) and those who advised Joe to stay in his IT job (right column). The quotes in each cell are examples of each theme. As with the career aspirants I interviewed, the connection between following one's passion and a "good life" was central to many people's responses to Joe's situation. Among those who said they would advise Joe to leave his IT job, 71% explained their reasoning in terms of the importance of passion-seeking for Joe's quality of life (left column, Theme 1), for example, "Life is too short to stay working every day of your life in something you don't love doing unless it's an obligation. If he can accept the pay cut, then why not." Also, among those who recommended that Joe follow his passion, 18% explained their affirmative response in terms of the hard work they presumed would accompany the passion driving Joe to be successful as a restaurant manager, for example, "If you like a job you will be better at it" (left column, Theme 2).

Among the respondents who said that Joe should remain in his IT job (34% of the total sample), half justified their response by noting that Joe's move out of IT would be too risky in terms of job security, for example, "Restaurants are likely to fail in the first year" (right column, Theme 1). About a third of those advising Joe to stay in his IT job explained their answer in terms of avoiding the financial hit that Joe would take by leaving the IT job (right column, Theme 2).[51]

Overall, the open-ended survey responses to this concrete example corroborate the more abstract conceptualizations of ideal career decision-making in the interview and survey results above. Most respondents endorsed the idea that Joe should follow his passion, even if it entailed significant financial sacrifice and job insecurity. Their justifications were in line with those expressed by the college student respondents: Joe should pursue his passion because it would lead to a better life and because passion would motivate him to work hard as a restaurant manager. Those who advised Joe to stay in his IT job did so primarily out of concern for his economic stability.[52]

CONTEXTS THAT CHALLENGE OR AMPLIFY THE PASSION PRINCIPLE

Above, I focused on respondents' own cultural logic regarding career decision-making. Yet these career aspirants are embedded in social and institutional contexts—families, schools, communities—that may presume, encourage, or challenge particular cultural models of career-seeking. Some of those contexts may amplify messages about the passion principle's desirability; others may offer alternatives or challenges to this guiding principle. There are hundreds of possible contextual factors that might impact respondents' adherence to the passion principle, from media to religious practices to geographic region, that are outside the scope of this book. I focus on the contextual influences that emerged as most salient in my interview data: family pressures, peer and curricular structures, and career-advising professionals.[53]

Table 2.1 Themes and example responses from respondents for why they would advise Joe to leave his IT job to follow his passion or stay in his IT job

Yes, Joe should leave his IT job *(66% of the sample)*	*No, Joe should stay in his IT job* *(34% of the sample)*
Theme 1: Passion-seeking leads to a good life (71%)	**Theme 1: Job security is important; restaurants are too risky (52%)**
— "You got to be happy with what you do for the rest of your life."	— "IT and restaurant management are two entirely different things. Just like IT, you have to learn how to be a restaurant manager. This is risky for both Joe and his friend. This is a terrible idea."
— "Life is too short to stay working every day of your life in something you don't love doing unless it's an obligation. If he can accept the pay cut, then why not."	— "I would advise Joe to stay with his current job until he has sufficient financial security to risk jumping into a situation which has no guarantees of success. In this case Joe is relying on his friend's financial success in hopes of finding his own success. Risky business at best."
— "Life is too short and so many hours are spent working that it's a waste to be in a job that you dread. I would tell Joe to pursue his passion."	
— "If Joe dreads going into work most days and finds no enjoyment at all from his current job, he should try something else that would give him a better sense of fulfillment."	— "He has no restaurant experience. The restaurant may not survive. People work jobs they don't like often."
Theme 2: Liking one's work = being good at the work (18%)	**Theme 2: Money is important (33%)**
— "Being unhappy at a job is not good for the company or your health. The restaurant will let Joe know if that is what he really would like to do and gives him a chance to develop new skills and streach [*sic*] himself."	— "Unless he's prepared to take the pay cut and have a little instability in his life, I wouldn't recommend taking the restaurant job."
— "Joe will ultimately be more successful at a job he has a passion for."	— "Better to have a solid, well-paying job than be out on the street with nothing in a year."
— "If he is unhappy where he works, he will not be very productive. If he is interested in a new career path, then go for it!"	— "Not sure if he can financially afford to take a pay cut."

Table 2.1   (continued)

Yes, Joe should leave his IT job (66% of the sample)	No, Joe should stay in his IT job (34% of the sample)
Theme 3: Money isn't a good enough reason to stay (11%)	**Theme 3: Seek other restaurant manager opportunities (15%)**
— "Life is not all about money. What good is it if you are not happy in work."	— "Most restaurants fail. If you are truly interested in becoming a manager at a restaurant I would find an established one to work for to learn the job."
— "Better to do something you love for less than something you hate for more money."	— "Work part-time at the restaurant b4 quitting IT job."
— "Work that makes you happy is more important than money."	— "More responsible to stay in current job. Look for another job while keeping current one."
— "If Joe is not enjoying his current job, then he should pursue his passion, even if it is a pay cut. He can always find lifestyle changes to accommodate the pay cut."	

Family Pressures

Career aspirants' families were an important source of career decision-making advice. Some students' families tolerated or even encouraged passion-seeking. Others strongly advised pursuing career fields that would maximize economic security down the line. In interviews with the parents of college-age young adults, the sociologists Jennifer Silva and Kaisa Snellman found that many parents expressed anxiety about their children's financial futures.[54] The students in my sample described feeling varying degrees of such pressure from their parents. Most middle-class students' parents, like the parents Silva and Snellman interviewed, saw a college degree as a safety net that would prevent their children's downward mobility. Consistent with Margaret Nelson's and Allison Pugh's research on white-collar parents' encouragement of their children to find meaning in their career paths, the middle-class students I interviewed typically noted that their parents encouraged them to follow their interests when choosing a major, as long as they finished their degree.[55] These students' parents "pushed them to engage in self-discovery early,"[56] so they had a robust sense of their interests even before they entered college and selected a major.

Working-class and upper-class students were more likely than middle-class students to report parental pressure to prioritize financial security—but for different reasons. Upper-class students received subtle messages to choose fields that would maintain their class standing and continue their "comfortable" lifestyles. For example, a chemical engineering student at MSU explained that he followed his parents' advice and chose his major in large part because he believed engineering would help him continue to live at a certain economic level: "I feel somewhat guilty about it, but . . . I value my comfort quite a bit. . . . You find a job after six months [and] have economic comfort. Enough of a salary to comfortably live, for me anyway" (upper-middle-class white man).

Isaiah, a UH pharmacy student, explicitly followed his parents' wishes to choose a lucrative field rather than follow his interests.

> My parents are Nigerian, and they both grew up poor. So their only way out of poverty was to make it rich and become something of themselves. . . . I don't necessarily want to be a pharmacist, but . . . I chose pharmacy because it would make my parents happy. . . . I could live a nice life and all that stuff, especially to please my mom. (Upper-class Black man)

Working-class and first-generation students were encouraged more often than their peers to choose fields that would contribute to a "mobility project"—the goal of using one's college degree for upward socioeconomic mobility—by providing a middle-class income and stable employment.[57] For example, an international relations student at Stanford explained the pressure from his working-class immigrant family to find a stable career.

> I guess my background is different from a lot of other people's backgrounds. Like, my mom, . . . she's an immigrant, . . . she knows like, okay, doctors, lawyers. . . . If she hears something outside of that, if she doesn't know it, then she'll be, like, what are you going to do with that? . . . She definitely wants me to do something that's stable and, you know, makes a lot of money. (Working-class Black man)

About half of working-class and first-generation students reported such family pressure to make sure they would not be strained financially once they entered the workforce. The other half explained that their families supported any major they chose as long as they attained a postsecondary degree in the end. As a UH sociology student put it, "They're just happy to see that I'm in college and gonna graduate college—because, you know, that's a big thing" (working-class Latinx woman).

Despite pressure from family to focus on income and stability, the majority of first-generation and working-class students—like their more privileged peers—prioritized finding career paths that would be fulfilling to them (see Figures 1.4 and 1.5). Selena, a human biology student at Stanford, explained that her mother had "very set ideas about what kinds of things make legitimate majors" and wanted her to be a doctor. But she decided to follow her passion into public health instead. She rehearsed what she planned to say when the time came to update her mother about her plans.

> I'll tell her that I still want to be involved in public health. . . . I just don't want to be a doctor. . . . And I'll also tell her, like, it's a really flexible major— I could definitely use it to support myself. It's really respectable, but it's also a lot of fun, and I think I'm really invested in it and that I find myself being passionate about it and it's something I really, really, really want to do. (Working-class Black woman)

Public health work is not typically in the same income bracket or at the same prestige level as being a physician, but Selena planned to reassure her mother that she would be able to provide for herself nonetheless. Selena's justification leaned heavily on the passion principle's validation of her personal interests as a legitimate basis of decision-making.[58]

Although obtaining a college degree itself represents social and economic mobility for many first-generation and working-class students, most were not motivated primarily by maximizing the mobility potential of their degree—even if their parents were more likely than the parents of middle-class students to encourage them to do so. First-generation students in particular were more likely than their more economically privileged peers to have mobility projects, but most (10 of 19) saw a degree in any field as sufficient for such mobility goals.

Why did adherents to the passion principle typically resist parental pressures? Most framed pressures from family members as a problematic encroachment on their individualism: parents, although well meaning, "do not know what is good for you," and acquiescing to family expectations amounted to "living someone else's life." For example, a Stanford student explained that she was going to "follow [her] heart" into creative writing even though her mother wanted her to get a "stable job." Her mother, she said, is "resigned to the fact that I'm probably going to do something that doesn't make a lot of money, and she's going to have to worry about her own [retirement] plan, because I'm probably not going to contribute to it" (middle-class Asian woman). Many rejected family pressures as a legitimate basis for career choice in general and often pushed back on such pressures from their own families.

These classed patterns of parental pressure were echoed in the PPS data. I asked these college-educated workers to reflect on their college major selection and the messages they received from their parents about their field of study. As with the college students, PPS respondents from both upper- and working-class backgrounds were more likely than their peers from middle-class backgrounds to have been encouraged by their families to prioritize their future salaries and employment stability. Specifically, respondents from upper- and upper-middle-class families were more likely than those from less privileged families to report feeling pressure from parents to "choose a career field that would make a lot of money," that would "lead to employment opportunities," or that would "lead to a prestigious career."[59] Similarly, respondents from working-class families were more likely than other respondents to have considered their ability to financially support their parents or other family members in their decision. PPS respondents from working-class backgrounds were also less likely than their peers from wealthier families to have been encouraged by their parents to "pursue [their] interests regardless of the pay and prestige of the field."[60]

I also found differences in family pressures by race/ethnicity and immigration status. Specifically, Asian respondents in the PPS data were more likely than their white peers to report having felt pressure from their parents to choose fields with opportunities for high salaries and prestige and less likely to have felt encouraged to follow their interests when selecting a career path. Asian respondents and those born outside the United States were also more likely than their peers to note that their ability to financially support family members influenced their career decisions.[61] This is consistent with social science and higher education literature suggesting that Asian and immigrant students feel greater pressure than their peers to prioritize financial stability and family assistance in their career choices.[62] Yet, despite these differences in parental pressure, the majority of Asian respondents in the PPS data highly valued passion-seeking, and more than half prioritized passion-seeking over economic considerations in their abstract beliefs about good career decision-making (see Figures 1.2 and 1.3).[63]

However, like the college student interviewees, the pressures to prioritize financial and stability concerns that PPS respondents recalled from their parents had little effect on their own adherence to the passion principle. Specifically, regardless of their race/ethnicity and socioeconomic background (and other demographic measures), college-educated workers in the PPS who reported that their parents encouraged them to prioritize employment opportunities, salary, or prestige were *not* less likely than their peers to endorse the passion principle. In other words, college-educated workers' adherence to the passion principle does not seem to have been thwarted by their parents' emphasis on financial stability when they were students.[64] However, college-educated workers who reported that their parents encouraged them to follow their own interests when choosing a major *were* more likely than their peers to endorse the passion principle as working adults.[65]

Curricular and Peer Influences

The curricular structure and peer interactions that students encountered in college were also salient in students' embrace of the passion principle. First, in general, the curricular structures at UH, MSU, and Stanford helped facilitate students' passion-seeking. All three institutions allowed students to explore academic subjects for two years or more before declaring a major. Each school offered over fifty different majors, and all had formal programs to help students craft their own path of study if their personal interests were not precisely matched by established programs. These schools are not alone. Academic institutions have been expanding the number of majors, minors, and certificates available to students, allowing them even more flexibility to tailor their training to their interests and priorities.[66]

Further, the schools' admissions processes likely selected for students who were passion-oriented. Like many US colleges, the essay portion of the admissions applications to these schools asked students to paint a picture of their sense of self and future plans.[67] This requirement may have privileged students who most convincingly articulated their passion and the way the college could facilitate their pursuit of that passion.

In addition, students' day-to-day interactions with one another often reinforced the value of passion-seeking. As students recounted them, their conversations with friends and roommates about their future careers were often recitations of the passion principle: classmates prodded one another about their interests and values and brainstormed together about what career paths might be best suited for a friend's unique constellation of preferences and self-understandings. A Stanford student who had not yet chosen a major contrasted the career-related conversations she had with her parents to those she had with her classmates.

> So, when I go to my parents I'll be like, "Oh, so I want to do CS," and they're, like, "What can you do with CS?" Talking with my friends, I'll be, like, "Oh, this is fun." And they'll be, like, "Okay, go for it." . . . [My parents] want to make sure that in the future they won't have to worry about me, about a stable job. Whereas, my friends are more, like, "Well, make sure it's something you do like so you're not miserable for the rest of your life." (Middle-class West Asian woman)

Similarly, a senior who served as a residence hall adviser talked about mentoring first-year students about their majors: "I've talked to a couple freshmen, and I think for the most part they are all choosing things that they're really interested in and things that they love. . . . It's exciting to hear how passionate they are about what they intend to study" (middle-class multiracial woman). Passion was frequently a taken-for-granted touch point in the interactional contexts of students' classrooms and friend groups.

At the same time, some Stanford students described prestige expectations that were in tension with the passion principle. Unlike MSU and UH respondents, a few Stanford students noted the pressure they felt to get "big, flashy jobs . . . like founder of a startup or working on Wall Street" to live up to the "Stanford name." Scholars studying Ivy League students interested in business and law recorded similar prestige expectations.[68] Expectations of prestigious jobs reflect the elite firms (e.g., McKinsey, Google) that regularly recruit on the Stanford campus. For example, a Stanford design student explained that she wanted "something where I feel like I'm . . . revolutionizing something. . . . I want to feel important, . . . to be recognized for what I do eventually" (middle-class white and Asian woman). At elite institutions like Stanford, elite professional service (EPS) firms routinely woo students into their entry-level positions through lavish events and intensive recruiting fairs. At Harvard, for instance, 31% of graduating seniors followed the siren song and took jobs at EPS firms.[69] However, sociologist Lauren Rivera found that most students who took these jobs did not envision them as their career end goal. Instead, they saw them as "golden doorstops" for their future career paths. Rivera explained that career aspirants "who did not yet know their passion or how to attain their career goals saw employment in EPS firms as a way to delay decision-making" or simply to help pay off student loans before pursuing less lucrative positions more in line with their passion.[70] EPS firms were widely seen as "finishing schools" for elite graduates, not long-term career destinations.

The Stanford students I interviewed with aspirations outside of business and law were less affected by prestige expectations and the lure of EPS firms. A biology student, for example, said, "I don't feel it as directly as some of my friends who are interested in business . . . because I'm looking more into something that's health related that doesn't really lend itself quite as much to that" (upper-class white woman). Both the pressures and the opportunities for prestigious work in high-flying firms are particular to elite institutions like Stanford. There was little comparable pressure among MSU or UH students, nor did MSU or UH students have access to the same golden doorstop opportunities that accompanied Stanford students' institutional privileges and pedigree.

As I showed in the previous chapter, despite institutional differences, the prevalence of the passion principle was largely consistent across students in these schools.[71] Students at Stanford were just as likely as those at MSU and UH to articulate passion as a priority in their career decisions, suggesting that variations in institutional context, while important, may be overshadowed by the dominance of the passion principle as a frame of career decision-making across the schools.[72]

Career Counselors and Coaches

Most colleges have dedicated career counseling staff who advise students about selecting their majors and planning their career paths after college. All three schools in my study had well-funded career counseling centers to help students "define their professional career path and pursue their interests and aspirations" (MSU Career Counseling Center website). The career counseling offices at these institutions varied in terms of the resources they offered to connect students directly to employment opportunities after college. Stanford had more extensive career coaching and a denser network of connections to alumni and prestigious potential employers than the other two schools. The centrality of passion in career advising also varied somewhat by institution. According to UH's career counseling center website, the center focused on the mechanics of applying for jobs but still offered a number of programs to "pinpoint [student's] vocational interests, personality preferences, and ideal work environments." Stanford's career counseling center website, on the other hand, offered an explicit institutional articulation of the passion principle centered on the importance of "meaningful work."

> *Welcome to BEAM, Stanford Career Education!*
> *What Is Meaningful Work?*
> The core of our career education model embodies meaningful work. The phrase "meaningful work" means different things to different people. It is work that adds value, significance, and purpose to an individual's life. It is customizable and unique to every individual that aligns with the true interests, values, and skills of that individual. Meaningful work could include:
>
> - Work that brings a positive sense of self
> - Work that is engaging and exciting
> - Work that brings a sense of balance[73]

This perspective was not lost on Stanford students, and several explicitly noted the emphasis on passion at their school. Yet the core goals and messaging of career counseling were generally consistent across the three schools.

What cultural perspectives would students encounter if they sought advice at these career counseling centers? Although only a minority of US college students seek the advice of career counselors, these professionals' perspectives on career decision-making is important both symbolically and practically.[74] Nationally, first-generation and working-class students are more likely than their more privileged peers to seek the advice of career counselors.[75] Thus the narratives promoted by advisers may be especially salient for such students. Beyond these university-based career counseling offices, a rapidly expanding sector of private career coaches caters to clients in college (especially those from wealthy families), as well as clients who are already in the professional workforce.

These career-advising professionals have undergone special certification or earned a degree in this field.[76] Their professional mission is to guide career aspirants and workers to identify their career goals and work systematically toward those goals. How does the passion principle factor into career-advising professionals' perspectives on career decision-making and how they guide their clients?

To explore this question, I conducted interviews with 24 professional career counselors and coaches. Seven were employed at the three institutions where the students I interviewed were enrolled, 7 were connected to other institutions of higher education, and 10 were in private practice in the Houston and Detroit areas and worked with both college students and college-educated clients already in the workforce (see Appendix A). Although they worked with different kinds of clientele and were based in different local labor markets, there were several important themes that emerged in their perspectives and advising approaches.

Like the career aspirants they advised, most of these career-advising professionals emphasized the importance of meaningful, self-expressive work. Vince, a Houston-area career coach who counseled both college students and working professionals, explained the value he sees in his clients pursuing work they are passionate about.

I believe the work you are doing if you are passionate about it will be more fulfilling. If I was doing work, let's say, I signed up to do something where everyone would say it's very clearly making an impact, like building wells in Africa for disadvantaged people, . . . the value of being of service and all of that is there, but is the work itself something I'm passionate about? Probably not, I'm not a builder of things. I think passion is about the full expression and application of your unique person. . . . I believe if you are able to more fully and authentically incorporate or apply a full expression of self through work then its more fulfilling and it represents something you are passionate about. (White man, mid-30s)

This emphasis on passion-seeking was evident in both the standard intake procedures many of the career-advising professionals used with new clients and their personal value orientations to good career decision-making. Most of the professionals I interviewed used some type of assessment tool with new clients, such as the Strong Interest Inventory or Gallup's StrengthsFinder Tool.[77] Although each assessment tool is different, all share the same underlying approach: the client answers a set of multiple choice questions about whether a set of character traits "fit" them and the assessment outputs recommendations for specific task areas (e.g., management, data analysis) or specific occupations that "match" the client's self-conceptions based on algorithms developed from profiles of workers in those occupations. A university career counselor, for example, noted that assessment tools gave her and her client a place to start their conversation.

Not that [an assessment tool] is *the* truth, but it could be *a* truth, and then from there we understand what is *their* truth. So passion and interest is psychometrically sound, and what [the assessment] does is identify, hey, if there are people with the same passion and interest in XYZ jobs, . . . you might want to think about [those jobs]. (Black woman, 40s)

In practice, these assessment tools attempt to quantify respondents' self-expressive interests and tie them to existing occupational paths. Few assessments account for other considerations like risk tolerance, hobbies, student loan debt, relationships, or family priorities. Even if career advisers don't see these assessment tools as the "the truth," starting new client relationships with them places passion-based factors at the center from the very beginning of the advising relationship.

Beyond these intake tools, most career-advising professionals highly valued passion-seeking as a guiding principle in career decisions. Some even encouraged their clients directly to prioritize their passion over financial considerations. For example, Frances, a private career coach in southeast Michigan, explained that she sometimes explicitly asks the college students she counsels to rethink their prioritization of money or salary.

> Follow what you are really passionate about. . . . I had a number of students who grabbed a well-paying job that they knew from the get-go that that wasn't something that they were really into, but they had loans to pay and so on, and they figured the money would make up for everything else. And I would tell them, "Money does not buy happiness." Money is necessary for happiness, no question, but it's not sufficient. If all you have is money . . . you'll just be chasing more and more money, or just be this bottomless pit who thinks that, "Okay, if I have another million, then I will be really happy because I can buy a fifth house on the Riviera," but those are not really happy people. (White woman, mid-50s)

In a follow-up question, I asked her what role students' financial and security concerns should play in those decisions.

EAC: What about money or job security? When do those things supersede passion?

FRANCES: Well, I'm an optimist. I believe that if someone is pursuing their passion, and fully expressing or doing that full expression of their self, . . . then money will be there, as long as you don't have some superficial idea of I need to make X amount of money. . . . A life measured by fulfillment and impact and happiness in that sense rather than amassing wealth. If you look at money from that context, I don't think it's in competition with passion or the pursuit of passion. Sometimes you have to back people out of that mind-set.

In the same vein, Dalia, a UH career counselor, explained her view that the state of the economy and resulting job opportunities should be secondary to "internal factors" when students are making career decisions.

EAC: What do you think are not so good factors to take into account [in students' career decision-making]?

DALIA: I think the economy is not. I think that's always a big factor for people . . . oh, the economy, it's a terrible time. It's like whatever. It's never a good time. But you only need one job, you don't need a hundred jobs. . . . [Also] what your parents tell you that you should do—I think that's terrible. I don't think external factors are as important as internal factors. . . . I know everybody is trying to get into STEM now, . . . okay, but first you have got to figure out if they have some connection to STEM. In what area of STEM would they . . . feel the most fulfilled in. I think it's okay to consider STEM, but it's solely after you consider the internal factors. (White woman, early 30s)

Many career-advising professionals, like the career aspirants discussed above, believed passion-seeking was a useful guiding principle for career decisions because passionate workers would ultimately be better at their jobs. For example, a Houston-area career coach explained:

When you do work that feels meaningful, you can be happier and you're going to be a better employee. Even if you're not getting paid what you want, even if you're not in an environment that you love, if the work is meaningful, to me, that's the crux of it. You can pretty much tolerate a lot of other stuff if what you're doing is meaningful. . . . You will work harder to find a position or to make money if you can do that than you will if you're just doing something because you were told to do it, or you fell into it. (White woman, 40s)

Also, like the career aspirants, the majority of professional career advisers (18 of 24) tied the importance of having work in one's passion directly to notions of a good life. For example, Heather, an MSU career counselor, explicitly stated that money was a bad reason for students to make career decisions. As long as they can "hit the basics" of food and shelter with their wages, in her view, they should not chase a high salary for its own sake.

EAC: And what do you think are some not so great reasons for making a career decision?

HEATHER: Money.

EAC: Money, and why is that?

HEATHER: I'll give the example of somebody who's come out of school, let's say with a biochemical [engineering] degree, and they go to work for a pharmaceutical company. . . . But if you've known all along your passion is somewhere else, but you've jumped into a job where you make a lot of money, you get used to that lifestyle and then you continue making decisions that support the lifestyle. . . . And I'm not negating the fact that you do have to make decisions, you've gotta be able to pay your basic bills, you've gotta be able to eat, you've gotta be able to have a house or some kind of shelter. So, yes, if you talk about, like,

Maslow's theory, we gotta hit the basics here, [chuckles], okay?. . . .
But making career decisions to chase the dollar, unless that is your
top value, that's not always the best decision. I can tell you, being a
career counselor, this is not the way to make a bunch of money.
[*Laughs*] . . . But I love what I do. . . . When you've met your basics,
following the money is not always the best way to make a career decision. (White woman, mid-40s)

A Houston-based career adviser who worked with both college students and professionals explained why encouraging her clients' passion-
seeking was part of her *own* passion for her job.

I can tell you that I am very passionate [about career advising]. But I hon-
estly think that this is my mission—people should not be unhappy at their
jobs, because a job can be the easiest way of happiness, because it has every
potential. It's an activity which has everything for self-realization and for the
happiness. . . . Well, just imagine that I have enough influence to change so
many people's minds! (White immigrant woman, mid-40s)

The professional career advisers above echoed many of the student narratives presented earlier in this chapter: passion should be prioritized over
money and job security considerations, and passion is a good guiding
principle for career decision-making in part because passion-based investment of effort in one's work will drive success and a sufficient salary for
survival. Implicit in many of their comments was a sense that uncertainty
and work precarity immediately after college is a normal part of the career
launch process. A Stanford-affiliated career counselor explained that the
time immediately after college should be used for investigating work people are personally connected to.

Finding a job is different than going to school. And so what I emphasize is,
and I believe this to be true, is pretty much our twenties, assuming that we
finish college at twenty-one or so, our twenties are about exploring. So you
don't wanna define this as, "I must get this [job] right now, and if I'm not
doing that, there's something wrong with me." No! What you're doing is
you're exploring, this is your exploring time. Take advantage of it. [*Chuckles*]
Because you can't explore forever. And so people will say, "I'm not sure where
I wanna go." Great! Start reaching out . . . [and] sit down with somebody
who does that. (White woman, mid-60s)

I discuss in the next chapter the sorts of safety nets and springboards that often are required to weather the precarity of this exploration.

A handful of the career counselors and coaches I interviewed emphasized alternatives to passion-seeking. Two mentioned that monetary considerations were important alongside fulfillment from work. For example, a career counselor at UH noted that while she used to emphasize passion with the students she advised, she now sees financial stability as a vital part of career decision-making.

> Yeah, I guess early in my career, . . . my goal [with clients] would be finding something where you're excited to wake up every day and to do that job. [Now,] I do think, and this is just, I think it's just from my perspective right now as I'm trying to buy a house with my husband, and I'm realizing that sometimes I think that money is a very important value for that position as well. (White woman, 30s)

A few others encouraged their clients to consider alternative paths to passion-seeking, such as pursuing fulfilling endeavors outside of work. Corrine, a career coach in the Detroit area, explained that she helps her clients interested in the arts find a middle ground between working full-time in their passion and giving up art entirely for a different line of work.

> There are people who . . . like to do something that they're very good at, but nobody will pay. That's the fate of artists. And what I usually tell artists, and I've had artists for clients, is, "You should continue with your art, but you need a day job, because you can't count on your art. Someday, maybe [it will] pay a lot of money, but [until then] . . . They feel like it's a choice. They either do art, whether it's music or sculpture, whatever, or they just take a job where they're condemned to be unhappy. And even in the day job, they can find something that is compatible with them. Very often, . . . if they're in a situation where what they do is appreciated and where they work with people that they like to work with, then they [do well.] (White immigrant woman, mid-50s)

Similarly, in response to a hypothetical scenario about someone whose passion would not support them financially, Shae, a career coach in the Houston area, explained that she encouraged clients to think strategically about the earnings potential of pathways that they were considering, especially if they had a family.

EAC: What about somebody who is really excited about being a chef but is a little bit uncertain and has a family to support and isn't sure that [being a chef] is going to be able to support them financially at the level that they want. How would you advise that person?

SHAE: Well, is there any way that you can pursue the chef career on a part-time basis? . . . Because I don't want you to not do what you enjoy so much, but at the same time, you have to be able to feed your family. Can you do that? Are you willing to do that? One is going to pay the bills, and the other one is passion. If you don't have a family, then you could do both. But, I say, do you have children? Do you have a family? . . . If you have a family, you have to feed your family. You have to face your responsibility. (Black woman, mid-50s)

A career counselor at the University of Michigan similarly encouraged her clients to "set realistic expectations" about what career paths to pursue.

So a lot of people believe that [their career path] must be something that you're passionate about, and I don't necessarily believe that. . . . Work-life balance is important. I think it just really depends on the type of life and the lifestyle that they want to have. Does it help you reach your goals? . . . Does it help you to use whatever your strengths and your skills are? And if it doesn't meet your passion, does it allow for you to make time for your passions outside of work and not just for your family or friends, but say you are really good at drawing and painting. Does it allow for you to make time to do that? Is it stressful? So I guess it's just like, . . . does that career help you to reach whatever goals that you might have career-wise and outside [of work]? (Latinx woman, 20s)

Six of the 24 career-advising professionals offered perspectives that tempered the moral primacy of passion-seeking. They sometimes nudged clients to consider a more holistic set of factors such as financial stability, family responsibilities, and even the level of stress a career path might entail. However, these alternatives to passion-seeking were offered by only a segment of the career counselors and coaches I interviewed. Although this is not a systematic sample of career-advising professionals, the results illustrate ways that career counselors and coaches may reinforce the value of passion-seeking among their clients. Most promoted the importance of seeking self-fulfilling work to their clients, and some even openly encouraged clients to make financial sacrifices or weather employment precarity in pursuit of their passion.

Echoes of this are evident in the PPS data as well. Looking only at college-educated workers under forty years old (as the career counseling profession has changed greatly over the past twenty-five years),[78] I find that college-educated workers who were advised by career counselors in college were more likely to be passion principle believers than workers who had not visited career counselors while in college.[79] Although this does not implicate career counselors as the *origin* of these beliefs, it suggests that college-educated workers who sought these professionals' advice in college were not any more likely than their peers to develop skepticism for passion-based career decision-making.

CRITIQUES OF THE PASSION PRINCIPLE

To better understand the resonance of the passion principle as a cultural schema, it is instructive to consider the perspectives of those who were skeptical about passion as a guide for career decision-making. During interviews with career aspirants, I routinely raised counterpoints about non-passion-related decision-making priorities, including job stability, salary concerns, skill, and work-family balance. In doing so, I offered interview respondents an opening to critique passion-seeking as a guiding principle or to offer alternatives to the prioritization of passion. Even then, few respondents took advantage of that opening.[80] Only eleven of the one hundred students I interviewed offered any sort of implicit critique of passion-seeking, even when asked to directly compare passion-seeking with other priorities. Overt criticism of the passion principle was even rarer among the career aspirants I interviewed.

Critiques of the passion principle were oriented along four broad lines. The first and most common critique was resistance to the idea of prescribing *anything* to another person. These respondents believed that people should be free to make their own decisions about their career priorities— whether passion, salary, or free time. A computer science student at MSU explained his resistance in this way.

If you wanted to have a family and you wanted to settle down and get married, then if you wanted to do those things, then you'd want to choose a career that allows you to do that, i.e., something that has a good—has stability, has enough of an income that will pay. . . . I'm firmly in favor of figuring out what *your* goals are as best as you can, and I don't particularly think any set of goals is terrible. So, like, if your goal is to get really rich, then you should go work at Wall Street or something, or if your goal is to help impoverished people, then you can go work at a not-for-profit organization. (Upper-class white man)

Second, a few respondents argued that passion-seeking was overblown and that career aspirants ought to prioritize financial stability and job availability instead because important benefits like healthcare and material comfort are tied to jobs. A UH sociology student, for example, told me:

I think choosing your major based off the job availability is just as fun as choosing it based on something you want to learn about. It might seem nicer if you're, like, "Oh, you're really doing what you love." It sounds nice and romantic, but people need to work, and so, . . . and there's those jobs can be filled, and those jobs will eventually help me indirectly somehow. . . . So I don't think there's really a bad reason. I think it's all relative because, I mean, maybe your parents are making you do that [career], but I feel like that's just—it's on the same level as choosing something because you really want to learn about it. . . . They're all good reasons. (Working-class West Asian woman)

These critiques resonated with those offered by some of the career counselors who were critical of the passion principle and some of the survey respondents who disagreed that Joe should leave his IT job and take the restaurant manager position. Their main point of contention was that passion-seekers sacrifice too much to follow their passion and may later find themselves in an economically precarious position that would be worse than having a job they didn't like. Here respondents are making evaluative claims that economic insecurity is just as bad, if not worse, for life satisfaction than the grind of work one dislikes.

The third line of critique was a skepticism about the long hours that respondents believed passion-based work might entail, in lieu of time spent with family and friends. Such critiques were uncommon but meaningful: they resisted the idea that work should have such a large footprint in one's life. Three students noted that one's relationships are more important than any job. For example, Tyler, a business major at MSU, explained:

> People who think that a career should be pretty much what defines them, or people who try to find a career that will fill some ideology, . . . that [career choice] methodology is indulgent and harmful, because it doesn't allow for balancing out [work] with other things such as a personal life, family, friends, expendable income, things like that. . . . Life isn't about working. Or it's not all about working. . . . It's about the relationships you have and create. . . . It's, like, even with college—yeah, I graduated, but if I was just focused on graduating the entire four and a half years that I was going, then I wouldn't have enjoyed it as much as I did. . . . Even at school, I just loved spending time with people and making relationships. Those are some of my best friends, and they'll be lifelong friends. (Middle-class white man)

Similarly, his MSU classmate, Joseph, an English major, made a case for why work as the center of one's life may undermine the quality of one's relationships.

> I'm so glad that I have lifelong friends out of college [rather] than a 4.0 [grade point average]. . . . It's kind of like the same way with work. I don't want to work, only work 60, 70—however many hours a week—and then look back even 15, 20 years from now and be, like, "Oh. Wow. I have a wife and I have a kid that's 8 years old and I don't even know who his friends are." Those are the important things to me. (Middle-class white man)

For Joseph and Tyler, guiding principles that encourage overinvestment in work, especially those that lead to work being "taken home with you all the time," competes with workers' ability to maintain lasting, high-quality relationships with their families and friends.

Finally, two students offered a more radical critique that gets at the heart of the passion principle's self-expressive goals: they believed that "work should not be the centerpiece of one's identity." Sara, an accounting major at UH, explained that people should be more than their jobs. She is working to live, not the other way around.

> I know a lot of my peers, I'm sure their [output] at work is way higher 'cause they're gonna clock in those hours, they're gonna stay extra late. By the end of the day, I just have to remind myself it's just a job. I don't live to work, I

work to live. Whenever I'm done, it's okay to just go home. . . . Like, it's gonna seep into other parts of my life. . . . I mean, my negative attitude that could come from that is gonna seep into other aspects of my personal life. I just make sure to stay balanced and well-rounded 'cause it's where it got me, and I just want to continue being that well-rounded person. (Middle-class white and Asian woman)

Sara challenged the idea that one's identity should be wrapped up in their paid employment; her goal was to be a well-rounded person.

There are three notable patterns in these critiques. The first is their striking rarity. A number of careers aspirants believed factors like salary and employment security were more important than passion-seeking in their personal careers, but very few questioned the premise of the passion principle itself. It was especially interesting that for most passion principle adherents, passion-seeking was an all-or-nothing endeavor. There were few suggestions of compromise, like working part-time to make time for hobbies outside work.

Second, these critiques still fit comfortably within hyper-individualistic, neoliberal understandings of labor force participation—that everyone should be free to make their own decisions within the current economic structure and live with the consequences of whatever they prioritize. Even if skeptics disagreed that passion should be the best approach to career decisions, their responses assumed that it is the individual's responsibility alone to navigate the labor market. Few held employers or institutions accountable to support workers by reducing the economic inequalities between career paths, eliminating demands for overwork, or providing family leave and caregiving provisions. In the end, only two individuals raised the possibility that "finding ourselves" in work might be problematic.

Third, no clear or robust counternarrative to passion-seeking emerged among these respondents; there was no culturally viable, equally valued alternative to prioritizing passion. Even those who prioritized salary and employment security in their own paths acknowledged that they were diverging from the presumed norm of passion-seeking (see Chapter 1). Of course, the realities of the labor market provide plenty of counterexamples of how people ultimately prioritize financial security, family responsibilities, and so on, over passion—lessons these career aspirants may learn as they navigate the unequal institutional structures of the workforce. And, as I show in the next chapter, the most fervent criticisms of the passion principle came from people who were failed by its promises. Yet criticism of the passion principle is not value-neutral, and it means fighting against the gale-force winds of the American ideals of individualism, self-expression, and work ethic. The allure of passion-seeking, and the lack of coherent counternarratives, suggests that the passion principle may preclude the "thinkability" of alternatives among college-educated career aspirants for conceptualizing what "good work" might mean.[81]

IMPLICATIONS OF PASSION-SEEKING'S APPEAL

This chapter examines why many career aspirants and college-educated workers found the passion principle compelling and the structural and cultural contexts (family pressures, peer interactions, curricular structures, professional career advisers) that challenged or amplified this schema. There are several important implications of the findings presented here. First, the two primary reasons that passion-seeking was seen as a compelling guide for career decision-making (motivation for hard work and a predicate for a good life) were couched as solutions to problems respondents perceived in lifelong participation in the white-collar labor force and the pressure of living up to ideal worker expectations. Respondents often expressed anxiety about the prospect of spending one's work life stuck in self-estranging jobs. They gave clear-eyed critiques of the demands of overwork and the potential for self-estrangement in the capitalist labor force and tended to recognize, in turn, its risks of precarity. Passion-seeking promises the possibility of avoiding "losing" oneself at work by means of self-expressive investment in the content of that work. Adherents to the passion principle acknowledged that all jobs include some tedious or boring tasks but believed that if they have work that aligns with their passion, they can spend much of their working hours doing what "fits" and "fulfills" them.

The respondents' existential concerns about a lifetime of paid work, like those of Alejandra quoted at the beginning of the chapter, were not unfounded. Demands for long hours and dedication among professional workers have amplified over the past decades, and work takes up a bigger footprint in our lives.[82]

Yet passion-seeking is an individual-level solution to these structural problems of the paid workforce. "Loving your job" may motivate people to invest the hard work and long hours necessary for career success, and finding meaning in work may make some aspects of paid work feel less like drudgery. But such actions leave the overall structure of the white-collar labor force—the very structure that demands long hours from ideal workers and may entail self-estrangement—unchanged. On the contrary, passion-seeking and the cultural valuation of the passion principle may actually help perpetuate the exploitative cultures and structures of white-collar work. The passion principle seems to quell respondents' critiques of the precarity and overwork rampant in the white-collar labor force, casting poor pay, long hours, and job instability as potentially tolerable and even necessary trade-offs for engaging in work that aligns with one's passion. The popularity of the passion principle among career aspirants may help replenish the professional labor force with new cohorts of dedicated workers who are personally invested in their jobs and willing to comply with the overwork expectations that are central to the exploitation of white-collar workers. Rather than foster reflexive distance from the labor force processes of which respondents were so critical, the passion principle may actually anchor aspirant workers more firmly to the labor force and its ideal worker demands.

Ironically, then, the passion principle may serve as the ballast of postindustrial white-collar capitalist work while simultaneously satisfying cultural demands for opportunities for individualistic self-expression. By framing the pursuit of fulfilling work as a highly desirable solution to the problems of labor force participation and by making it individuals' own responsibility to find a self-expressive place in that labor market, the passion principle helps diffuse career aspirants' critiques of the capitalist work structure—critiques that might, under other circumstances, kindle collective demands for shorter work hours, more equitable pay, or better work-life integration.[83] The dominance of the passion principle may also foreclose alternative perspectives on labor force participation, such as prioritizing work that supports self-expressive hobbies, work that allows one to maximize time with family and friends, and/or work that is driven by the needs of one's community rather than one's idiosyncratic interests. In short, attachment to the passion principle is not irrational, given the structural and cultural contexts in which career aspirants and workers are embedded. And yet what seems to be an ideal individual-level solution to the labor force may help prop up those very labor force problems they are anxious to avoid.

3 The Privilege of Passion?

PASSION-SEEKING AND SOCIOECONOMIC INEQUALITY
AMONG CAREER ASPIRANTS

A-a-aye, I'm on vacation
Every single day 'cause I love my occupation
A-a-aye, I'm on vacation
Every single day, every, every single day
If you don't like your life then you should go and change it
. . .
Hard work, it pays off
I'm happy now, it's paying me
I love the life I live and enjoy the ride along the way
"I make a living out of living," yeah, that's what I say
. . .
My lack of the lazy has let me do shit that I love on the daily
Get to do this shit I love upon the daily
Everybody go and live your daydreams up

Dirty Heads, "Vacation"

One October morning, the students in my sociology of work class and I were discussing the early results of my passion principle research. One student raised his hand and said, "Hey, do you know that the Dirty Heads have a song that is about the passion thing you're talking about?" An internet search later, the class and I were laughing and shaking our heads at the music video of "Vacation." It seemed the passion principle had even found its way to the alternative-reggae-ska music scene.

In this chapter, I catch up with the career aspirants after they have left college. Do they "love [their] occupation"? Did their commitment to following self-expressive and fulfilling career paths remain steadfast, or did encountering the realities of the labor market lead them to prioritize more practical factors like employment opportunities or financial stability? What does passion-seeking look like after college? And is the likelihood of landing stable employment in one's passion equitably distributed?

My goal is to uncover whether the passion principle was just an idealistic cultural belief students indulged during college and discarded thereafter or whether it actually helped shape their strategies of action as they negotiated their next career steps. Career aspirants at this stage have many decisions to make about what options to pursue, what opportunities to foreclose, what trade-offs they would be willing to make between secure, fulfilling, and/or high-paying work, and how to balance those considerations with other factors like student loan payments and personal relationships. Here I track respondents' shift from *passion-planning* in college to possible *passion-seeking* after college and the factors that enabled and constrained that shift.

I conducted follow-up interviews with 35 of the original career aspirants three to five years after they left college (see Appendix A for details). These interviews allowed me to explore whether respondents' adherence to the passion principle in college stayed with them or faded as they left campus and how they balanced passion-seeking with other priorities.[1] To my initial surprise, I found that the majority remained committed to prioritizing fulfilling and self-expressive work as they transitioned into the labor market.[2] Nearly three quarters of those I reinterviewed prioritized passion-related considerations when navigating their postcollege paths, and over half (21 of 35, or 60%) had entered jobs or advanced degree programs that they saw as solidly in line with their passion.

Prioritizing passion after graduation often came at a price, however. Passion-seeking frequently meant enduring employment delays and precarity. Only some passion-seekers (13 of 35, or 37%) were able to launch into stable jobs or promising advanced degree programs in their passion. The respondents who were most successful in this were typically those from wealthy or middle-class families. Socioeconomically privileged students had more access to resources that helped them navigate the challenges of passion-seeking: these respondents' parents provided more robust *safety nets* of financial support as they looked for passion-based work, as well as *springboards* in the form of cultural, educational, and social capital that helped them navigate the next stages of their career. As such, the ability to launch into secure jobs or promising advanced degree programs in their passion was neither randomly nor equitably distributed.

The interviews revealed that passion-seeking, especially when it entailed big shifts in career trajectories or sacrifices of job stability or salary, could be especially risky for working-class and first-generation college graduates. Not only were both groups less likely to secure gainful employment or admission to advanced degree programs related to their passion, but their passion-seeking often led to more unstable employment, often while they juggled tens of thousands of dollars in student loan debt. Working-class passion-seekers were just as committed to success in their passion as their more privileged peers, but lacking the safety nets and springboards available to middle- and upper-class career aspirants, their career outcomes often looked qualitatively different.

Wealthier career aspirants who attempted to follow their passion but fell short often still ended up in fairly well paid, stable positions outside their passion. Working-class and first-generation passion-seekers who tried and failed to find work in line with their passion more frequently ended up underemployed or precariously employed. Although springboards and safety nets would be advantageous for career aspirants regardless of what they prioritized in their career decisions, I show that the employment delays, financial sacrifices, and precarity that often accompanied passion-seeking (as opposed to accepting available, stable, and/or well-paying employment that one is qualified for but may not fit one's passion) are particularly impactful for the entrenchment of socioeconomic disadvantage.

I end this chapter by discussing the implications of these results. Passion-seeking was more than just a pipe dream among college students; most career aspirants attempted to launch themselves into fulfilling career paths, even if that meant sacrificing higher salaries or employment stability along the way. However, wealthy and middle-class respondents were more often successful at launching into stable work in their passion, while working-class and first-generation respondents were more likely to end up in jobs that were precarious, distant from their passion, or misaligned with their education level, or all three.

Although the empirical results presented in this chapter focus on socioeconomic differences, they have implications for race and gender inequality as well. Socioeconomic capital (whether educational, social, cultural, or economic) is one source of privilege. But racial and gender structures also provide differential access to stable employment and plum jobs.[3] While my data cannot compellingly speak to such patterns, white cisgender male status may act as its own sort of springboard, amplifying the socioeconomic privilege of wealthy white men career aspirants and making it even more difficult for women and people of color from working-class backgrounds to find footholds in stable jobs aligned with their passion.[4]

Overall, this chapter points to the more nefarious side of the ideal of passion-seeking—the ways it can, in the aggregate, entrench socioeconomic inequalities among those who seek meaningful, self-expressive work. I discuss in the conclusion the broader implications of these findings for educators and policy makers in higher education and beyond.

PASSION PURSUITS AFTER COLLEGE

As Chapter 1 revealed, most students in the first round of interviews prioritized passion in their choice of academic major and had planned to seek paths in line with their passion after graduation. Many presumed that a college degree would provide a floor of economic stability below which they were unlikely to fall, regardless of the degree they pursued. And most prioritized passion-related considerations above maximizing financial earnings or security in both their abstract conceptualizations of good career decision-making and their career planning after college.

This prioritization of meaningful, fulfilling career paths generally persisted even as these respondents graduated and entered the workforce; most of the career aspirants I reinterviewed continued to prioritize passion in their career decision-making once they left college. Nearly two-thirds actively pursued passion-based paths after college.[5] And many succeeded in following career paths in line with their passion: over half were employed in (with varying levels of financial stability) or actively pursuing their passion two to five years after college.

As examples of the most straightforward transitions from passion-planning in college to passion-seeking after college, consider the trajectories of Maria, Devon, Dave, and Claire. Although their interests and circumstances vary, all four highly valued passion as a career decision-making factor when they were students and prioritized passion-seeking after college. Maria was a first-generation college student and a junior in sociology when I first met her at UH. She explained at the time that passion was a central factor in her future career plans.

> I wanted to pursue something that I was very interested in, that I knew that I could do well with academically and then take it out to the workforce. So I knew that I've always enjoyed working with people and learning about people through sociology, that really has inspired me to keep going. (Middle-class Latinx woman)

As a student, Maria described her plans as follows: "I would like to go back and do work for either a nonprofit organization or religious-based nonprofit organization, . . . maybe the Department of Human Services or CPS [Child Protective Services] or something."

As she had hoped to do, Maria earned her master's degree in social work two years after graduating from UH and accepted a job as a social worker at a nonprofit in South Texas. In the follow-up interview, I asked her whether she felt she was following her passion. Maria explained:

> Yeah, I am. . . . It doesn't pay a lot and the benefits or the rewards are often behind closed doors. You don't get a whole lot of recognition, . . . but [when a client is in a] crisis situation and they're telling you, "I've never told anybody this" or "Thank you so much for listening to me," . . . all of those things just really make you feel like you are providing a valuable service. . . . I feel that, yes . . . I am—I am doing something that I'm very passionate about. (Middle-class Latinx woman)

Although her job paid modestly (about $39,000 a year) and didn't offer much formal recognition, Maria was grateful to be doing work she found fulfilling.

Devon was a business major at MSU when I met him; he was similarly interested in following his passion after graduation.

> What's most important to me would probably be just keeping my passion for [my work] and just reminding myself every day why I'm here. . . . Passion is important because when you're doing a job, if it's a job you don't like, then you're not going to do nearly as well of performance because you're kind of just doing it to . . . get it out of the way. (Middle-class Latinx man)

As a sophomore, Devon had planned to start his career in the air force and then work in marketing for an international company. When I caught up with Devon after he graduated, he had indeed taken a job in the air force. Although his job involved more hands-on flight training than he had expected, he was pleased with how his career path was unfolding, and he was keeping on track with his long-term plans to work in marketing in the private sector when his air force service commitment ended.

> My passion is in business, but also I'm also here to serve my country and I really enjoy what I do here in the air force. So even if I do decide to separate [after] my six-year commitment, I wanna go into a business career field after this. . . . My overarching passion is to make a difference—to serve my country and make a difference. So the air force is absolutely accomplishing that. . . . Now, once I roll into a business career, yes, I'll still be making a difference, but by that point I'll really feel like I served my country. . . . In terms of more of a micro passion, I would say, I'd be marketing. So right now, my current career field does not satisfy that micro passion, if you will. So that's why I'm also trying to get started with my online MBA in marketing as I do my current job to keep my mind fresh with that passion that I have for marketing.

Devon describes his "broad" passion as making a difference by serving his country in the air force and his "micro passion" as business marketing, which he was investing in for the future through his enrollment in an online MBA program.

Dave was a geology student when I first met him at Stanford. Like Devon, Dave had expressed his career priorities as an undergraduate as "something I can enjoy and I could see myself wanting to learn more about and not just waking up and being like, 'Oh, I have to go into the office and fix something.'" After graduating, Dave took several temporary geology-related jobs at the Bureau of Indian Affairs and the Department of Energy. He then moved to Colorado to begin a graduate program in geology. Although he was frustrated with the level of funding in his graduate program, he was happy with his decision to enter graduate school because it would allow him to teach at the college level down the line: "I decided that I wanted to teach one day and you need a PhD to do that" (Middle-class Native American and Latinx man).

Finally, Claire, described in the introduction, was a history and anthropology major at UH when I first interviewed her. She explained at that time that passion was the most important consideration in her future career path.

> If you aren't really passionate about it and you're just dreading going to work and you're dreading staying late or anything and you're driven just by money, and then if you get laid off or even if the company goes under, you're left with nothing because you never pursued what you wanted. (Middle-class white woman)

In line with her passion, Claire took a job at a major Houston natural history museum after graduation. Asked why she sought this job, Claire replied:

> I wanted to pursue something that I truly care about and think is very interesting and that I can learn from. I didn't want to pick something just because it's a really popular field that has a lot of jobs. . . . I feel like if I had to pick a job just because it was a job, then it would just be boring to me, and I wouldn't be able to really excel at it because I just wasn't passionate about it.

Even though she was working part-time without benefits and made less than $18,000 a year, Claire was delighted with her museum job. She explained that she's not really concerned about her current salary: "I'm pretty fiscally responsible, so in my mind I'm like, as long as I don't make less than I do now, I know I'll be able to maintain my lifestyle." As shown below, financial assistance from her parents helped make the maintenance of that lifestyle possible.

The paths of Maria, Devon, Dave, and Claire represent an idealized form of passion-planning and passion-seeking after college. They each prioritized passion in their career plans as students and sought out paths aligned with that passion after graduation.

The process of passion-seeking after college could be linear or winding. Some career aspirants identified a passion early in life and followed it through from high school to college to employment. Katelyn, for example, entered MSU intending to be an elementary school teacher. After graduating with an education degree, she began working as a high school teacher in a small town in northern Montana. At our second interview, she reflected on her path this way:

> I feel really happy knowing the way that I exist in the world. I think that I offer things to my students and I help them to feel better and really that's all I could ever ask, to help other people in their life. It's a cool feeling. It's really good to know that I'm making a difference and really happy doin' it. . . . I can still wake up in the morning and feel like good things are gonna happen. (Upper-class white woman)

In contrast to Katelyn's linear path, other respondents went down one path thinking it was their passion but realized in college or shortly thereafter that it wasn't the right fit for them after all.[6] For instance, Rohan, a UH graduate, explained that he originally pursued an engineering degree but realized he wasn't really that interested in engineering. He switched first to a business major and then to construction management.

> I think when we first talked, I think I was an engineering major. . . . I did that for a year or two, and I just didn't really see myself [sitting] a desk drawing all day. . . . I like more of the business aspect of it. So I switched into business, and after I got into business, I felt like—I just didn't enjoy it at all, because I didn't feel like it interests me. . . . I was kind of lost in terms of school until I found construction management, . . . a good mixture of both. It's a lot of business, a little bit of engineering, a little bit of architecture involved. It was very interesting. I looked into it and then, honestly, it was an overnight decision. Like, I dropped all my business classes and signed up for as many construction classes as I could take and started from there. (Upper-class West Asian man)

At the time of our second interview, Rohan had taken a job at a local construction company in Houston doing work that excited and interested him. The content of his passion had shifted, but his prioritization of interesting work remained constant.

Similarly, Theresa, a Stanford graduate, had not been sure about what career she wanted to pursue, so she took a job at a consulting firm in New York City. However, Theresa found the work wasn't "particularly meaningful" to her, and she wanted a change.

> I think one of the biggest drivers was that looking around, I didn't see anybody that I wanted to be like in five to ten years. . . . Another part of it was the work itself. I was not really feeling it, so it wasn't particularly meaningful. (Upper-class Asian woman)

After a yearlong job search and intensive networking, Theresa found a lower-paying job at a start-up in Chicago focused on educational software. She found this new line of work much more fulfilling. Whether these passion-seekers' paths were linear or winding, they made good on their commitment to prioritize finding meaningful work after college.

In contrast to those respondents, several of the career aspirants I reinterviewed (5 of 35) prioritized economic security and job opportunities in their postcollege career decisions. For example, Trevor, a UH graduate who enrolled in a physical therapy (PT) school, explained that PT wasn't really his passion, but it allowed him to take advantage of the GI bill to fund his postgraduate training after his service in the military. Trevor saw PT as a "safe route" to stable employment.

> Unfortunately, no, [PT is not a passion]. Not really. . . . I really admire people who start their own business or, in any other way, follow what their true passion is. I'm attracted to physical therapy, and I respect it. It's not my passion, though, not by any means. . . . Financially, I've always been pretty cautious and conservative. I think that's why I'm choosing maybe a safe route rather than, oh, I want to open a vegan grocery store, or I want to, I don't know, do something that I'm actually passionate about. (Middle-class white man)

A few career aspirants shifted their priorities from passion to financial and employment stability concerns on entering the labor market. For example, Zhang, a Stanford computer science graduate who had originally prioritized passion, ended up seeking out programming jobs with good employment prospects and a good salary to help her attain the financial "lifestyle [she] wants to lead" rather than pursuing a PhD in a topic that interested her.

> You have to be able to see like, how much the industry needs people there and what's the long-term job prospects, because I think, well, money isn't everything, but you definitely have to think about it. To me I guess that that's one critically important thing, how desirable and well paid the field is. Another is obviously I need to be at least willing to learn about it and interested and not just be in it for the money. I need to have some sort of motivation there, personally, or it's really hard to do well. (Middle-class Asian woman)

Even though a good salary had become her central priority, Zhang noted that she at least needed to have some interest in the work for her to consider taking a job.

Two of the 35 respondents explained that family and work-life balance were top priorities for them as they entered the workforce. Sara, an accountant who graduated from UH, explained that she chose accounting because it would allow her the time and resources to pursue "extracurriculars." As an employed accountant, she saw herself as a "champion" of her own work-life balance.

> Even though [accounting] wasn't something that particularly really interested or challenged me coursework-wise, . . . I knew that if I was good at it and I excelled in it, then that would free up a lot of time for me to pursue other extracurriculars and other passions. . . . It's a good fit for my personality type and my other long-term goals. . . . Like I said, I champion my own work-life balance. (Middle-class white and Asian woman)

Sara explained that she routinely communicated to her supervisor and coworkers her desire to limit how much she worked on evenings and weekends to give her time for her hobbies and volunteer work.

Tyler, who graduated from MSU in business finance, had prioritized passion in his career decisions when I met him as a sophomore. However, his priorities started to shift during his final years in college. After graduating, he decided he wanted to focus on "self-growth" and the "relationships in [his] life" rather than dive head-first into a professional career. He traveled around for a year after college and ended up in New Zealand, where he was working odd jobs to cover his living expenses.

Through school, I was still, like, knowing the importance of work-life balance. I don't wanna just be consumed by my work. I wanna really pay attention to the people in my life. . . . I'm so glad that I didn't jump into a nine-to-five, or something more along those lines, because I could have got consumed by it pretty quickly. (Middle-class white man)

Tyler wasn't sure what would come next for him, but he was grateful for the time and energy he now was able to invest in his friends and family.

On the flip side, a few respondents who had prioritized financial security and stability in their career decisions as students came to regret not following their passion. For example, Isaiah, the pre-pharmacy student discussed in Chapter 2 who followed his parents' wishes to choose a well-paid and respected career path as a pharmacist (even though he believed strongly that people should be passionate about their work), was having second thoughts.

Even though pharmacy school has opened doors for me and stuff like that, I still haven't found the "passion." I'll always hear people say, "You gotta be passionate about your job." . . . I never really became passionate about pharmacy. It was just something where, okay, when I graduate, I'll have a stable career. . . . It wasn't until when I actually became accepted into the pharmacy program where, in my head, I had already become in too deep, in a sense. I couldn't just escape. . . . I felt that I couldn't just . . . leave pharmacy school. I'm not tryin' to paint a negative picture about pharmacy, but I always felt I had an entrepreneur spirit. (Upper-class Black man)

Isaiah had his eye out for opportunities to start his own business, but at the time of the interview, he felt locked into pharmacy for the near term.

Overall, the commitment to passion-seeking among the college graduates I interviewed echoed their perspectives as students. Some prioritized salary, stability, or work-life balance, but for many, passion-planning in college became passion-seeking in the labor force.

CHALLENGES OF PASSION-SEEKING

Although pursuing work they believed would be fulfilling, self-expressive, and meaningful was a career decision-making priority for many respondents, doing so often entailed challenges and sacrifices. First, pursuing passion often required *tolerance of precarity*: many graduates who pursued passion-related work endured months or even years of employment instability as they searched for jobs, navigated part-time or underpaid work, or identified and applied for advanced degree programs that fit their passion.

Brianna, the UH journalism graduate, spent two years working as a sales associate at a mobile phone store before she felt prepared to apply to master's programs in journalism: "I did have a deadline [about how long to wait after college before moving on]. It was three months, and it went to six months. Then it went to a year because I knew [broadcast journalism] is what I always wanted to do" (upper-class Black woman). Brianna was eventually admitted to a prestigious journalism program and was delighted to "follow [her] dream." Like Brianna, other respondents worked temporary jobs as baristas, rideshare drivers, or car salespeople as they pursued potential avenues in their preferred career paths.

Second, pursuing passion could entail extensive *delays in full-time employment*—months or years in limbo as career aspirants "figured out" what career paths aligned best with their passion or waited until the right job came along. Jasmine, an upper-middle-class Stanford graduate in human biology, spent the better part of three years "waiting it out" until she identified her next career move.

> It has taken me a while to figure out what that passion is career-wise. . . . I had the mind-set of, "If [a job] is not in what I want to do right now, then I don't wanna do it." So I think after graduation . . . I was like, "Oh, maybe something else will come up, and I don't want to commit to something else that would prevent me from doing something that I really wanna do." One reason why I didn't have a job right after college was that I wasn't sure. I didn't know what exactly it would look like. . . . I was thinking that there would be something that matched more perfectly to what I want to do [that would] come up. (Latinx and white woman)

Jasmine purposefully limited her job searches so as not to settle for jobs that might not be aligned with her passion. After traveling for six months and volunteering at a community health program for two years, she decided that community mental health was her passion; she eventually applied to and enrolled in a master's program in public health.

Similarly, Brianna, the UH journalism graduate, described the months of uncertainty and unemployment she experienced after finishing her master's degree in journalism.

> I started my job applications before I graduated from [journalism school], applying to multiple jobs. I would get a couple of interviews but nothing set in stone. I ended up moving back to Houston just to keep the job hunt going. I didn't get a job until like four months later. . . . Once I moved back home, my full-time job was applying to jobs. I was online just every day sending out my résumé—filling out applications to multiple stations. Four months later, I finally got a job. . . . I thought about maybe being a producer and try to work my way into on-air in front of the camera, but I just knew like, okay, I only have one life to live. I want to do what makes me happy. . . . I just kept on trying. I was just too determined to just give up that easy. (Upper-class Black woman)

Brianna noted that it would have been much easier for her to find a job on the production side of broadcast journalism, but she had her "heart set on" being in front of the camera. Brianna eventually landed a job as a newscaster at a regional TV station in the Midwest. Dave, the geologist mentioned above, similarly rotated through a series of temporary positions before applying to graduate school. Employment delays like Brianna's and Dave's sometimes involved periods of part-time, low-paying employment in the service sector or no employment at all.

Third, pursuing passion sometimes meant *deprioritizing economic advancement* in favor of passion-related paths. Respondents were clear-eyed about the financial sacrifices they were making to follow their passion. Samantha, a Stanford graduate who was an employee at a tech start-up, for example, explained that her creative role was more important to her than a high salary in her future role in the company.

> EAC: How would you rank those two things, [meaningful work] content versus the salary?
>
> SAMANTHA: Probably the content creation part. . . . Salary is important, but I think I have enough—I'm young and I think I have time to grow into more of a high-salary position, and willing to learn right now and grow from the ground up, sort of. I think the role itself, the creative part, is more important. (Middle-class Asian woman)

Maria, the social worker who graduated from UH, echoed this, noting that salary would not be an immediate priority for the next step in her career: "A lot of time social workers don't make a whole lot of money—I know that a lot of my colleagues complain about that. It's not something that I have complained about myself" (middle-class Latinx woman).[7] And Theresa left a consulting firm job for a start-up paying $20,000 a year less to do work she found more meaningful and fulfilling.

Chapter 1 showed that college students who adhered to the passion principle often devalued peers for whom financial concerns and economic mobility were of central importance. Similarly, in the follow-up interviews, many respondents disapproved of former classmates who were enticed by higher salaries over work they found fulfilling. Rohan, the construction manager who graduated from UH, explained his reaction to friends who changed jobs to secure better salaries.

> I know people who would switch jobs for a few thousand [dollars] here and there more than their current paying job, but then when they switch, they're like, "Man, I really hate this. . . . I don't like the kind of work I'm doing or people I'm working with." I think money is one thing, but your happiness and your satisfaction with your career or your life in general is more important. So, yeah, even if you're making less doing something, but you're happy, I don't think you should switch for more money. (Upper-class West Asian man)

Encountering precarity and employment delays is not, of course, exclusive to passion-seekers; career aspirants who seek stable employment or a high salary may also encounter time delays and unemployment as they search for jobs that meet those criteria. However, the postgraduation paths of those who prioritized employment opportunities and/or salary over fulfilling work often looked quite different from the paths outlined above. Career aspirants who prioritized economic security typically took advantage of the career opportunities available to them, even if those opportunities were not aligned with their passion. Lynn, for example, graduated from MSU with an accounting degree and took a job as an accountant at the headquarters of a large box store where she had interned. She wasn't especially excited about the company or the work, but she took the offer without looking for other jobs because, she said, "it's hard to find jobs after graduating" (working-class white woman). Accounting is a far cry from her passion, working with young children: "I helped my mom at her preschool when she had it, and I loved that portion of it, just seeing how all the kids grow and how excited they get when they accomplish something." But Lynn explained that the economic stability of accounting kept her from leaving to pursue teaching: "In the past I've thought of going into teaching, but it would be a tough switch, especially due to I would take a significant pay cut. That is a large factor in that."

Trevor dreamed of opening a vegan grocery store but chose to enroll in physical therapy school instead because it was an opportunity afforded to him by the GI bill. Lynn and Trevor wished their career paths were more fulfilling, but they had seized the financially viable opportunities available to them given their particular circumstances. In contrast, those prioritizing passion sometimes turned down or left financially viable employment opportunities in their attempt to better align their unfolding career paths with their self-expressive interests. Several passion-seekers were willing to make considerable sacrifices to pursue work in their passion. Jasmine avoided applying for jobs that would have taken her off track from her passion. Brianna stuck with applying for newscaster jobs when behind-the-camera work was more plentiful and better paid. Samantha knowingly sacrificed better-paid job opportunities to stay with the content creation work she found meaningful. And Theresa left a better-paying position in an established firm to take a lower-paying job at a software start-up that offered work that was more fulfilling. Passion-seeking thus typically entailed greater financial sacrifices and carried greater risks of precarity than the prioritization of other factors in career decision-making. These career aspirants' passion-seeking goals were not always reflected in what they were able to achieve in the labor market, however. Below I explore the uneven distribution of those risks across career aspirants.

THE INTERSECTION OF PASSION AND STABILITY

Two factors—passion and economic stability—were sometimes in tension in career aspirants' navigation of their postgraduation career paths. These factors can be represented by a two-dimensional axis, as depicted in Figure 3.1. In this figure, the horizontal axis represents the extent to

Name	SES	Gender	Race/ethnicity	Post-college position
Cynthia	Upper	Woman	Black	Project manager at a startup
Lindsey	Upper	Woman	Multiracial	Engineer; project management
Isaiah	Upper	Man	Black	Pharmacy school
Zhang	Middle	Woman	Asian	Programmer
Trevor	Middle	Man	White	PT school
Sara	Middle	Woman	Asian and white	Accountant
Elijah	Working	Man	White	Airline manager (left college)
Lynn	Working	Woman	White	Accountant

High Stability

Name	SES	Gender	Race/ethnicity	Post-college position
Rohan	Upper	Man	West Asian	Construction engineer
Tara	Upper	Woman	Asian	Med school
Theresa	Upper	Woman	Asian	Management tech consultant
Katelyn	Upper	Woman	White	High school teacher
Miles	Upper	Man	White	Air force
Devon	Middle	Man	Latinx & white	Air force
Dave	Middle	Man	Native Amer & Latinx	Geology graduate program
Connor	Middle	Man	White	Medical laboratory technician
Ryker	Middle	Man	White	Air force
Maria	Middle	Woman	Latinx	Social worker
Jasmine	Middle	Woman	Latinx & white	In MS in public health program
Samantha	Middle	Woman	Asian	Educational technology startup
Madison	Working	Woman	White	Chemical engineer

▨ Upper Class SES background
☐ Middle Class SES background
☐ Working Class SES background

No Passion ←　　　　　　　　　　　　　　　　　**→ High Passion**

Name	SES	Gender	Race/ethnicity	Post-college position
Rebecca	Upper	Woman	White	Employed at local nonprofit
Tyler	Middle	Man	White	Unemployed; traveling
Ellen	Middle	Woman	White	Barista
Michael	Middle	Man	Latinx	Warehouse worker
Thomas	Working	Man	White	Brewery worker
Kevin	Working	Man	Latinx and white	Recruiter for tech company (part time)

Name	SES	Gender	Race/ethnicity	Post-college position
Brianna	Upper	Woman	Black	Broadcast journalist
Claire	Middle	Woman	White	Natural history museum worker (part time)
Sam	Middle	Gender non-binary	Black	Film program at community college
Aliyah	Middle	Woman	Black	Dance instructor (left for another university)
Kiara	Working	Woman	Black	Contract employee for video content website
Andrew	Working	Man	White	Gym owner (left college)
Lupita	Working	Woman	Latinx	Social worker (part time)
Santiago	Working	Man	Latinx	MS program, engineering (non-prestigious program)

High Precarity

Figure 3.1 Schematic two-dimensional axis representing workers' degree of passion for their work (horizontal dimension) and the stability or precarity of their labor force position (vertical dimension), and the location of follow-up interviewees on this passion-stability axis.

which one's career position aligns with their passion, from no passion to strongly passionate. The vertical axis represents the economic stability or precarity of one's career position.

Along these axes, normatively ideal career positions—those that align with one's passion and also offer economic stability—are situated in the top right-hand quadrant. Less desirable positions are those that are in one's passion but are precarious (bottom right) or those that are stable but not in one's passion (top left). The least normatively desirable positions are those that are neither stable nor in line with one's passion (the lower left quadrant).

The labor market position of each career aspirant I interviewed can be roughly categorized into one of these four quadrants: those with stable jobs or who are in promising postgraduate degree programs that align with their passion (top right), those in jobs or training programs that align with their passion but are precarious (bottom right), those with stable jobs far from their passion (top left), and those who are in precarious labor market positions with little connection to their passion (bottom left). "Precarious" work is that which is unstable, pays less than a livable wage, and/or is temporary or seasonal, informal or "under the table."[8] Precarious training opportunities are those in low-ranking or for-profit universities or those that offer more limited employment opportunities than higher-ranking programs.[9] While an oversimplification, these axes provide a useful heuristic for understanding divergent career paths among passion-seekers.[10]

Figure 3.1 displays four tables nested within the stability-passion axes. The tables in each quadrant present demographic information (class background, gender, race/ethnicity, postgraduation path) for each respondent.[11] The dark gray rows represent respondents from the most privileged socioeconomic backgrounds; the lighter gray rows, middle-class respondents; and the unshaded rows, respondents from working-class backgrounds.[12] Overall, socioeconomically privileged students more often ended up in jobs in the top right quadrant—the most normatively desirable quadrant—than their less privileged peers. Among wealthy students, 9 of 10 (90%) attempted to follow their passion after graduation, and 5 of those (50%) were able to secure stable employment in their passion. Most of the middle-class respondents in the medium-shaded rows (14 of 16) also tried to pursue their passion, and 7 of the 16 (45%) were able to secure stable employment in their passion. Finally, three-fourths (7 of 9) of the working-class respondents tried to pursue their passion, but only one was able to secure stable employment in their passion. Further, although middle- and upper-class career aspirants in this sample across race/ethnicity were similarly likely to land secure jobs, white career aspirants were more likely to come from middle- and upper-class backgrounds in the first place and therefore to have access to the safety nets and springboards that helped launch them into secure employment in their passion.

Although these interview data suggest classed patterns in who lands in the most and least normatively ideal quadrants, this is a small sample with limited generalizability. I therefore examined the National Survey of the Changing Workforce data to test whether these patterns were evident among the college-educated workforce more broadly. Indeed, in the US labor force overall, college-educated workers from working-class families were significantly less likely than college-educated workers from wealthy families to be employed in stable jobs they were passionate about, net of demographics, education level, occupation, and sector. Specifically, 31% of college-educated workers from upper-class backgrounds were employed in stable jobs in their passion, compared to 25% of those from working-class backgrounds.[13] In contrast, college-educated workers from working-class families were significantly more likely than their peers from upper-class backgrounds to be employed in precarious jobs they were not passionate about (22% vs. 14%). In addition, workers from wealthy families were twice as likely to be in stable jobs aligned with their passion than to be in unstable work outside of their passion (31% vs. 14%).

I also found in the NSCW data that women were more likely than men to be employed in precarious work in their passion. This is consistent with the undervaluation of women-dominated and feminine-typed occupations such as care work and primary education.[14] There were not similar differences by race/ethnicity in the likelihood that college-educated workers would be in precarious non-passion-based work or stable passion-based work. But consistent with broader trends in the United States, this classed story is a racialized one as well: nonwhite college-educated respondents were significantly more likely than whites to be from working-class families.[15] As I note in the conclusion of this chapter, the patterns among passion-seekers have particular implications for racial/ethnic minority college graduates, who are less likely than their white counterparts to have grown up in wealthy families and to have access to springboards and safety nets.

Previous research has carefully documented the ways that socioeconomically privileged, college-educated career aspirants benefit from the economic, social, and cultural resources of their families.[16] Rivera, for example, demonstrated how elite professional service firms often utilize biased hiring procedures, such as recruiting exclusively from elite universities and emphasizing upper-class interactional styles and pastimes (e.g., polo) in interviews.[17] Armstrong and Hamilton found that US universities' fund-raising priorities and unrealized commitments to mobility create divergent "pathways" for women students depending on their economic and social capital. While middle- and upper-class women on the "professional pathway" do well after college, low-income students on the "mobility pathway" often struggle with student loan debt and lack sufficient social capital in their job searches. The affluent "party pathway" students who prioritize the college experience over academic pursuits tend to do just fine on the job market by relying on their financial resources and social networks.[18]

In contrast to these institutional and organizational processes, I focus here on the resources that are especially consequential for passion-seekers as they negotiate the challenges and sacrifices often required of passion-seeking.[19] In the follow-up interviews, I found that socioeconomic privileges helped more advantaged career aspirants navigate the challenges of passion-seeking. Two types of resources were particularly useful for (and more available to) socioeconomically privileged passion-seekers: safety nets and springboards.

SAFETY NETS AND SPRINGBOARDS

Middle- and upper-class respondents were not insulated from the challenges of passion-seeking as they sought paths after graduation. However, they were often better equipped with more robust safety nets and springboards to help them negotiate these challenges and to find promising employment paths that aligned with their passion.

Safety Nets

As they sought paths in their passion after college, many career aspirants relied on a number of financial safety nets provided by their families or institutions. These resources protected passion-seekers from financial uncertainties as they traversed the terrain of unemployment and employment precarity, giving them more freedom to take their time securing a path in their passion or to take more risks to find fulfilling work.

The most beneficial safety net was the direct financial assistance some career aspirants received from their families. Samantha, the upper

-middle-class Stanford graduate, reflected on what it meant to her that her parents were able to pay for her education, recognizing that this safety net gave her freedom to follow "the passion route."

> I went the passion route; history and anthropology aren't exactly the moneymaking majors, clearly, but it's something I was good at and something I felt good about. . . . I could have struggled through science classes, for example. I was pre-med for a very little, brief bit. . . . I recognize more that I had the freedom to do that because I didn't have student loans, [and] . . . my parents are really supportive of whatever I do. I think if I'd been in a different situation where money was more of a concern, yeah, I would definitely have chosen money over passion. (Asian woman)

Claire, the upper-middle-class UH graduate employed at the national history museum, explained that her parents also supported her financially through college, and for six months after she graduated. This helped her get on her feet after graduation and establish herself in a new role without the burden of student debt.

> [My parents] paid for my tuition. They let me live with them for free. . . . I paid for food and got my books, but the rest of it was taken care of. Because my mom and dad told me if I went to school in Texas . . . they had saved enough money to afford [my] in-state tuition. (White woman)

This assistance allowed Claire to maintain a middle-class lifestyle while earning less than $20,000 a year at her museum job.

Beyond big-ticket expenses like tuition and rent, many wealthier respondents also said that their parents assisted them after graduation in less obvious ways, such as keeping them on their health insurance, buying them professional clothes, or paying their mobile phone or medical bills. As Dave explained, "I got a concussion over the summer, and the hospital bills were pretty high. So my parents helped me a little bit with that" (middle-class Native American and Latinx man, Stanford graduate).

Respondents who relied on their parents' financial help after graduation were often uncomfortable with this arrangement but saw it as a necessary trade-off for continuing the pursuit of their passion. Brianna, the broadcast journalist from an upper-class family, explained that financial help from her father was vital for her ability to continue doing work she loves.

I love what I do . . . but it's hard sometimes. I'm twenty-nine and still sometimes have to have help from my dad because this job doesn't pay as much. . . . I'm almost thirty and still not officially cutting that umbilical cord. I don't wanna bug my dad, but it's just I don't have another choice. (Black woman, UH graduate)

Katelyn, the passionate high school teacher and MSU graduate, described how her wealthy parents supported her financially through college. Katelyn took for granted this financial support until she accepted her first teaching job and established financial independence. The new independence was a stark indicator of how much she had depended on that safety net when she was a student.

I chose a career field that I have to budget wisely and I live within my means. . . . I've been living independently supporting myself for two years now. . . . It's funny how all of a sudden everything is different. Three years ago you'd ask me, "How worried about money are you?" [And I would say,] "I'm not, everything's great. My parents have everything paid for me." It wasn't that I wasn't grateful for that, I'm eternally grateful for my parents and realize just how much they gave to me, but it's funny how adulting just changes your mind-set of things. I'm at the store and looking at a candy bar and I'm like, "Oh, I can't pay two dollars for that, no way." (Upper-class white woman)

Like Katelyn, many upper-class and upper-middle-class respondents took their parents' financial support for granted; they believed that if they "got in a real pinch," their families would be able to assist them.

One safety net that was less obviously class-differentiated was moving back in with one's family after college. Many graduates who pursued passion, especially those facing precarity as they searched for jobs or got their foot in the door of work in their passion, lived at home for a while after graduating. This typically saved them rent money as well as some of the cost of food and utilities. Seventeen of the 35 respondents—about half—lived with family after graduation. Some stayed with their parents for a few months as they searched for jobs. Others were still living with their parents when I interviewed them several years after college.[20] Rohan, the construction manager, lived with his parents throughout his time at UH and planned to do so until he gets married.

I still live with my parents. I plan on living with my parents until I get married. I plan on getting married, hopefully, next year. I have a girlfriend. I'm trying to save up as much money now, so when I do get married next year, I can go ahead and buy a house. (Upper-class West Asian man)

Many working-class respondents also lived with their families for a time after graduation. Yet these individuals were more keenly aware than their wealthier peers of the financial burden this placed on their parents. However, drawing on family support was a matter of survival. An MSU engineering graduate suggested just how tenuous her living situation would have been had she not had access to this safety net.

I mean, I didn't have any money when I left Montana State. All of my part-time work went to books and food, and so if I hadn't had family take me in, I don't really know where I would have gone after that. I could see that happening to a lot of kids, and then going [down] some crappy roads. (Working-class white woman)

A third safety net was only recently accessible to the Stanford graduates: jobs in elite professional service (EPS) firms. As at other Ivy League schools, elite banking, management consulting, and law firms aggressively recruit Stanford undergraduates for entry-level positions. MSU and UH students, like the vast majority of four-year college students, were shut out of these positions because they lacked what EPS firms saw as the right educational "pedigree." As I explained in Chapter 2, landing an EPS job was rarely career aspirants' end goal. Rather, EPS jobs were enticing and highly lucrative stepping-stones for launching into career paths in graduates' passions. These "golden doorstops," as Rivera called them, allowed Stanford students who graduated not yet knowing what their passion was or not yet having clear opportunities in that passion to acquire skills, build their networks, pay off student loans, and pad their bank accounts. "Once these employees find their passion," Rivera notes, "they are poised to move into desirable positions in corporations, non-profits and politics. . . . The shared perceptions of EPS jobs as important placeholders and stepping stones made these positions safe options that kept doors open, allowing students' passion to enter."[21] Theresa, introduced above, did just that. She worked for an EPS firm in New York for a few years until she identified a job in educational software that aligned with her passion.

For those who could access them, then, these three safety nets provided passion-seekers the luxury of time to figure out what jobs would best align with their passion, to undertake multiple rounds of job hunting or graduate school applications, or to just "wait it out" until a job that aligned with their passion came along. For example, Jasmine, the Stanford graduate from an upper-middle-class family who eventually applied to a master's program in public health, was secure in the knowledge that her parents would help her financially if she could not find work that aligned with her interests. Over a three-year period, she volunteered and worked part-time jobs while she figured out her next step. She even took a gap year to travel abroad, paid for by her parents.

> I heard a little bit about [gap years] from my aunt. She had asked me, "Did you ever consider taking a gap year?" She's like, "That's something that you do." Defining [my] passion, I think it didn't have to look like something in particular and I didn't have to know what it was quite yet. . . . So after Stanford I didn't have a job; it was another reason why I went back home, was kind of unclear with what I wanted to do with my degree, and just also needed a break, felt pretty worked out. . . . I spent three months in Morocco in an Arabic-language school at the end of 2013. (Upper-middle-class Latinx and white woman)

Jasmine's family's support gave her the time she desired to "take a break," "define [her] passion," and identify postgraduate education options that aligned with that passion.

In contrast, Kevin, her working-class classmate at Stanford, with a cognitive science degree, did not have the luxury of time. He too did not have clear plans after graduation, but he doubted his family would have had the financial resources to support him for more than a few months.

> [After graduating], I figured I'd take some time off and go back home, spend some time with the family. I wasn't really sure how to line up next steps, and I had some chats about getting into some labs here and there but largely hadn't heard back from the lab managers or the professors or anything that I had reached out to. I even offered volunteer-basis stuff, but, unfortunately [it did not happen]. . . . I was able to do this [exploration] without asking [my parents] for any money, which who knows that they had. (Working-class Latinx and white man)

Safety nets were not exclusive to the most financially privileged career aspirants. Some working-class students, like Kevin, did move back home with their parents for a bit to try to secure their next career steps. But these safety nets were more extensive and more available to socioeconomically advantaged career aspirants, who often took them for granted. The privileged passion-seekers enjoyed financial support from their families and the luxury of not having to jump immediately into employment or "settling," enabling them to weather the precarity—sometimes even for years—of searching for career paths that aligned with their interests without worrying too much about whether their early jobs were financially viable. Stanford students had the added luxury of access to golden doorstops in EPS firms. Respondents without these safety nets, as we will see, more often had to abandon their passion for other lines of work or navigate employment precarity while burdened with student loan debt.

Springboards

Not only did the most privileged passion-seekers tend to have access to financial safety nets that helped them weather employment delays and precarity, but they also often had access to springboards, in the form of nonmaterial resources or "capital," that helped them launch over this uncertainty into stable, well-paying jobs in their passion. The sociologist Pierre Bourdieu differentiated several types of nonmaterial capital.[22] I discuss three types that were particularly beneficial to passion-seekers: *cultural capital,* or familiarity with the informal rules of engagement with powerful persons and institutions; *social capital,* or social connections to persons with important institutional knowledge and decision-making power; and *educational capital,* or formal qualifications via certification or degree acquisition that benefited career aspirants' job opportunities. Access to cultural, social, and educational capital was not uniform across middle- and upper-class career aspirants, nor were these types of capital absent among all working-class respondents. Nonetheless, those with privileged socioeconomic status tended to have access to springboards that allowed them to leap beyond potential precarity and secure stable jobs in their passion.

Scholarly attention to social, cultural, and educational capital is not new; indeed, much research has been dedicated to understanding just how social class differentially prepares career aspirants to be successful in the job market.[23] I focus here on the forms of capital that helped more privileged passion-seekers avoid or overcome the particular challenges of passion-seeking.

Beyond the class-based factors I discuss below, race/ethnicity, gender, and immigration status likely also play a role in career aspirants' ability to launch into work that aligns with their passion. Being white and a man and having been born in the United States are also springboards that advantage these career aspirants as they navigate racist, gendered, and nativist academic institutions and labor markets. Although the size of the interview sample I draw on here is ill equipped to examine these nuances, such processes are almost certainly at play in advantaging some career aspirants and disadvantaging others as they attempt to start their careers.

CULTURAL CAPITAL

The first springboard that wealthy and upper-middle-class passion-seekers were more likely than their peers to benefit from was cultural capital. This type of capital often involved tacit knowledge instilled by family members about how to get the most out of college, how to navigate the job search process, how to be comfortable in a professional role, and how to orient oneself most advantageously in the job search or graduate school application process.[24] Tara, a medical school student and UH graduate, explained that her exposure to the medical field through her family solidified her passion at a young age. Tara's parents, older sister, and brother-in-law were all doctors; her family members helped her prepare for the demands of medical school and navigate the application process.

> My parents . . . always encouraged me to pursue [medicine] further. I went to a medical high school in Houston. It's pretty much geared towards carving high school students into the medical field. You do everything, like you start hospital rotations in high school. You do a bunch of medical-related courses. . . . I got guidance both from my dad mostly and from my older sister. Because my older sister did take a similar route, at the time her and my brother-in-law were both in [medical] school in Boston. . . . I listened a lot to them. . . . [They said,] "You have to do well. You have to have research. You have to have your volunteer stuff." (Upper-class Asian woman)

Thanks to her family, Tara learned early how to orient her learning in high school and college to set herself up for the best chance of admission to medical school.

Tara's upper-middle-class UH classmate Claire noted that her parents—both professionals—encouraged her to volunteer at the zoo and the natural history museum when she was in middle school to get her foot in the door.

> Well, my parents were both in a medical field, so I've always had a biology background. . . . We gardened and we went outside, and my mom told me about medical stuff. . . . I've always really loved animals, and when I was a teenager, instead of taking summers off, my mom encouraged me to volunteer at the zoo, volunteer at the museum. I volunteered at both for five years, until I was eighteen. I started when I was thirteen. (White woman)

The connections Claire developed volunteering at the museum as a teenager gave her a competitive edge in the internship selection process later on.

> When we have our interns, they're like, "Oh, the application process was terrible," and I was like, "I'm so sorry." [*Laughs*] I feel bad being like, "I didn't actually apply. I didn't apply for my job." They were just like, "Oh, there's a position open. Do you want it?" I feel like it's been easy for me. . . . I have been really lucky in my ability to get into the career I'm in now. (White woman)

In contrast to these respondents, whose parents often imparted knowledge about the professional labor market through their own experiences in the white-collar workforce, career aspirants without such cultural capital often described tensions with their parents as they searched for jobs. An MSU graduate who was working as an engineer described her mother's lack of understanding of the postcollege job search process.

> Yeah, my mom was really frustrated with me when I didn't have a job [after graduation], which was really tough. I wasn't living at home, I stayed in Louisiana and just kinda lived off of my savings for most of the time and a little bit of unemployment. It was just really difficult for my mom and dad. . . . They didn't really understand the job process, I guess. I mean, if I had known someone, I would have used that cushion, but I didn't . . . it's a lot harder to get your résumé through. I probably should have found a

professional résumé writer or somethin' like that to help get it through the computer [job application] systems. (Working-class white woman)

Lupita, a first-generation UH sociology graduate tried to shield her family from the challenges she had getting a social work job because her mother and sisters were so proud of her and she feared they "wouldn't understand."

> I'm a first-generation college grad, so it was new to my whole family. My whole family didn't know. I didn't want them to know what was going on [with the job search]. They were, like, "Oh, my daughter graduated." It was a big deal. The whole intricacies of finding a job, I didn't want that to be known to them, because my mom was yelling it from mountaintops, you know? (Working-class Latinx woman)

Career aspirants like Tara and Claire, whose families imbued them with cultural capital that helped them navigate their transition from college, were better prepared to weather the precarity of passion-seeking and more easily launched into career paths in their passion than their working-class peers. In these instances, cultural capital fulfilled in the job search process what passion alone could not: familiarity with the postgraduation career launch process and an understanding of how to gain a competitive edge in accessing job opportunities.

SOCIAL CAPITAL

More privileged passion-seekers also benefited from social capital, or social connections to influential persons or institutions in their career paths.[25] Career aspirants from wealthier families were more likely than their working-class peers to have social connections that helped them navigate the job search process and gain experience.

Access to internships through social networks was central to many respondents' competitiveness in the job market.[26] A third of respondents (12 of 35) had internships during college. Five of those 12 internships were unpaid, and all 5 students who had unpaid internships were from upper- or upper-middle-class families.

Many of the more privileged passion-seekers obtained their internships through their family or friend networks. Rebecca, a Stanford graduate working for a nonprofit organization, said, "Pretty much all of my jobs came from knowing other people," and "the internship I originally got, my dad was involved with the organization" (upper-class white woman). Those internships helped her break into the Bay Area nonprofit sector. Similarly, a Stanford student explained that she was able to secure an internship at a large technology company because her mother worked there (upper-class multiracial woman).

In addition, respondents' social networks helped them assess what career options were available to them and explore what jobs might best align with their passion. Jasmine described her upper-middle-class parents' concerted efforts to introduce her to people in their networks who might be useful contacts as she investigated paths aligned with her interests.

> So after graduation, I was at home. . . . It's through a connection with my dad that I got my first job back in the Bay Area. We have some friends at my parents' church who work in public health, and [my parents kept] bringing them up, they'll want to introduce me. . . . [My parents would introduce me to them, saying,] "Oh, this person works in public health." And I'll be like, "Okay, cool." (Latinx and white woman)

In contrast to the social capital connections of his peers, Trevor, a lower-middle-class UH graduate, noted that he did not have any connections to help him acquire the observation hours needed for his PT school applications. Instead, Trevor emailed professors out of the blue based on their websites.

> I went to the College of Human Health and Performance Web page, and I looked at the professors' research interests. I saw one that aligned with mine somewhat, and I harassed him until he allowed me to volunteer in his lab. I ended up getting two letters of recommendation from him, so it paid off, and a small scholarship. (White man)

Beyond these personal connections, institutional socialization at Stanford emphasized the importance of cultivating social connections with alumni. Students were encouraged to strategically use their own network of classmates, as well as the Stanford alumni networks, for job connections and advice.[27] Lindsey, a Stanford graduate from an upper-class family, was an astute observer of this.

Going into Stanford, I was pretty idealistic. I would probably have said, like, "Yes, all you need is passion." And I thought, like, "If I apply to some job online, I have an equal chance as everyone else who's applying," but over time, you realize that people who are getting the jobs are the people who know the recruiters, who get their résumé personally handed to a hiring manager, etc., who may even get jobs. . . . People just get jobs that aren't even posted online because they know a person who can create a job for them. . . . Stanford has a lot of privileged people, and just seeing how they're accomplishing things, I soaked that up. (Multiracial woman)

Neither UH nor MSU graduates had access to robust alumni networks, nor did they encounter such institutionalized encouragement to use alumni connections to get jobs.[28] However, as Kevin's story attested, simply having a Stanford degree didn't automatically confer tangible connections to career opportunities.

EDUCATIONAL CAPITAL

Wealthy and upper-middle-class respondents often also had access to supplemental educational and training opportunities that improved their competitiveness in job applications and graduate school admissions or just gave them time to figure out their next steps without a "hole in their résumé." For example, Jasmine enrolled in a yearlong post-baccalaureate program at Stanford for recent graduates of her department. This program did not offer a formal degree. Rather, it promised to provide her with structured opportunities to access internships and other social connections related to health and healthcare.

There were a fair number of recent grads in the program. . . . A cohort, I think, was like twenty-plus people, and at least half [had] graduated [from Stanford] within the last five years. And so there's a lot of us together thinking about what we wanted to do next. . . . 'Cause there was an internship component, and I ended up having an internship at a school. . . . And so after that program . . . someone else from the program who was older . . . . was working at this start-up, and she was like, "Do you wanna come work for us?" And I was like, "Yeah, I would love to." (Latinx and white woman)

Jasmine's educational program not only provided her with an additional certification but also fostered connections that helped her extend her social network and gain access to employment opportunities.

Graduate certificate programs, which advertise their ability to "help you demonstrate your expertise" and "help you stand out in the crowd," have become increasingly popular over the past decade.[29] For example, a Stanford graduate enrolled in a pre-med program after college to help her shore up her medical school applications, and an MSU graduate enrolled in a lab skills training program that would make him more competitive for the medical technician jobs he was excited about. These programs were especially beneficial to passion-seekers who were interested in advancing their chances of employability in a specific field. Yet, unlike PhD programs, students in graduate certificate programs are not typically eligible for federal financial aid.[30] Most enrollees pay out of pocket, and costs range from $300 to $1,300 per credit hour. Thus these programs are often only viable for socioeconomically privileged passion-seekers.

Although cultural, social, and educational capital were useful for career aspirants regardless of whether they prioritized passion or other factors in their career decisions, springboards were especially beneficial to passion-seekers who did not want to take just any job for which they were qualified but were focused on maximizing the alignment of the content of their work with their interests and sense of self. In summary, passion-seeking was not always a direct path from school to job. It often involved employment delays, job precarity, and deprioritization of financial considerations. Passion-seekers from more privileged socioeconomic backgrounds tended to have more extensive safety nets—in the form of monetary assistance from parents and the ability to live at home without fear of straining their family's finances—that allowed them the luxury of time to apply to jobs or graduate school programs in their passion (or even figure out what they were passionate about). More privileged passion-seekers also had springboards—educational, cultural, and social capital—that helped them gain the experience and connections to launch them from school to career.[31] With the help of these resources, wealthy and middle-class career aspirants were more likely than their working-class peers to be gainfully employed in their passion.

These patterns were echoed among the college-educated workers in the Passion Principle Survey. Among those who agreed that pursing their passion was the top priority in their postcollege career paths, 69% of those from upper- and upper-middle-class backgrounds reported that their families helped pay for their college tuition and living expenses, while only 46% of those from working-class families reported such safety nets. In addition, evincing class differences in springboards, 29% of passion-seekers from wealthy backgrounds said their families or college alumni connected them with internships during college, compared to only 6% of those from working-class families.

HOW THE PURSUIT OF PASSION PERPETUATES SOCIOECONOMIC DIFFERENCE

In Figure 3.1 above, the most normatively desirable location is the top right quadrant: stable employment with a good salary in one's passion. With the help of safety nets and springboards, some students, especially the most socioeconomically privileged, were able to launch into this quadrant. But what about career aspirants who encountered employment uncertainty or precarity or jobs that were far outside their passion or both? I argue that not only were career aspirants from less privileged backgrounds more likely to end up in the other quadrants, but the pursuit of passion itself was generally riskier for them than for their peers.

Passion in Precarity

Many career aspirants sought work in their passion but ended up precariously employed or unemployed. For respondents from less privileged class backgrounds, passion-seeking came with greater risk of landing on a precarious path—a path that was unstable, temporary, poorly paid, and/or lacked feasible advancement opportunities. These socioeconomic differences were particularly evident among career aspirants who drastically shifted career trajectories after college. I consider three illustrative examples of respondents who changed trajectories in pursuit of their passion and how their lack of safety nets and springboards hampered their ability to land stable opportunities on their new paths.

Aliyah was originally a math major at UH. Because she found math unfulfilling, she left UH to attend a small private college in Texas to pursue a dance degree. Her decision to change fields and schools was a tumultuous one that spanned more than a year. She explained her transition to dance this way:

> I guess I felt like I was running away from something, and it wasn't until I got into dance that I noticed a void that I didn't know was there was filled. I noticed that I enjoyed dancing. . . . I think that was kind of the trigger of fulfillment. This is what it means to be in a career and not a job because you're enjoying what you're doing. (Middle-class Black woman)

Later on in the interview, just to be sure, I asked Aliyah whether she would say she was pursuing her passion. She emphatically replied, "Definitely. Definitely. Definitely. Definitely. Definitely. I wouldn't change it."

At the time of the follow-up interview, Aliyah was a dance instructor at a local high school. She had a yearly contract with the school, but her job only paid about $25,000 a year and she had to supplement her income by working as a barista on evenings and weekends. Although she had followed her passion, she lacked the cultural and social capital to begin her career at a more prestigious and better-paying private school or as a full-time instructor at a dance studio like some of her classmates. And because of her family's limited ability to contribute to her educational expenses, she finished her undergraduate education with over $40,000 in student loan debt.

Andrew, whom I first interviewed when he was an engineering student at MSU, ended up leaving college altogether—with over $70,000 in student loans—to pursue his dream of opening a fitness facility.

> I realized fairly quickly that I would not be able to have a career as an engineer. . . . I wouldn't be able to do that and be happy. . . . It was just working and grinding for the sake of working and grinding, and that was just a bad move. . . . If I was going to be in a job that I wouldn't be able to do it and be happy, or at least get some kind of reward or return, it just, it wouldn't work for my self-care and all that.
>
> [Running a fitness facility] is incredibly difficult, it's extremely time-consuming, but I like it. . . . It requires a lot of—a very intimate relationship with all the athletes that I coach. . . . There's the technical aspect, and the programming, and the numbers, and tapering for meets, and all that, but yeah, it's good. It fills a lot of holes, and it lets me be myself, and also be in charge of that little corner of the world, which is good for me. (Working-class white man)

Although the fitness facility was just breaking even, Andrew and his fiancée had poured all their savings and credit into the business and worked feverishly to keep it afloat.

Two other respondents took similarly giant leaps to pursue their passion. Kiara was on a clear path to medical school and was admitted to a prestigious pre-med fellowship the summer after graduating with a human biology degree from Stanford. One week into the fellowship, she decided medical school wasn't for her.

> I started a pre-med pre-doc. I left that at the end of the first week. . . . I had a panic attack, told my mom I didn't wanna go to med school. I studied for the GRE instead, thinking that I was going to go do a master's in public health, basically like a . . . halfway compromise. I took the GRE, got pretty good scores, . . . [but] I was still not doing quite the right thing and not doing it for quite the right reasons. . . . I did informational interviews, with friends, or friends of friends. . . . I asked them like, "You're in a grad program learning how to make puppets," and "You're a writer," and asking them what their lives were like. . . . At the time, I don't know what drove me to do this or how I had the presence of mind to do it, but . . . I wanted to have a creative career, like make a go of it. (Working-class Black woman)

Over the next two years, Kiara worked a series of part-time jobs at media start-ups. She eventually was accepted into a coveted six-month fellowship at a popular online video production company. Unfortunately, there wasn't a full-time job waiting at the end of the fellowship as she had hoped. At the time of the follow-up interview, Kiara was working as a contractor for the same video production company, working only the days she was needed. When she could get work, usually just a few days a week, she typically made about $150 a day (about $19 an hour).

> In a way, I still work for [the video production company], and [it] is really my main employer, but I wasn't totally on the payroll anymore and didn't have a real title. I was like, okay, this is great, actually. It's given me flexibility to work days I wanna work and not work days I don't wanna work. It means I have to be on my email all the time, looking for and posting for a gig, but that's not that hard. I'm on my email anyway. (Working-class Black woman)

Although it was extremely challenging financially, Kiara downplayed the precarity of this sort of on-demand employment as a necessary sacrifice to follow her passion.

Sam (who uses they/their pronouns) left UH after struggling with mental health issues, partly as a result of their deep unhappiness with their career path. After taking some time to recover, Sam moved to Los Angeles to start classes in a film program at a community college. Although Sam was following their passion, they were unclear about what the next step might be. Sam had about $40,000 in student loan debt from UH.

> I did all these years of psychology [classes at UH]. . . . I got just really bored with it. I did it 'cause my mom wanted me to do it and wanted me to be a doctor. I was thinking about being a psychiatrist. I had no more passion for it at all. I really wanted to write and do cinema, or music, or something entertaining. . . . I moved to LA last year. I'm pursuing film now, 'cause it's what I've been wanting to do, . . . combine all my music passion, my writing. . . .
>
> [Before leaving for LA,] I contacted all my friends to see if I can get some money for a plane ticket, a one-way plane ticket, just a small backpack and some clothes in there. I flew to LA. The first night I slept on the streets, and then into a shelter, and then I got into transitional housing. . . . I'm right now in transitional housing at the Salvation Army.
>
> [Switching career paths] really just came to dedication to work. . . . You just wanna make money off something you really love. You couldn't go [to work] and hate yourself. There's nobody left. You're never gonna obtain success by following somebody else's path. You gotta learn, keep learning, and keep being passionate about your craft, and just really keep improving. I think that cuz I love writing. I love film. I love music. (Working-class nonwhite gender nonbinary person)

Sam's mom pressured them to pursue a career in a medical field. That pressure, plus Sam's unhappiness with their experience at UH, led Sam to ultimately leave UH and seek out another path that better aligned with their passion.

Aliyah, Andrew, Kiara, and Sam all followed their passion after college—sometimes at great financial risk. Their complex and sometimes tumultuous paths likely would have been easier with the safety nets and springboards their privileged peers enjoyed. With a wider safety net and the social and cultural capital of his more privileged peers, Andrew might have had access to loans or investments from his personal networks when he opened his business, Aliyah might have gotten a better-paying and more stable job as a dance instructor, Kiara might have been able to transition into something more permanent or financially viable, and Sam might have been able to afford a more prestigious film school or at least have the resources to make a security deposit and pay rent on an apartment before moving to Los Angeles. At the very least, each would likely have been carrying less student loan debt.

Not Passion but Stable Employment

Not all respondents who tried to pursue their passion at the outset ended up on a path that aligned with that passion. Some ended up in a stable job outside of their passion, while others ended up in temporary or precarious positions with little connection to work they found fulfilling. Whether passion-seekers working outside of their passion ended up in stable or precarious work was bound up with their level of socioeconomic privilege.

Wealthy respondents who were working outside of their passion typically still ended up in stable, well-paid jobs. Cynthia, a Stanford graduate from an upper-class family, started off as an engineering major but decided not to pursue an engineering career because it didn't "fit" her. She sought other paths, obtaining a master's degree in management science and then an MFA, hoping to find something she was passionate about. At the time of the interview, Cynthia was working as an operations manager for a small start-up in Singapore. This job provided a decent salary and good growth opportunities, but it was not her passion. She had found the job by using the job-search-related cultural capital she learned from her family.

> So I had family members who recommended needing to reach out and find people who worked there rather than trying to apply online. . . . I wasn't sure what I was really good at or what my passion would be. So I wasn't sure what would make me happy. Even now, I think part of why I switch so often roles is I don't believe I can predict what's gonna make me happy, so I'm always willing to just try something out and then see how it goes. (Upper-class Black woman)

Cynthia planned to wait it out in her job until she found a next career step that would "make [her] happy."

Connor, an MSU graduate from an upper-middle-class family, moved across the country to participate in an expensive graduate certification program for which he paid out of pocket. Connor then started a lab technician job that seemed to align well with his interests. He loved the microbiology aspects of his work but found the job structure and interactions with colleagues much less enjoyable than he had expected. He was thinking about leaving in the future but was staying put in the near term because he was "making decent money" (around $55,000 a year).

> Being in the academic world for so long, it's been that transition of seeing how things are done in the clinical lab, and some of the things that I find oddly done compared to what I'm used to, and the changes I'd like to see, and not being able to make those changes . . . is a frustrating thing. While I do enjoy it . . . both of my degrees are practically microbiology, and I'd hope you'd enjoy what you get if you get two degrees in it, but it's not entirely what it is that I had built up in my head. (White man)

Although Cynthia and Connor were unsuccessful at landing work they were passionate about, they were securely employed. Both young professionals were well equipped to transfer to work they were more interested in, should the opportunity arise. But for the moment they were comfortably situated in stable labor market positions.

No Passion, No Stability

The least normatively desirable quadrant in Figure 3.1 (above)—unstable employment outside of one's passion (bottom left)—was dominated by respondents from working-class and lower-middle-class backgrounds. Respondents in this category valued and sought out passion-based work after graduation but could not secure employment. Instead, they had to resort to work in the service or blue-collar sector to provide for themselves.

Ellen, a lower-middle-class MSU graduate in elementary school education, tried for eighteen months to get a job in the local school district. She worked part-time in the service industry, hoping that she could make ends meet until she was hired in her degree field: "I've been working as a barista at the [bookstore] café for a year and a half. That's just what I plan on doing until I get a teaching job." She earned about $11,000 a year as a barista and did not have benefits. She didn't have much experience in the classroom and lacked network connections in the district; Ellen was crossing her fingers that her degree didn't go stale before she secured a teaching job.

Kevin, the Stanford cognitive science graduate, tried for as long as he could to follow his passion. He applied to graduate school while working without pay at a tech start-up that was trying to get off the ground. The start-up enticed Kevin with the promise of a well-paid, full-time job if it monetized. Kevin worked odd jobs for two years (e.g., tutoring foreign students) to bring in a little money in the meantime. But he was never accepted into graduate school, and the start-up was never funded.

> After graduating, . . . I was doing an internship for this company that does online therapy modules . . . It never got off the ground. I never got paid for anything. And so I told them I can't keep doing this. But if I have to pay bills, I'm gonna have to take these other jobs, . . . freelancing and doing conversational help with Chinese students looking to study abroad. (Working-class Latinx and white man)

Believing he would have plenty of cognitive science–related career opportunities in New York City, he took the savings he had scraped together and moved there without a job.

> Honestly, when I came to New York, things were really rough. . . . When I came out [to the city], I had like $2,000, just a little less, and I was like, "Oh yeah, it would be so easy to find a job here. They grow on trees. That I'll just walk in and within a week, I'll have a job." But that was not the case. It took many months of working hard, not being able to afford a lot of things, and I think that gave me . . . a perspective on how hard it can be and how hard a lot of people do have it . . . holding on and hoping things will get better and . . . eventually they did.

Lacking social capital connections or the cultural capital to understand the labor market in New York City, Kevin struggled to find work related to his passion. Kevin eventually took a job working thirty-eight hours a week without benefits as a recruiter for a large social media company. The job had little connection to his interests. Kevin read cognitive science research in his spare time to maintain a connection to his passion and hoped he would eventually be able to transfer to something closer to his interests.

But at the time of the interview, he quipped, he was working in a job that helped connect others with jobs in their passion.

Thomas, an MSU graduate with a music degree, moved back to his home state of Minnesota after college to start his own private music lessons business. Although he was initially successful getting clients, he could not get on top of his student loan payments fast enough and ultimately had to give up on his business and find another job. At the time of the interview, he was working at a brewery making around $30,000 a year and had over $60,000 in student loan debt.

THOMAS: I had high hopes of going into music education, . . . but reality set in pretty quickly.

EAC: What do you mean by "reality"?

THOMAS: Finances, bills, how not marketable my degree was, and it just didn't really make sense to take on more debt to pursue a . . . [master's] degree. . . . Once my student loan kicked in, my reality set in pretty fast, and I actually went back to my college job, which was working in a warehouse through UPS. I worked there for three years. . . . The last two years I actually started as a craft brewer. I'm kinda the first one in my family to ever go to school. . . . I went kinda back to blue-collar [work], . . . which is my whole family. I guess family history says that I don't belong at a desk, and I don't.

I come from a farming family. I'm not scared to work hard at all, but I don't have any family support. I took on a crap ton of debt. . . . There's that saying where I'll lift myself up with my boot straps, but I don't have any straps. It's so easy for a dude that's successful to look back and say, "Oh yeah, you just gotta work hard, and put your head to the grindstone." For example, . . . [I was] making $11 an hour working in warehouses. It's really hard, and you're not even making enough money to go look for another job. [*Laughs*] You know what I mean? [I'm] so poor I can't even put gas in my car to go look for another job.

My goal right now, as I mentioned earlier, is getting me out of debt, and then saving as much as we can, and we're gonna get the hell out of the city. . . . Cuz the system kind of ate me up and spit me out and took advantage of me. I have bitter feelings about all that. (Working-class white man)

Thomas regretted how much debt he accumulated in college and how his loans hamstrung his ability to manage employment precarity as he attempted to get his music lessons business off the ground. His job in the brewery neither required nor used his postsecondary education and was certainly a far cry from his passion for music education.

For these career aspirants, safety nets of financial assistance would have lightened the burden of student loans, provided a little money to get set up in a new location, or offered more time to invest in applying for jobs or graduate school. Such safety nets might have allowed Thomas to successfully launch his music lessons business in Minneapolis. More cultural or social capital might have helped Ellen get her foot in the door of the local school district, and more financial support would have allowed her to volunteer or substitute teach to gain experience rather than work as a barista. Greater cultural capital might have helped Kevin apply more successfully to graduate school and better understand the employment market in New York, while more financial resources could have given him more time to look for jobs that aligned more closely with his passion. We cannot know, of course, if the safety nets and springboards accessible to their more privileged peers would have made the difference to launch these career aspirants into stable employment in their passion. But in the language of averages, not having those springboards and safety nets put these career aspirants at greater risk of being on paths to precarious employment—either in their passion or far from it. Without extensive safety nets and springboards, less socioeconomically privileged career aspirants *risked the most* and *lost the most* when they couldn't land stable work in their passion. For Ellen, Kevin, and Thomas, pursuing passion effectively entrenched their socioeconomic status of origin, with the added burden of tens of thousands of dollars in student loan debt.

The Emotional Toll of Searching for a Job in One's Passion

Less socioeconomically privileged passion-seekers were disadvantaged in another way: the job search process often took a bigger emotional toll on them than on their peers. Many respondents whose families had extensive familiarity with white-collar and professional work coached them on the length and difficulty of the job search process after college—consoling them when they didn't get offers and encouraging them not to take it personally. Many of the working-class and first-generation respondents were deeply demoralized by their job searches in the white-collar labor market, often internalizing their failure to find work as a sign of their own short-comings.[32] Lupita, a UH graduate who eventually landed a part-time position in social work in Houston, explained how difficult it was for her after college and how she wished she had understood how common her experience was among other recent graduates.

> Thank God, I finally ended up getting something related to my field. . . . I get a lot of my self-worth from being able to work and help my family. [Before the social work job,] I was getting depressed for a while. I was like, "What's wrong with me?" I'd get an interview and I'd never get a call back. . . . I think in retrospect, I should have known that it wasn't going to be easy finding a job, but I did think that maybe getting a degree would earn me some sort of respect. . . . I wish somebody would have told me. [I said on] graduation day, "Oh, it's the best day of my life." And then you get a sense of the real world. They don't want to hire you, 'cause you don't have experience. . . . I kept wondering what was wrong with me. . . . I was like, "Man, I wish I knew that I wasn't alone back then." I think a lot of students experience the same thing I did. I'm not an anomaly, you know? (Working-class Latinx woman)

On top of the personal difficulties she was having with the job search process, Lupita had to explain to her mother why she wasn't getting any job offers.

> I would just [say], "Mom, generally, this is the struggle. Everyone goes through this. I know eventually it's gonna happen. Right now, I'm working at [a department store], but I'm trying to get this good job and this is just part of the process." She was always so supportive. I try to keep her in the loop but out of how I'm feeling. I just try to reassure her that I'm totally fine.

Similarly, Michael, a UH history graduate, explained how disappointed he was that his multiyear job search didn't net him anything except for a couple of interviews.

> Well, after graduation, I tried looking for a job for a while, which didn't work out. Pretty hard to get a job these days just no matter what you study or anything. . . . I had my aunt who was working in human resources for a long time, she helped me put together my résumé, signed up for all the different job sites, . . . tried to apply in all places that said they took in-person applications. . . .

It's hard to get experience if no one will hire you. . . . I would get an interview every now and then, and nothing would come of it, or I'd just get a robot email saying, "Thank you for applying. We wish you luck in your job search," or whatever. They never tell you why. (Lower-middle-class Latinx man)

At the time of our conversation, Michael was working part-time in a manual labor job at an Amazon warehouse sorting facility. He hadn't had any work experience before graduating and was overwhelmed to realize that his degree would not provide much leverage for him on the job market. Both Lupita and Michael, like many of their peers, believed as students that a college degree would provide a floor above which they would be able to access stable, decently paying jobs and build their careers (see Chapter 1). While most respondents overestimated the sturdiness and levelness of that floor, Lupita and Michael had to find that out firsthand. Working-class and first-generation respondents often internalized the lack of immediate success in the labor market as their own personal failures.[33]

THE UNEQUAL CONSEQUENCES OF PASSION-SEEKING

Most career aspirants I reinterviewed remained committed to the passion principle as a decision-making guide as they entered the workforce, translating their earlier passion-planning into passion-seeking after college. However, pursuing passion-based paths was easier for some career aspirants than others. A few, especially those with professional degrees in education or accounting, for example, were able to move in a linear fashion from school to a job in their field. For others, the experience of passion-seeking was more erratic, as they explored which jobs or advanced degree programs would best suit their passion or switched to other fields.

These career aspirants' experiences reveal the sacrifices that prioritizing passion in one's work often entailed. In particular, those who prioritized passion often tolerated precarity, delays in employment, or economic instability as they launched their careers. Passion-seeking sometimes meant walking away from more stable or better-paying options or even taking great risks to change course entirely. Those who prioritized financial security and stability, in contrast, typically took advantage of good opportunities in front of them, even if those opportunities didn't necessarily align with their personal interests. Compared to those who prioritized security or salary, many passion-seekers were willing to make real financial sacrifices in order to find fulfilling work.

Career aspirants were not equally well equipped for this passion-seeking, however. Respondents from wealthy and middle-class families typically had access to financial safety nets to help them weather the unemployment, precarity, or uncertainty that often accompanied passion-seeking. They also were more likely to have access to springboards—cultural, educational, and social capital—that helped smooth their transition from college to passion-related work. Less privileged students had fewer safety nets and springboards and were less likely to have landed stable employment in their passion. These socioeconomic differences were not due to the crowding of wealthy students into more "marketable" fields with greater job opportunities but to their greater access to these springboards and safety nets.

Broadly, then, enactment of the passion principle may help perpetuate career aspirants' socioeconomic status of origin. The passion principle, and the act of passion-seeking itself, relies on—and often presumes—economic and cultural resources that are only typical of middle- and upper-class career aspirants. Previous research has illustrated the importance of social networks and cultural capital for accessing employment after college and the way in which transitioning from education to employment, especially in competitive fields with low demand, often requires economic support for extensive job searches, underpaid or unpaid internships, or employment trial periods.[34] Wealthy and middle-class students had greater access to these safety nets and springboards and thus were better equipped to translate their passion into stable work or promising postgraduate education.

Although the interview data were ill equipped to identify systematic racial/ethnic or gender differences in how these passion-seeking patterns played out along these and other social categories, the patterns revealed are nonetheless highly salient for the experiences and opportunities of career aspirants across many axes of disadvantage. Nationwide, Black, Latinx, and Native American college graduates are significantly more likely than their white peers to come from working- and lower-middle-class backgrounds.[35] They are also more likely to graduate with substantial student loan debt.[36] As such, the class patterns are racialized in important ways that my interview sample is too small to adequately tease out. For example, the social capital that helped more privileged students launch into stable positions in their passion is likely inflected by racial as well as class disadvantages. Whiteness could itself be considered a springboard that helps white career aspirants navigate the labor market in ways their equally passionate and skilled peers cannot.

These patterns are likely gendered as well. Although the springboards and safety nets did not seem to differentially benefit men and women, women may be disadvantaged by less consistent inclusion in powerful social capital networks and by presumptions that they are willing to sacrifice more or endure more precarity for work they are passionate about. In addition, the fields where women are most overrepresented (e.g., education, social services) tend to have lower average pay than those that are dominated by men or gender balanced.[37] At baseline, these differentials in access to high-paying, stable jobs likely amplify the inequalities among passion-seekers across sociodemographic categories.

The book's conclusion and epilogue review the implications of these findings for educators, policy makers, and career aspirants themselves, but two things are important to note here. First, the tendency to moralize passion-seeking in higher education and beyond, and to devalue those who prioritize economic factors in their career decisions, may help entrench patterns of economic privilege and disadvantage that accompanied students when they entered college. University faculty and administrators should think carefully before encouraging students to follow their passion without being mindful of the unequal distribution of cultural and social capital, the inadequacy of leveling mechanisms in higher education, and the devaluation of career aspirants who prioritize financial considerations above their passion.

More than these individual-level processes, the results in this chapter point to important places where higher education institutions can intervene to even the playing field for passion-seekers, helping to ameliorate differences in safety nets and springboards. Reducing the burden of tuition costs through increased aid in the form of grants and scholarships is an obvious starting point. In addition, colleges could, for example, offer or expand scholarships that allow low-income and first-generation students to take unpaid internships. And they could pressure the companies and organizations who take on their students as interns to pay those interns livable wages in the first place. Colleges could also provide more structured alumni networking opportunities and do a better job of making explicit employment search–related cultural capital.

However, even if universities succeed in reducing student debt and equalizing access to internships and employment opportunities, there are still deep-rooted inequities in labor market processes. Discrimination and nepotism in hiring practices advantage the most sociodemographically privileged graduates.[38] In turn, weak welfare provisions and employment-linked healthcare deepen the financial risk of precarity for the least privileged career aspirants.[39]

These inequalities afflict disadvantaged groups regardless of what they prioritize when looking for work. However, as I have argued in this chapter, passion-seeking entails greater exposure to employment delays and precarity as one attempts to situate oneself on a path related to one's passion. For example, if Kiara hadn't prioritized her passion and had instead continued her pre-med fellowship, her career advancement wouldn't have required additional social capital to access full-time work in the online video company. Springboards and safety nets are beneficial for career aspirants regardless of what they prioritize when it comes to employment, but they take on a more crucial role when career aspirants prioritize work that aligns with their passion rather than stable work with a decent salary for which they are qualified.

The point, though, is *not* that socioeconomically disadvantaged career aspirants should be given different career advice than their more privileged peers.[40] On the contrary, they should have the same right and encouragement to prioritize whatever factors make the most sense to them. The message to educators is to encourage all students, regardless of their background, to weigh a number of factors in their decisions, including fulfillment and economic security but also work-life balance, the ability to contribute to the collective good, and opportunities for leisure time, and to be equipped to resist pressures they may feel from others to prioritize passion-seeking. I speak to these issues in greater depth in the concluding chapter.

Second, the results in this chapter highlight places where literature on the labor market "success" of college graduates needs to be recalibrated.

For example, much has been made of college graduates' seeming lack of readiness for employment.[41] This supposed unreadiness needs to be reconsidered with the passion principle in mind. Some career aspirants prioritize passion-based work over financial stability and knowingly sacrifice stable opportunities in favor of work they are personally committed to. Although scholars' assessments of these trends in postcollege career launch decisions may count such career trajectories as failures, the graduates themselves may not make meaning of their experiences in this way.

In addition, literature on postcollege career trajectories has long documented the differential resources available to college graduates and how universities differentially launch career aspirants. It is no surprise that career aspirants who come from the most privileged backgrounds often have access to the best, most economically stable employment opportunities.[42] But what this literature typically misses is the *goal orientations* of these respondents—especially the role of passion-seeking. Most career aspirants here did not elevate stability and security in their jobs above all else, and many made decisions that ran counter to their short-term economic interests. These differential trajectories are a story of how career paths play out when career aspirants are prioritizing other goals—when they are not explicitly intending to seek out the most economically secure jobs possible but rather ones that align with their sense of self. Yet, even when prioritizing noneconomic factors (e.g., passion), more privileged career aspirants *still* make out better. Strictly economic accounting of these trends may misinterpret the career outcomes of college graduates by seeing economic stability as the only basis for "successful" career launches. Decisions that seem irrational, unwise, or inexplicable through the lens of economic security maximization may make perfect sense when viewed through the lens of career aspirants' own priorities.

If we do not account for the role of passion-seeking in postgraduation decision-making, we risk mischaracterizing both the patterns in career aspirants' decisions and the patterns of inequality among them. The book's conclusion discusses the broader implications of these patterns among passion-seekers. The next chapter broadens the examination of the passion principle from a guiding principle for individual action to considering it as a prescriptive and explanatory schema.

The Passion Principle as Prescriptive and Explanatory Narrative?

HOW THE PASSION PRINCIPLE CHOICEWASHES WORKFORCE INEQUALITIES

"Oh, he must really love bricks!"

On a visit to rural western Mexico in 2019, a small group of visitors and I, led by a local guide, stopped along the roadside to meet a brickmaker named Andrés and admire his craftwork. Andrés was slicing rectangles into the clay-laden earth and carving them out of the ground one by one. He worked with remarkable precision, even in the hot midday sun. Our guide explained that brickmakers like Andrés are paid by the brick. The bricks are sold for three pesos apiece, and brickmakers earn one peso per brick. "Simple capitalist exchange," the guide said. Andrés must make around six hundred bricks per day, working up to sixteen hours, to earn a livable wage.

Sherrie, a white upper-class American woman in her mid-fifties, made the declaration above. Her tone implied that she had figured something out about Andrés. She used the lens of a love for work to make sense of the brickmaker's experiences and motivation. She imposed on Andrés the presumption that he was driven by some inner connection to the product of his work—bricks—and that this love had led him to brickmaking in the first place. Perhaps Andrés really did love brickmaking, but that's beside the point. If Andrés was anything like the brickmakers that Tamar Diana

Wilson studied,[1] he might indeed enjoy the lack of direct supervision and the freedom to set his own hours, but the work is physically demanding and can be brutal in the heat of summer and the chill of winter.[2] Sherrie used a narrative originating from her privileged socioeconomic position to interpret the intentions of a piece-rate manual laborer. This sort of move is an example of cultural framing that uses the passion principle as a tool for interpreting the circumstances of others in a way that minimizes or erases the structural processes that deeply affect their economic and social opportunities.

In this chapter, I explore the ways that the passion principle can serve as a cultural scaffold to understandings of the labor market that diminish the deeply rooted inequalities that lie within. Sherrie is not alone in dismissing others' structural constraints by filtering them through the passion principle.

In the previous chapters, I shined a spotlight on the cultural schema of the passion principle, illustrating why many college-educated career aspirants and workers were compelled by this perspective and how differential access to safety nets and springboards perpetuated class differences among passion-seekers after college. In this way, the passion principle can serve as a guide for individual decision-making that can help reinforce career aspirants' socioeconomic status. However, that is not the only way that the passion principle might help perpetuate processes of inequality. As a cultural schema, the passion principle may be part of a larger web of beliefs that promotes a particular way of understanding workforce processes. In this chapter, I widen my spotlight to illuminate the web of cultural beliefs in which the passion principle is entangled. Using interview data and the Passion Principle Survey (PPS) data, I explore the ways the passion principle, as a cultural schema that helps its adherents make sense of the world, may be connected to other well-documented beliefs about the labor market—particularly beliefs that help to uphold existing unequal economic and social structures.

Specifically, I argue that the passion principle is deeply entwined with two powerful and well-documented beliefs: the meritocratic ideology and the personal responsibility trope of neoliberalism. The *meritocratic ideology* is the belief that the labor market is fundamentally fair and equitably rewards those who are sufficiently hardworking and talented.[3]

Neoliberalism is a political and economic ideology that advocates radical free market capitalism under the presumption that economic and social well-being is best achieved by scaling back social programs and resisting collective or redistributive processes that would restrict the free market in any way.[4] A core tenant of neoliberalism is the *personal responsibility trope,* the belief that individuals should be held solely responsible for their own economic success and failure and that government assistance and social provisions are demotivating and unnecessary.[5]

These two ideologies are related and reinforcing but conceptually distinct. The meritocratic ideology is a *descriptive* perspective—a meaning-making framework about how people believe the labor market actually operates. Neoliberalism's personal responsibility trope is a *prescriptive* belief—a narrative that prescribes that individuals take responsibility for their own advancement and for governments and organizations to scale back social programs that might enable those who seek a "free ride." I argue that these beliefs help legitimate the passion principle as an approach to career decision-making, and the passion principle, in turn, helps to scaffold meritocratic and neoliberal perspectives on the labor market.[6]

Together, the passion principle, the meritocratic ideology, and the personal responsibility trope provide an enticingly individualized cultural model of career success—one in which individuals are responsible for navigating a complex and increasingly risky labor force and where social institutions have little role or responsibility to address systemic occupational inequalities. I also argue that the passion principle may help mask existing structural inequalities, portraying them as the benign result of—or easily overcome by—individuals' passion-driven hard work.

THE CULTURAL SCHEMA OF THE PASSION PRINCIPLE

As we have seen, the passion principle is a cultural schema that elevates passion-seeking as the most desirable guiding principle in career selection. Cultural schemas are shared cultural models for "viewing, filtering, understanding, and evaluating what we know as reality."[7] Schemas are not only cognitive models; they help structure our moral and emotional responses as well.[8]

Cultural schemas don't always shape the way people approach the mundane tasks of their daily lives. During "settled" times, our actions tend to rely on our semiconscious habits more than on our conscious martialing of cultural or moral beliefs.[9] However, cultural schemas may powerfully shape people's actions as they approach life crossroads like career decisions. When individuals are at an impasse in consequential life decisions, they often lean on deeply held cultural beliefs to inform those decisions.[10] This action-inspiring facet of the passion principle is evident among the career aspirants discussed in Chapters 1 and 3. When Aliyah left math for dance, for example, and Rohan switched from engineering to construction management, they drew on the passion principle as a guide for how to progress through those difficult decision points.

But inspiring individuals' career decisions is not the only way this cultural schema might be consequential. Cultural schemas can also serve as interpretive frames that help people make sense of the broader social and structural processes in which they are embedded. Schemas can help people conceptualize what is, and what should be, in a complex social world.[11] Cultural schemas of inequality, for example, provide mental models that help people explain systemic patterns of difference like residential segregation or gender wage gaps. People with cultural schemas of inequality that acknowledge structural biases are more likely to interpret systems of ascriptive difference as immoral and unfair.[12]

Here I examine the mutually reinforcing relationships between the cultural schema of the passion principle and two common ideologies about the labor market: the meritocratic ideology and the personal responsibility trope. I argue that the passion principle is buttressed by these ideologies and that the passion principle, in turn, does important cultural work to scaffold these beliefs. After examining these interconnections, I explore whether people who strongly adhere to the passion principle are more likely to dismiss structural gender, class, and race-based obstacles in the labor market. These analyses illustrate that the cultural schema of the passion principle is neither isolated nor benign; it is part of a larger web of cultural beliefs that downplay or deny structural barriers in the labor force and blame individuals for the constraints they encounter along their career paths.

I focus on the ideologies of meritocracy and personal responsibility in particular because, of all the popular beliefs about the labor market, they have perhaps done the most damage to reproduce socioeconomic disadvantages in the United States and to undermine sustained policy and activism that addresses inequality in the workforce and beyond.[13] The meritocratic ideology promotes the idea that the labor force operates fairly and a person's (or a group's) lack of success is the result of their own shortcomings. This blames the victims of occupational inequality and casts efforts to address inequality as "overreaches" or "reverse discrimination."[14] Adherents of the meritocratic ideology are unlikely to support policies and practices that address systemic patterns of workforce oppression because they already think that the labor force is fair.

Similarly, the personal responsibility trope of neoliberalism has quickened the erosion of worker power that began in the 1970s. Neoliberal policies at the governmental and organizational levels have amplified income inequality, reduced social support structures, gutted collective bargaining, and trumpeted the argument that workers should rely on their own efforts and industriousness alone to chart their economic course.[15] Although the passion principle might seem disconnected from the meritocratic ideology and the personal responsibility trope, an examination of the data suggests that the passion principle does important work to help perpetuate these perspectives—or at least helps make them more culturally tolerable.

Drawing on the PPS and the follow-up interviews with career aspirants, I show that passion principle adherents are more likely than passion principle skeptics to believe in the meritocratic ideology and the personal responsibility trope. In addition, adherents are more likely than skeptics to believe that passion is idiosyncratically derived and that structural gender, race, and class barriers can be overcome simply with hard work. I call this process *choicewashing*: the cultural framing of processes that are systematically classed, racialized, and/or gendered as the benign result of deliberate individual choices within equitably functioning and opportunity-rich social contexts.[16] By downplaying structural obstacles, the passion principle choicewashes obdurate patterns of occupational segregation and inequality of opportunity as the legitimate, fair outcomes of personal, passion-seeking choices.

These patterns have important consequences for public discourse about the need for—and the legitimacy of—policies aimed at mitigating occupational segregation and inequality. I argue at the end of the chapter that the passion principle may entrench individualized neoliberal views of the labor force and perpetuate structural obstacles. It may also undercut arguments for worker assistance programs, education, and training that seek to level the playing field for occupational success.

THE LABOR MARKET IS(N'T) FAIR: PASSION PRINCIPLE ADHERENCE AND MERITOCRACY BELIEFS

The belief that the labor force is fair is common in the United States. Many Americans deny the existence of enduring structural barriers or downplay them as a relic of earlier eras; instead, they see the labor market as a system of opportunities available for the taking to those willing to invest sufficient effort.[17] According to this meritocratic ideology, education and effort foster individual merit, enhance productivity, and are fairly rewarded with good pay and high status. In contrast, those deficient in the requisite training or motivation are believed to lack merit and will inevitably be surpassed by others.[18]

The meritocratic ideology is a dominant ideology in how Americans understand the labor force.[19] This belief has been relatively stable over the past four decades: since the 1980s, about 70% of the US population consistently reports that "hard work" is more important than "lucky breaks" or "help from others" in succeeding in the workforce.[20] It helps Americans reconcile their cultural commitments to formal equality with the vastly unequal labor market outcomes in the United States by class, race, gender, and other social categories.[21]

Consistent with the broad popularity of the meritocratic ideology, the college graduates I interviewed typically believed that the labor market is meritocratic. Most thought they would succeed if they held fast to their passion and put in sufficient effort.[22] For example, Rohan talked excitedly about where he saw his construction management career going in the near future and his belief that hard work and devotion will lead him to success.

> Now, I see a lot of growth opportunity here with this new role I'm transitioning into. . . . I see myself achieving an executive position really fast. . . . As

long as you're hardworking, you're smart, you can make it pretty far. . . . I feel like most of the time if you're hardworking and you devote yourself you can get what you want. Of course, there are some times where things are out of your control. Most times, I think if you work hard enough you can get what you want and get where you want to go. (Upper-class West Asian man)

Kiara, the online video freelancer described in Chapter 3, similarly said that hard work would bring her success, even in the uncertain world of the entertainment industry.

I wanna be a very successful show creator/actress and ideally have a really successful YouTube channel and then be moving into stage plays and shows. I just have lots of stories in my head that I wanna tell, . . . and I wanna ideally make good money doing it. That's the dream. . . . That sounds like a very arrogant, ambitious dream to have. But . . . that's what I'm working toward. . . . [I am] still firm in my beliefs that people have their free will and they can do whatever they want. . . . I know who I am and what I stand for and what I believe in. (Working-class Black woman)

Aided by her belief that her hard work would eventually deliver within what she believed to be a meritocratic system, Kiara was undeterred in the pursuit of her ambitious dream.

At the time I interviewed them, Rohan had a stable, full-time job while Kiara was a freelancer. Both assumed that they were (and would continue to be) fairly rewarded for their efforts and anticipated that their hard work and dedication to their craft would be their ticket to success.

Most adherents to the passion principle not only thought the labor market treated them fairly but also that it operated fairly as a general rule. Brianna, the passionate broadcast journalist, put it succinctly.

If you don't work hard, you won't get far. There are some people that are lucky. They might be born into wealth, . . . but for those who [aren't], you can still be successful if you are determined. You put your heart into it, and you work hard. I believe that is true. (Upper-class Black and Asian woman)

Taylor, a UH biotechnology major, explained that success will come naturally from pursuing a field one loves as long as one continues to work at it.

So I mean like, when you love something so much, no matter what obstacle's in your way, you're gonna get it done. . . . If you don't choose a major that you really like you will fail because you're not interested in it, you make bad grades and just skimming by. . . . Like, intensity always beat extensity every time, so if you're intense about something, even if you don't make that much money initially off of it, you keep workin' at it, keep workin' at it, eventually you're gonna hit the goal line. . . . You may not have it right away, like some engineers are, but if you really apply yourself, you know, really work it, you will like, fulfill yourself in that situation. So money should never be the object. (Middle-class Black man)

For Taylor, the connection between passion and success was obvious and reliable.

Many respondents not only understood the labor market as fair, but interpreted the lack of success of others as the outcome of their lack of drive. While working part-time as a line cook, Devon, the air force worker, explained how he came to the conclusion that people who remain in working-class jobs are just holding themselves back from advancement.

When I was nineteen, twenty years old . . . I can remember feeling almost trapped in that sort of environment and that sort of workplace. Then that also, like, drove me to do better academically. . . . I knew that I wanted to be better. Not to say anything of the people who were working there, because a lot of them were still my friends. I don't have a problem washing dishes. I knew I could become something more. . . . I [had] some drive, some resolve that [I] didn't see often amongst my coworkers and peers working at the food industry. This last summer when I was flipping burgers, I was a college-educated, military professional. My coworkers were drug addicts and high school dropouts. . . . I can remember just . . . being like, man, is my life that much different than yours, that this is your end goal? (Middle-class white man)

Of course, not every career aspirant believed the labor force is fair.[23] Isaiah, the pharmacy student whose parents are Nigerian, explained that his and his family's experiences of racial oppression in the United States made it clear that not everyone has an equal opportunity in the workforce.

I just feel like, although hard work is glorified, I feel like people are . . . able to achieve a certain amount of success based on maybe a person that they know or . . . they're just born in a well-off-to-do family immediately, so they kinda have advantages immediately from birth. Then there's also a systematic oppression regarding race and minorities that, even if you are the best within your class, there's always—there's a ceiling for us, especially for African Americans. . . . I think that, even though we had a[n] African American president, . . . I still feel like you chase your dreams and chase those things, but know that there are others who may not have to deal with the same type of oppression. . . . That's just the world that we live in right now. (Upper-class Black man)

Isaiah's questioning of the meritocracy of the labor force was not common among his peers. Passion-oriented career aspirants typically saw the labor force as fair not only for themselves but for their peers as well.

But, of course, the labor market is not fair. Although most institutions and organizations formally strive to enact fair hiring practices and publicly oppose nepotism and overt discrimination, systematic inequalities along the lines of gender, race, class, sexual identity, and disability persist.[24] Talent and hard work may amplify one's chances of success, but long-standing processes of discrimination mean that not everyone who is talented and hardworking will ultimately succeed.

Using the PPS data, I was able to more directly test for connections between adherence to the passion principle and assessments of the labor market as meritocratic. Specifically, I examined whether college-educated workers who adhered to the passion principle were more likely to believe that the workforce is fair.[25] Items A and B in Figure 4.1 suggest that this is the case: adherence to the passion principle is highly correlated with beliefs that the labor market operates fairly.[26] Passion principle believers (light bars) were 35% more likely than skeptics (dark bars) to agree, for example, that "opportunities for personal advancement are available to anyone who cares to look for them" (Item A). Believers were also more likely than skeptics to agree that "professional success is primarily the result of hard work and dedication" (Item B).[27]

At first glance, this might be surprising. These cultural beliefs seem quite distinct: the passion principle is a guiding principle about career decision-making prioritization, and the meritocratic ideology is a broader assessment of the fairness of advancement structures in the US labor market. The meritocratic ideology is tightly correlated with political conservatism, but the passion principle is not. Why would these beliefs be so strongly related?[28]

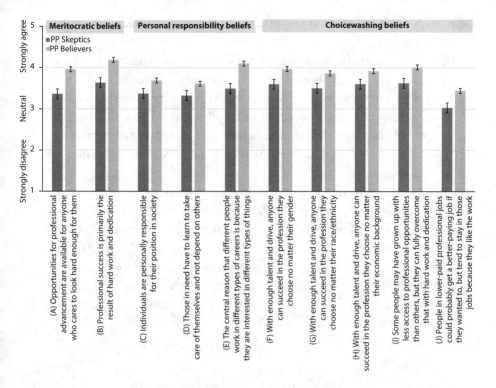

Figure 4.1 Meritocratic, personal responsibility, and choicewashing beliefs among college-educated workers, by passion principle adherence (PPS data).

It may be that passion principle believers cling to the idea of meritocracy in order to justify their own passion-seeking as a viable career option: they presume that labor market advancement is at least fair enough that their investment in their passion has a reasonable chance of panning out. Prescribing passion-seeking to others, in turn, may require an implicit belief that the labor market is predictable and fair and generally rewards individuals equitably on the basis of merit. The meritocratic ideology and the passion principle are, I posit, intertwined cultural beliefs, each of which helps scaffold the other's feasibility. The meritocratic ideology may prop up the passion principle, as the meritocratic ideology promotes the belief that it does not matter where someone comes from, that one can be successful in whatever their passion is as long as they put in the work.

Students I interviewed frequently made this connection as they talked about their own paths and about success in the labor market generally. If the labor market is a meritocracy in which hard work and training lead to career success, then following one's passion, which motivates hard work and training, seems less risky and maybe even a wise guiding principle for career decisions. In contrast, rejecting the idea that the labor market fairly rewards passion-fueled work makes pursuing one's self-expressive interests seem more risky and suggesting that others follow their passion seem like less sage advice.

At the same time, the passion principle may prop up a meritocratic view of the labor market. As Chapter 2 showed, passion is often conceptualized as a bottomless wellspring of dedication that is necessary to inspire the hard work needed for success. Passion feeds into this meritocratic logic: people follow their passion, passion catalyzes hard work and training, and that hard work and training, in turn, results in career success. I discuss later in the chapter the potential consequences this co-scaffolding might have for the reproduction of occupational inequality.

PASSION IS(N'T) ALL YOU NEED: BELIEF IN THE PASSION PRINCIPLE AND THE PERSONAL RESPONSIBILITY TROPE

In the broadest terms, neoliberalism is a political and social ideology that promotes free market capitalism and policies of privatization, deregulation, and austerity. Neoliberalism originally emerged in the last half of the twentieth century as a political and economic ideology that stressed the transfer of power from government to private markets and the constriction of social provisions like unemployment and welfare. This perspective expanded from strictly policy-based applications to encompass broader cultural beliefs that market-based solutions are the best way to solve social problems. In addition, it presumes that people's own social and economic fates are best left to competition within the free market.[29] Neoliberalism has become a hegemonic perspective on the labor market since the late 1970s—a "touchstone of rationality" of political and economic decisions.[30]

One of the central tenets of neoliberalism is the personal responsibility trope—the belief that "each individual is held responsible and accountable for his/her own actions and well-being. . . . Individual success or failure are interpreted in terms of entrepreneurial virtues or personal failings."[31] In the 1980s and 1990s, emboldened by the rising popularity of neoliberalism, legislators rolled back social support programs such as welfare and unemployment benefits and systematically attacked labor unions.[32] Neoliberalism's cultural appeal to individual freedom and responsibility were generally persuasive to the American public, disguising the gutting of social provisions and the resultant expansion of income and wealth inequalities as a matter of fiscal responsibility.[33] The personal responsibility trope is thus both a core principle of neoliberal policies and a legitimating ideology that does work to justify those policies to the public.

There is reason to suspect that the passion principle may be associated with the personal responsibility trope. As discussed in Chapter 2, many respondents understood pursuing passion as vital for success, because only passion could motivate the hard work that success requires. Ryan, a UH sociology graduate, for example, stated that "interest is definitely the most important [in choosing a career] because if you want to do something, then you'll be intrinsically motivated to be good at it" (middle-class white man).

Most college students I interviewed (63%) believed that passion was more important than skill for initial occupational success. These career aspirants often explained that it did not matter whether someone was skilled at their work at the start of their career; passion would provide the stamina needed to develop the requisite skills. For example, Autumn, a psychology and anthropology major at UH, said:

> I think in the long run interest might be more important [than skill] because skills I think you can build on if you're not very strong in one area . . . I think you can practice a lot, then you could maybe improve in it. Whereas interests, if you're not interested to begin with, it's gonna just be like an uphill battle and everything will be hard. (Middle-class white woman)

This sometimes took the form of a "pull yourself up by your bootstraps" notion of career achievement. As a music major at UH explained:

I don't care what it is, if you wanna do it and if you set your mind to it, then you can have the skills to do it. Skills can be built, . . . so if you like doing something and you think you're not good at it . . . you can get better at it; just surround yourself with the right people. (Middle-class white woman)

Here, career success is up to the individual; if one's drive originates in one's passion, one is more likely to succeed.

Respondents certainly understood that the "passion + effort = success" equation has boundary conditions. For example, a UH student noted that "not everyone is going to cure cancer," however passionate they are. Some people will not break a sprinting world record, no matter how hard they try. Even so, passion-driven work was understood by adherents as a reliable path to success for most people in most occupations.

Respondents frequently explained their *own* career outcomes as the product of their individualistic, passion-driven efforts. For example, Sara attributed her early success as an accountant to a series of deliberate decisions about which internships and job tracks she should pursue.

Usually when you get an accounting degree . . . the go-getters in college, they usually go Big Four because when you graduate, the idea is that if you start big, it's easier to go smaller than it is to go to a boutique shop and then work your way up. . . . I wanted to go to work for a big name. . . . I interned at [a large petroleum company] on their commodity trade floor. . . . I was a top performer and so they offered me a returning internship. . . . Then, when it came time to negotiate my salary and my benefits [for a full-time position], management there didn't see the need for a CPA [certified public accountant credential], they did not feel like they needed to pay for it. I told them that I would go into public accounting where the CPA was valued and I could further that personal and professional goal. That's why I went the public accounting and Big Four route. (Middle-class white and Asian woman)

Sara explained her trajectory, which involved several industry changes (from petroleum to public accounting to a Big Four firm), as a series of intentional choices. Yet her ability to follow this path was not the result of passion-driven choices alone; consistent with springboards described in Chapter 3, Sara's opportunities for making such choices were facilitated by internships she accessed via connections through her parents.

It is not surprising that respondents interpreted their success as the outcome of their own choices and hard work. More strikingly, many passion-seekers who encountered stumbling blocks along the way also framed these as the result of their own decisions, even when structural obstacles were evident. Ricardo, for example, was pursuing a PhD at an Ivy League school when he decided to leave his program and pursue a master's degree in bioengineering at a lower-ranked program. Although it became clear over the course of his interview that a major factor pushing him out of the program was the lack of support and resources from his racist adviser, Ricardo framed his departure as an individual choice driven by passion-seeking. The troubles he encountered in his PhD program were fateful, he said, in that they "opened the door" for him to contemplate more passion-based career trajectories.

> Deciding to leave my PhD was a tough one. It took a lot of soul searching, a lot of angry conversations, a lot of frustrated conversations with myself, a lot of wine, and really figuring out if it was the best thing for me. I thought if I'm struggling this much, then I probably don't belong in this program. That sort of opened the door for me to really become more introspective of how— what it is that I wanted and what was truly gonna make me happy. I was afraid that I had just given up on something and I was letting people down who supported my decision to go to [the Ivy League university] and were so happy and proud of me. (Working-class Latinx man)

Although he encountered clear structural barriers, Ricardo framed these struggles as evidence that he did not "belong" in the program—a realization, as he portrayed it, that ultimately advanced his goal of moving toward a field that better aligned with work he "really liked."

These messages are consistent with Jennifer Silva's research on working-class adolescents who were often reluctant to admit that structural barriers (even in the midst of an economic recession) prevented them from succeeding and instead tended to blame themselves for their shortcomings in the labor market.[34] The findings also resonate with Ofer Sharone's research on unemployed white-collar workers in the United States[35] and Allison Pugh's interviews with blue- and white-collar workers who had been laid off who often blamed themselves for their job loss and their inability to get work,[36] citing their personal lack of "fit" with the jobs they applied for.[37] Like these works, my study of passion-seekers revealed that career aspirants often put the responsibility for their school or labor market success or failure on their own shoulders. Even if respondents were able to recognize the existence of structural inequalities in the abstract, they were generally unable (or unwilling) to see how these might have advanced or stymied their own career outcomes.[38]

Are passion principle adherents, then, more likely to buy into the personal responsibility trope? The PPS data confirm that college-educated and employed passion principle adherents are indeed more likely to believe in neoliberalism's personal responsibility trope than their more skeptical peers. Item C in Figure 4.1 shows that passion principle believers are significantly more likely than passion principle skeptics to agree that people are personally responsible for their position in society, net of controls for education level, occupation, and demographics. They are also more likely than skeptics to believe that "those in need have to learn to take care of themselves and not depend on others" (Item D).

As with the meritocratic ideology, the passion principle and this personal responsibility trope appear to scaffold one another.[39] Neoliberal ideas of personal responsibility reinforce the passion principle's emphasis on individualism and the expectation that a person will pursue their own idiosyncratic path. In turn, the passion principle's prescription to dig deep and find motivation in one's unique, self-expressive interests in order to be successful plays into neoliberal notions that individual hard work drives success. I discuss the implications of this interconnection later in the chapter.

HOW THE PASSION PRINCIPLE CHOICEWASHES OCCUPATIONAL INEQUALITIES

The results above suggest that the passion principle is intertwined with beliefs that the labor market is fair (the meritocratic ideology) and that people are solely responsible for their own social positions (neoliberalism's personal responsibility trope). But the passion principle may also have more proximate connections to beliefs about inequality. Specifically, I argue that the passion principle may help choicewash patterns of occupational inequality and promote assumptions that individuals can overcome structural obstacles with enough passion-driven hard work. I explore here how the passion principle may individualize occupational segregation.

Then I examine the relationships between adhering to the passion principle and endorsing the belief that women, people of color, and working-class persons can overcome gender, race, and economic disadvantages if they are willing to work hard enough.

Passion Is(n't) Idiosyncratic

As I explained in Chapter 1, "passion" as I use it in this book is a self-expressive connection with and commitment to an occupational field or productive task realm. Notions of what we are passionate about rely on our self-conceptions, the theories we develop and nurture about ourselves regarding who we are and what we like. Although these self-conceptions are shaped by the cultures and structures in which we are embedded, self-conceptions, and the passions based on them, are typically understood as an outgrowth of one's idiosyncratic (i.e., personal, nonstructural) preferences and values.[40] The career aspirants I interviewed saw their passion as fundamentally individualistic, tied to their enduring personality traits, individual experiences, and/or deeply held personal values.

However, on closer examination of the "origin stories" of career aspirants' passion, it becomes clear that powerful structural processes also facilitated the development of their passion. Consider Chase's narrative about how he came to be passionate about physics.

> I've really always been pretty interested in [physics]. . . . Even as a little kid, I was always really interested in how stuff works . . . I remember asking my parents how light worked, as an elementary school kid. Looking back, they always told me, yeah, that was a weird question. . . . Now that I'm a scientist that works with light, it makes sense. It's something I've always been interested in. In my freshman year of high school, I guess, I had one science teacher that was super, super interesting and involved and enthusiastic. He turned me towards the professional path that made me realize that it was something I wanted to do. Then all through high school, I just naturally fell into the math and science classes. When I went into college, it was the next logical thing. There really wasn't much question about doing anything else. (Upper-class white man)

Chase described his interest as an enduring part of his personality. And his parents nurtured a narrative that the roots of this interest extended all the way back to his early childhood. Yet Chase also happened to have people around him who encouraged that interest. Without encouraging parents and the supportive teacher in his upper-class high school, Chase may have ended up on an entirely different path.

Similarly, Tara explained that she knew as a child that she wanted to be a doctor. Medicine was an important part of her identity and had long been her dream. Not coincidentally, both her parents were doctors. The imprint of her parents' professional status on her passion was undeniable.

EAC: How do you think you ended up on the path to a medical degree?

TARA: That goes back to ancient times, ever since I was a kid. . . . My dad used to get his doctor journals in the mail. I used to be so engrossed with them. I'd come home and get super excited every time there was a new one. . . . I would be disappointed if there weren't enough gory pictures for me. Gory in a sense where I was just so fascinated by it and I would ask my dad all these questions, like what happened to him, why is he like this, can you fix that, things like that. My parents . . . encouraged me to pursue that further. . . . I knew also that I would probably go that direction. (Upper-class Middle Eastern woman)

Tara's passion was sparked by the resources she had access to as a result of her parents' profession and the validation of her budding curiosity. She had the privilege of early exposure and parental encouragement, which led her to apply to a medical high school in Houston. This, in turn, led to her undergraduate biology major at UH and, later, enrollment in medical school.

Similarly, Melissa, a music education major from MSU, animatedly explained her enduring love of music: "I've just been in music since I can remember, just being little and singing. . . . It's just always been a part of my life. . . . That's what I love, is just creating music with people. . . . It just brings me joy in my life" (middle-class white woman). On further questioning, Melissa shared that her parents were capable of financing her piano lessons and choir participation. She was able to participate in school musicals, which involved months of intense preparation and rehearsal, rather than take a part-time job like many of her high school classmates. Melissa's parents' investment in her music interests provided opportunities that may not have been available to other students. Without such resources and sustained involvement in extracurricular music activities, her interest in music may not have unfolded the same way. Yet Melissa's narrative individualized her connection to music and leaves out the structural resources she had access to as an adolescent.

The impact of respondents' social circumstances on the development of their passion wasn't always tied to privileged status. Sometimes respondents' encounters with structural disadvantage helped shape their interests. For example, Maria explained how her interest in being a social worker originated from helping her mother navigate social services as a child.

> I grew up in a household in Central California. . . . Everybody—they're migrant farmworkers, multiple family farmworkers, [were] Spanish-speaking only. A lot of kids had to step in for their parents at a young age and provide that service of interpreting. . . . We would go out and we would interpret for families like at the hospital, at the doctor's office, at the school with the principal, anywhere that you can think of that there's professionals providing services. . . . At a very young age, I saw the importance of helping others and what a benefit that was. I always felt like I would work with the Latino population, and I am. (Middle-class Latinx woman)

Maria's childhood experiences in Central California made her aware of how much her community needed Spanish-speaking social service workers. However, Maria spoke about the growth of her passion in terms of her *own* social justice–oriented value system rather than as an outcome of her structural circumstances.

Most respondents explained that they discovered their passion on their own as a natural outgrowth of their idiosyncratic tastes and values.[41] These are retrospective narratives through which respondents made sense of their past partly through the lens of their present values and circumstances.[42] Yet it is clear in each instance that these passions were in part structurally nurtured or derived. In contrast to the dichotomous notion of passion typical of passion principle adherents, where one "knows" instinctually that a field is or is not their passion, passion development is highly dependent on one's constraints and opportunities. Part of the power of the cultural schema of the passion principle, then, is perpetuating the idea that being passionate about a career field is something that one just *is* rather than something one *becomes*.

I argued in Chapter 1 that self-conceptions are built through gendered, classed, and racialized structures and institutions—which means that when people seek self-expressive career paths, they often help reproduce class-, gender-, and race-based occupational segregation.[43] Beyond reinforcing actual patterns of occupational segregation in the labor force, the passion principle may also help individuals make sense of these patterns of segregation in ways that minimize their structural bases. If one believes that interests (their own as well as others') are idiosyncratic, then the obdurate patterns of occupational gender, race, and class segregation may seem like unremarkable or benign outcomes of individual passion-seeking. Passion principle adherents may be more likely than passion principle skeptics to explain away patterns of occupational segregation as the outcome of benign interest-following.

Using PPS data, I examined whether passion principle believers were more likely than passion principle skeptics to explain away occupational segregation as the outcome of individualistic choice. Overall, about three-fourths (75.7%) of the sample agreed that "the central reason that different people work in different types of careers is because they are interested in different things." The difference between passion principle adherents and skeptics is notable: while 85% of adherents agreed that people work in different careers because of divergent interests, only 61% of skeptics concurred. (See Item E in Figure 4.1.) Importantly, the values in the figure control for whether people are passionate about their own work, capturing the passion principle as a prescriptive narrative rather than simply a reflection of their own work experiences.

In general, then, adherence to the passion principle may not only encourage individual career aspirants to follow self-expressive paths that entrench patterns of occupational segregation (as I argued in Chapter 1); it also may lead them to frame occupational segregation as the benign outcome of people fulfilling their genuine personal interests. By framing passion as idiosyncratically derived and occupational segregation as the outcome of individual passion-seeking, the passion principle helps mask these occupational patterns and explain away their structural and cultural roots as the collective result of deliberate individual choices.

The Passion Principle and Understandings of Occupational
Segregation and Structural Inequality

The passion principle might not just interface with people's explanations of occupational segregation; it may also be related to how adherents understand the landscape of structural class, gender, and race barriers in the workforce more generally. Here I examine the connection between adherence to the passion principle and respondents' recognition or dismissal of structural barriers.[44]

I hypothesize that passion principle believers may be more likely than passion principle skeptics to agree that disadvantaged group members can overcome structural gender, race, and class obstacles by dedication and hard work alone. If passion principle adherents tend to believe that passion drives hard work, and hard work leads to career success, then they may also believe that structural disadvantages like sexism and racism can ultimately be overcome with sufficient personal effort. In this way, the passion principle may serve not just as a prescription for how adherents believe others should act but also as a lens through which they understand structural barriers and how easy or difficult it may be to overcome them.

Using the PPS data, I examined connections between adherence to the passion principle and beliefs regarding the ability of disadvantaged persons to overcome structural obstacles in the labor market. In each analysis, as above, I controlled for whether respondents are passionate about their *own* work as well as variation by demographics and job characteristics. This helps isolate the prescriptive features of the schema, regardless of respondents' thoughts about their own jobs.

First, I examined whether passion principle adherents in the PPS were more likely to agree that hard work and talent are enough to overcome structural obstacles. Holding constant variation by respondents' own gender, race/ethnicity, class, and other demographic factors and respondents' own level of passion for their work, I found that passion principle believers are more likely than passion principle skeptics to agree that with enough talent and drive, anyone can succeed in the profession they choose, no matter their gender (Item F, Figure 4.1), race/ethnicity (Item G), or economic background (Item H). In other words, passion principle adherents are more likely to believe that passion-driven hard work can overcome social inequalities.

Consistent with demographic patterns that other scholars have identified, women respondents were more likely to disagree that people can succeed with hard work alone despite gender, race, and economic barriers.[45] Black and Native American respondents in the PPS were less likely than white respondents to agree that people can overcome gender, race, and economic barriers with hard work. However, adherence to the passion principle was not differently related to these structural obstacle measures depending on respondents' gender, race, or class background.[46]

Next, I used PPS data to examine whether respondents believed that people choose to stay in lower-paying positions because they like their work (a sentiment akin to Sherrie's statement that the brickmaker "must really love bricks"). Overall, 52% of these college-educated workers agreed that "people in lower paid professional jobs could probably get a better-paying job if they wanted to but tend to stay in those jobs because they like the work" (see Item J). Yet the difference between passion principle adherents and skeptics on this measure is telling. Among passion principle believers, over half (54%) agreed with the statement, while only about a third (35%) of passion principle skeptics agreed.

These analyses further indicate that those who adhere strongly to the passion principle were more likely to believe that structural obstacles of gender, race, and class can be overcome with enough effort. Strong adherents were also more likely to justify the distribution of people across differently rewarded occupations as the outcome of individual choice.

Finally, I explored whether the passion principle is related to respondents' dismissal of structural inequalities, independent of their political beliefs. I ran regression models predicting each of the items in Figure 4.1, including a measure of respondents' political conservatism plus controls. As expected, I found that the effects of passion principle adherence on the denial of structural obstacles remained significant even after controlling for respondents' political conservatism. In other words, the effects of the passion principle on these outcomes is not simply that the passion principle somehow serves as a proxy for political conservatism, but rather that the passion principle has an independent relationship to respondents' likelihood of dismissing structural inequalities.

Choicewashing

The results above suggest strong connections between the passion principle and respondents' downplaying or dismissal of structural obstacles in the labor force. To put a name to this process, the passion principle contributes to the "choicewashing" of patterns of structural segregation and disadvantage. This is what Sherrie did in her comment about Andrés: she choicewashed the structural circumstances that the brickmaker faced and framed his manual labor job as his choice to work with things he loved.[47] Of course, not everyone who believes in the passion principle choicewashes structural barriers or individualizes success and failure in this way. Yet these ideas are empirically and conceptually entwined.

In the results above, evidence of passion principle adherents' tendency to choicewash inequality emerged from a couple of places. First, most passion principle adherents considered people's passions to be organically derived from their idiosyncratic tastes and sense of personhood. However, selves are social constructs, and following one's passion often reinscribes rather than challenges the social patterns of gender, race, and class that helped create those selves in the first place. Prescribing passion-seeking as an ideal method for career decision-making not only promotes segregation along these lines; it helps choicewash existing occupational segregation as the benign outcome of individual passion-seeking.

Second, passion principle adherents were more likely than those skeptical of this schema to believe that structural obstacles like gender, race, and economic background can be overcome through hard work in one's chosen occupation. This denies the enduring power of structural obstacles and shifts the responsibility for overcoming those obstacles onto disadvantaged group members themselves.[48] Interestingly, there was little difference in the relationships between the passion principle and these beliefs by respondents' own gender or race/ethnicity. Women and people of color were less likely overall to believe that structural obstacles can be overcome with hard work, but adherence to the passion principle similarly increased their likelihood of believing that structural obstacles are surmountable.[49]

But, of course, individual-level hard work is not the answer to structural barriers and believing that it is burdens disadvantaged group members with additional effort not required of their more privileged peers. And, of course, passion is not sufficient for career success. As described in Chapter 3, not everyone possesses the educational preparation, extracurricular internships, and social connections to be professionally successful, and status biases and discrimination continue to disadvantage underrepresented groups in higher education and the workforce.[50] To conceptualize passion as sufficient for success glosses over these structural and cultural constraints and places the blame for failure squarely on the shoulders of individual career aspirants who are presumed to simply have not worked hard enough.

STRONGER TOGETHER: HOW INDIVIDUALISTIC LABOR
MARKET BELIEFS SUPPORT ONE ANOTHER TO
REINFORCE THE UNEQUAL STATUS QUO

In a press interview in 2015, Richard Bolles, author of *What Color Is Your Parachute?*, said:

> Today's jobs are essentially adventures. You never know what's going to happen next. . . . You must find job satisfaction in the work itself. Your self-esteem must come from doing the work rather than from some hoped-for promotion, pay raise, or other reward—which may never materialize. . . . I truly believe that absent the victim mentality, everyone—regardless of background, education, or ability—can carve out a good path for themselves in this tumultuous workplace.[51]

This chapter showed that Bolles's belief that hard work and passion drive success even in the face of structural obstacles is common among many of the passion principle adherents I studied.

The previous chapters examined the passion principle as a guiding principle that individuals marshal to prioritize and make decisions about their own career paths. In this chapter, I explored the passion principle as a broader meaning-making schema. Using interviews with career aspirants and data from the PPS, I showed that as a widespread cultural schema the passion principle not only reaches into adherents' innermost sense of self (see Chapter 2), but it also helps them make sense of the operation of the labor force generally and can be used as a prescriptive account of how they think people should make career decisions. I found that adherence to the passion principle is not just an isolated cultural schema that stands apart from other beliefs about the labor force. Rather, it is embedded in a web of other powerful cultural beliefs—ones that tend to individualize career success and failure, portray the labor force as basically fair, and dismiss systemic inequalities as obstacles that can be overcome with sufficient hard work. Holding constant whether respondents were passionate about their *own* jobs (which might color how they see passion-seeking in general), respondents who adhered to the passion principle were more likely to believe in the meritocratic ideology and the personal responsibility trope.

The cultural beliefs discussed in this chapter are co-constitutive, and the processes of scaffolding unfold simultaneously. In concert, the passion principle, the meritocratic ideology, and the neoliberal personal responsibility trope present an enticingly individualistic story about labor force participation and advancement: people freely choose their career paths based on their passion, that passion intrinsically drives hard work, that hard work is recognized and rewarded by a fair labor market, and people find success as a result. Within such a logic, structural barriers are downplayed or dismissed, and individuals have the freedom and the burden of charting their own course in the labor market. Anyone can "carve out a good path for themselves" (in Bolles's words) in a field that speaks to their personal interests as long as they invest sufficient passion-driven work.

The passion principle thus helps scaffold a particularly atomized, choice-centric understanding of labor market dynamics and workers' fates therein. The passion principle fits comfortably next to meritocratic and personal responsibility–based notions of the labor force, where "the sanctity of individual choice is elevated to the highest priority; cost-benefit analysis provides guidelines for behavior, and the individual inadequacies [are] justified, functional, and inevitable."[52] Illuminating the passion principle's interconnection with the meritocratic ideology and the personal responsibility trope reveals the rhetorical power that is available from the interlocking of these beliefs.

Without understanding the role the passion principle plays in scaffolding—and being scaffolded by—meritocratic and neoliberal understandings of labor market success, scholars may underestimate the reach and persuasiveness of all three of these beliefs. The passion principle may make meritocratic and neoliberal notions of labor force participation more palatable to those with more progressive understandings of broader social processes of inequality. Those who otherwise recognize structural racism, sexism, and economic inequality may still promote passion-seeking as the best method of career decision-making and thereby implicitly promote these individualistic narratives of career success or even choicewash certain patterns of occupational segregation.

Broader Considerations for Inequality

The results presented in this chapter suggest three ways that the passion principle may legitimize and reinforce processes of labor market inequality. First, the passion principle helps choicewash patterns of occupational segregation and inequality. Strong adherents to the passion principle were more likely to explain away occupational segregation and interoccupation wage inequalities as the outcome of people following their idiosyncratic interests and were more likely to believe that structural obstacles could be overcome with individual effort. Like Sherrie's comments about the brickmaker at the start of the chapter, framing occupational segregation as the outcome of passion-seeking explains away these systemic inequalities. This outcome likely operates on both the individual level (affecting people's valuation of policies and actions that might address inequality) and the macro institutional level, shaping what avenues for action that public and private organizations and institutions see as culturally available to them.

Second, the passion principle helps scaffold core beliefs in the meritocratic ideology and the personal responsibility trope—two of the most effective beliefs at undermining workers' collective power and eroding public support for policies and programs that make labor market opportunities and outcomes more equitable.[53] The passion principle is an ideal input to an assumedly meritocratic system of career advancement where people are seen as solely responsible for their own career outcomes. This scaffolding does two things: (a) it undermines existing efforts and social services that seek to address those inequalities (e.g., welfare policies, affirmative action, need-based scholarships); and (b) it challenges the legitimacy of other structural and social changes (e.g., more progressive taxation) that might better address those inequalities.

The passion principle, in conjunction with the meritocratic ideology and neoliberalism's personal responsibility trope, allows for the telling of an even tidier, more seductively individualized story about labor force participation than the meritocratic ideology or neoliberalism alone. To the extent that the passion principle is a dominant cultural narrative about career decisions in education and the workforce more broadly, it may help legitimize patterns of occupational segregation in the eyes of educators, employers, institutional leaders, and lawmakers, as well as career aspirants. And the ubiquity of these views may make it difficult for policy makers and the public to imagine alternatives.[54]

Third, the passion principle may benefit dominant social groups by allowing them to frame their successes as the outcome of their own passion-based choices and the hard work that grew organically out of that passion. White wealthy men who do better in the labor market than other sociodemographic groups, may, like Steve Jobs and Elon Musk were apt to do, attribute their success to their passion-fueled tenacity, not their privileges and resources. They may have been passionate, but it was not passion alone that got them where they are. To be successful and to attribute one's success to one's passion is to win twice: one wins the economic success game *and* the cultural legitimacy game. A successful person who reaches the upper echelon of their profession and claims that their success is the result of their passion is an especially pernicious manifestation of the way the passion principle may serve to justify privilege.

Of course, not all passion principle adherents choicewash occupational inequalities or believe uncritically in the meritocratic ideology and the personal responsibility trope. And, in making sense of the world, people may draw on many, sometimes contradictory cultural narratives.[55] Yet beliefs about the labor force matter. Individuals and institutions who account for inequalities as the outcome of systematic structural factors are more likely to support policies and programs designed to undermine unequal opportunities or outcomes; those blaming inequalities on an individual's failings are more likely to reject such measures.[56] The passion principle may also help obfuscate the responsibility of educational institutions and employment organizations to more fairly distribute opportunities.

Overall, then, the passion principle is entwined with and contributes to a system of beliefs about the labor force that puts responsibility on individuals to pull themselves up by their bootstraps and denies the existence or severity of occupational inequalities. If Andrés is a brickmaker because he loves bricks and not because he has limited access to work that does not involve manual piece-rate outdoor labor, then there is little incentive for policies and practices to change the economic structures he labors within.

5 Exploiting Passion?

Project Analyst, Senior at Booz Allen Hamilton Inc.
Alexandria, VA

Are you passionate about helping organizations understand
and reach their goals? Do you live for that "aha!" moment
when your client realizes you just showed them how to
transform their organization? Many organizations know
where they want to go, but getting there can be a challenge.
We're looking for you: a strategy consultant who can identify an organization's long term goals and show it how to
achieve them.

Senior Software Engineer, DevOps at Capital One
Vienna, VA

The Capital One Engineering team is looking to hire a Full-
Stack DevOps engineer who is passionate about CI/CD [a
programming approach] and wants to be part of
the team that builds and maintains a centrally supported
set of scaled, integrated tools that enable the larger
software engineering community to accelerate development
of quality software and facilitate their automated
deployments.

Construction Safety Supervisor at FORMA
Construction Company
Seattle, WA

Are you passionate about safety and ensuring everyone
works in a safe manner and environment? At FORMA
one of our guiding principles is "Nobody Gets Hurt!"

We are currently looking for talented Safety Supervisors
who create, support, and will reinforce our commitment
to safety.

Monster.com job advertisements, retrieved May 20, 2019

When perusing online job advertisements or shop window help wanted
signs, the adjective *passionate* is hard to miss. The listings above appeared
among the first ten advertisements of over fifteen thousand results when
I searched for the term "passionate" on Monster.com. Indeed, organizations often list passion as a criterion when advertising for new employees.[1]
Why is this reference to passion so common? As long as workers do their
jobs well, why would employers be so interested in whether they find personal meaning and self-expressive fulfillment in them?

Chapter 1 illustrated that most college-educated career aspirants—and
US workers generally—highly valued having work that is self-expressive
and meaningful. Chapter 2 showed that part of this valuation is rooted in
the belief that passion facilitates sustained investments of time and attention that seem necessary for professional success. Passion, according to the
schema, provides a ready supply of intrinsic motivation to work hard and
stay invested—motivation that money or status alone cannot provide.

But what about the people and organizations that employ passionate
workers? Do they benefit from career aspirants' commitments to passion-
seeking, perhaps even to the detriment of those passionate employees?
This chapter investigates the *demand side* of the passion principle:
whether employers benefit from, prefer, and even take unfair advantage of
job applicants' and employees' passion for their career fields.

As we have seen, passion-seeking among career aspirants is often
accompanied by a willingness—even expectation—to trade higher salaries
and job security for work they "love." Even more, passionate workers voluntarily put more effort into their jobs than is expected of them and as a
result may be preferred by employers over workers motivated by salary or
career advancement.[2] I find not only that employers benefit from passionate workers but also that people with hiring authority are more interested

in passionate applicants because they seem more likely to bring extra commitment and effort to their jobs without demanding additional compensation for it. Employers, in other words, may knowingly take advantage of passionate workers' personal investment in their work without compensating them accordingly.

IS PASSION PART OF WORKER EXPLOITATION?

Before exploring the demand side of the passion principle, it is helpful to take a brief detour to review two bedrock characteristics of capitalist workplaces central to the concerns here. First, workers have to be motivated in some way to put in effort at work—either by indirect or direct coercion or by personal investment in the outcomes of their work. Second, profit in capitalist economies is the result of workers being paid less for the goods and services they produce than the worth of those goods and services on the market. As I explain below, the former insight is a key feature of Weberian ideas of modern economic relations; the latter is a cornerstone of Marxist theories of capitalism and worker exploitation.[3] Employees' passion for their work can serve a role in both processes in ways that may handsomely benefit employers and shortchange passionate workers.

For Max Weber, one of the central puzzles of the capitalist labor market is the issue of worker incentive. For work efficiency to be optimized in an organization, Weber believed, workers must have an "inclination" to work. Such an inclination can come from indirect or direct compulsion: workers may be compelled to work in order to provide for their families, in order to avoid punishment or shame, or because they are supervised and surveilled. Another way workers can be "inclined" to work is to be *personally* invested in the act of work itself, where a laborer "adapts a set of attitudes toward work where it is performed as if it were an absolute end in itself."[4] As discussed in Chapter 1, the Protestant ethic is one such moral imperative to work hard, irrespective of indirect or direct compulsion. The Protestant ethic's religious roots have given way today to the secular idea of "work devotion," or the expectation to demonstrate dedication to hard work and commitment to one's organization as an indicator of moral worth.[5] Such cultural or religious imperatives to work hard are effective ways of getting workers to invest effort in their jobs but require a "long and arduous process of education and socialization."[6]

Passion for one's work is an alluring alternative to the moral imperative of hard work for its own sake. Passion promises to inspire the inclination to work hard that is expected of employees in a capitalist economy, without requiring either extensive external compulsion by employers or the moral imperative of hard work for its own sake. Being a diligent worker is a much easier sell when work is one's passion. As I saw among the passion-seeking college graduates discussed in Chapter 3, dedicated labor force participation can feel like an act of self-expression and self-actualization. Instead of relying on "moral socialization" into the virtues of hard work, or belief that one's work, no matter how mundane, contributes to a broader social good, passion furnishes its *own incentive*.[7] As such, employers may especially value employees who are passionate about their work because, in theory, they would require less compulsion, less supervision, and less discipline to work hard.[8]

In contrast to Weber's interest in worker motivation, Karl Marx was concerned with the exploitation of workers in capitalist economies. Marx explained that exploitation is a "process by which labor effort performed by one group of economic actors is extracted and appropriated by another group."[9] The difference between the economic value of what workers produce and the amount they are compensated for their work is called "surplus value." For Marx, exploitation occurs when this surplus value is taken by employers in the form of profit. Those who provide more surplus value to their employer, either voluntarily or through compulsion, face greater exploitation. Importantly, exploitation is not just a characteristic of the transactional relationships between individual workers and their employers; it is embedded in the nature of the capitalist economic structure itself.[10] As such, exploitation can take place even when individual workers do not *feel* as though they are being exploited.

Others have extended these traditional notions of exploitation, which emerged from Marx's analyses of European industrial workers of the nineteenth century, to other populations. C. Wright Mills, for example, extended this analysis to white-collar and professional workers in the United States. Even though white-collar workers have qualitatively different working conditions from those of the factory workers Marx wrote about, they, too, encounter alienation and exploitation. White-collar workers are often "interchangeable parts of the big chains of authority, . . . sell[ing] their personalities" as well as their time.[11] This type of exploitation can occur not only in for-profit companies but in public and not-for-profit sectors as well.[12]

Workers' physical and mental efforts are not the only things that can be exploited. Arlie Russell Hochschild illustrated that workers' *emotional* labor, or workers' regulation of their emotions during their interactions with supervisors, customers, and colleagues, can be unfairly co-opted as well. When the labor that workers provide is required to be done with certain emotions (e.g., interpersonal warmth expected of flight attendants), those emotions can be appropriated as part of that labor.[13] Hochschild calls this process "transmutation," whereby private acts (like smiling and good humor) fall under the sway of employing organizations.[14]

I argue here that passionate workers' personal enjoyment of and curiosity about the substantive tasks of their career field can similarly get transmuted into outcomes of interest to their employing organizations, benefiting the latter in ways that employees are not fairly recognized or compensated for. In Chapter 2, we saw that many college-going aspirants believed that passion-related work would allow them to be more successful because passion would provide the intrinsic motivation to put in extra hours and effort beyond a standard forty-hour workweek. Yet such passion-driven labor nonetheless produces extra value for employers—even if it does not feel alienating to workers—and employers may be well aware of that fact.

SACRIFICING FOR PASSION

The passion principle prioritizes the pursuit of passion-based work over the pursuit of high salary or occupational prestige. Adherents to the passion principle often expressed readiness to sacrifice pay and economic stability for a career field they found fulfilling. Many passion-seeking students articulated their expectation and even willingness to work long hours, "eat ramen noodles," and be "comfortable being like a really poor twenty-something" if it meant that they could do work they are passionate about. A communications major at Stanford explained, "I had resigned myself a long time ago to know that I just wanted to write, so I knew I wasn't going to make any money" (working-class Black woman). Similarly, in response to a question about bad reasons for making career decisions, Lilly, an engineering major, noted:

> Honestly, right off the bat is like for money. Because even though money is a necessary thing in life to live on this planet and in our society, it's not like, it shouldn't be a driving force in your decision-making, because you can find a way to make it work. If you don't make as much money in your career, like your salary, it'll be okay. . . . If you apply yourself in whatever your passion is, it'll work out. (Middle-class Asian woman)

This willingness to sacrifice for work they "love" was similarly prevalent among students from different class backgrounds. A Stanford earth systems major from a wealthy family put it this way:

> I'm sort of the opinion, if it pays at all, I can make it work. I think maybe later as life goes on it can be more important to make more money, . . . but certainly when you're just starting off you can be very careful with your spending and it's not a big deal if you don't make a lot. I think as long as you're making enough to live on, you're fine. (Upper-class white woman)

An MSU biology student from a working-class family said that he knew he could live on a modest income as long as he liked his work.

> I grew up dirt poor, like getting boxes of clothes from Goodwill every other month kind of poor. So honestly like, my husband and I talk about this all the time. We'll have enough money when we can go to the store, buy the $4 loaf of bread and not feel guilty. . . . Both of us are used to living on nothing, so even a lower-class income will be fine for us. (Working-class white man)

Even many graduates who pursued passion and landed in precarious employment or low-paying work believed their sacrifices were worth it. Recall that Claire, the UH graduate who was working part-time at a Houston natural history museum for less than $20,000 a year, said:

I didn't want to pick something just because it's a really popular field that has a lot of jobs. Because, yes, finding a job is incredibly important, but it would just hurt me to totally abandon my more science, more anthropology, liberal studies background, just to find a computer sciences job that was really popular.

Claire was clear-eyed about the sacrifices she was making in terms of stability and income but explained, "I'm pretty fiscally responsible, so in my mind I'm like, as long as I don't make less than I do now, I know I'll be able to maintain my lifestyle."[15] These responses were echoed in J. Stuart Bunderson and Jeffery Thompson's research on zookeepers, who talked about their commitment to their job and the sacrifices they were willing to make. One zookeeper noted, "Even if I wasn't getting paid, I would still be here."[16]

Analyses in Chapter 2 using nationally representative NSCW data demonstrated that being passionate about one's work has some upsides for well-being: passionate employees are less stressed than their colleagues and are less likely to have depressive symptoms and sleeping problems than those in similar jobs who are not passionate about their work. Other research has found that workers who are passionate about their career fields are more satisfied with their jobs and with their lives than their less passionate peers.[17] Thus, working in one's passion does appear to have personal benefits, at least when compared to the experiences of similar employees who are not passionate about their work.[18] However, those benefits do not necessarily mean that passion-based employment is beneficial all around, as the overwork that may accompany passion-driven work has its own health challenges.[19]

In short, college-goers and college graduates who adhered to the passion principle generally expected, or at least expressed willingness in the abstract, to sacrifice financially for work they were passionate about.[20] This readiness to sacrifice for one's passion is likely good for employers' bottom line: like these respondents, people who are motivated to find personal fulfillment and meaning in their work may be willing to accept positions with lower pay or less stability than they might otherwise be able to secure with their credentials. But do passionate workers benefit their employers in other ways?

DO PASSIONATE WORKERS WORK HARDER?

As I illustrated in Chapter 2, adherents to the passion principle typically assumed that people who were passionate would work harder than those motivated by money. In terms of Weber's theory of worker incentives, respondents typically believed that passion provides more compelling and robust personal motivation for hard work than salary.

But is this true? Does passionate investment in one's work really translate into better job outputs than indirect or direct compulsory pressures such as needing to maintain a certain salary level or the fear of being disciplined by managers? Although passion and job engagement likely co-occur—workers who are personally invested in their careers are often also engaged in their day-to-day tasks—they are conceptually distinct.[21] Passion is a personal commitment to one's career field, which may or may not come with industriousness or conscientiousness in the way one engages in one's tasks on a day-to-day basis.[22] One could be passionate about the substantive area of work but be highly disengaged with their colleagues and most of the tasks their jobs entailed. For instance, Claire could be passionate about her curatorial work but dislike and slack off on the paperwork and administrative responsibilities of her job. In turn, one might be engaged with one's colleagues and dedicated to one's organization but not be passionate about the specific subject matter of the work.

National-level data on federal employees from the 2016 Merit Principles Survey (MPS) shows that workers who are more passionate about their work are more likely to be engaged in their jobs than less passionate workers. The top set of bars in Figure 5.1 presents the means for passionate (54% of the sample) and non-passionate (46% of the sample) federal employees across a number of engagement-related questions.[23] Indicating that passionate federal employees are more engaged in their jobs than their colleagues, passionate employees are significantly more likely to say they try to innovate, look for possible problems, and look for ways to help and motivate their colleagues.[24] These patterns are robust to variation in education level, demographics, job type, and industry.

There is a similar pattern in the 2008 NSCW data: employees who find their work meaningful and feel like they can be themselves at work (49% of the sample) are significantly more likely to feel personally responsible

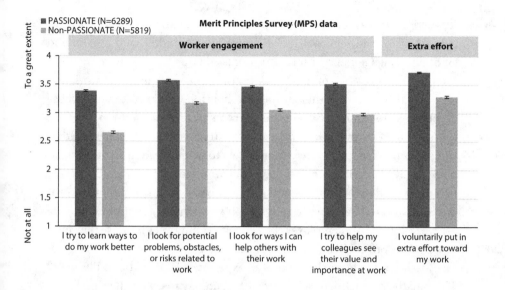

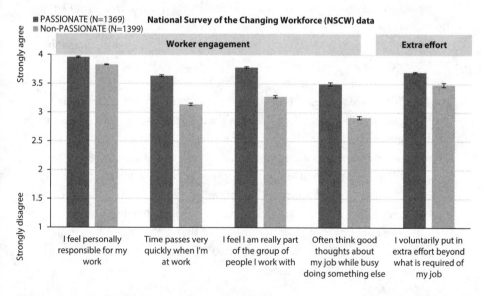

Figure 5.1 Means on worker engagement and voluntary extra effort measures for passionate and non-passionate US workers (MPS and NSCW data).

for their job tasks and to feel they are part of the team they work with (bottom set of bars in Figure 5.1).[25] Suggesting their additional mental and emotional engagement with their job, passionate workers are more likely than non-passionate workers to say that time passes quickly at work and that they think positive thoughts about their job when not at work. These differences are robust to worker demographics and job variation.[26]

Both the MPS and NSCW data showed that respondents who were passionate about their work were more likely to be engaged in their jobs and more likely to report acting in ways that were helpful to their coworkers and organizations. Engagement has long been a factor tied to work productivity and worker retention—both of which greatly benefit employing organizations.[27] And employers like engaged employees because they tend to be more productive.[28] I also found that passionate workers are less likely to intend to leave their jobs—an expensive problem for employers.[29] These patterns are mirrored in social psychology research that has found that passionate employees are more proactive and entrepreneurial than their less passionate peers.[30]

Passionate workers aren't just more likely to be engaged in their jobs, however. Analyses of the MPS and NSCW data show further that these passionate workers were also more likely than their peers to report that they voluntarily put in effort beyond what is required of their jobs (rightmost set of bars in Figure 5.1). In both data sets, these patterns hold net of differences by demographics such as gender, race, age, and industry, employment sector, and hours worked.

Overall, then, passionate employees are especially beneficial to the organizations they work for: they are more likely than their colleagues to be engaged in their tasks and more likely to report that they voluntarily put in more effort than their jobs demand of them. This provides employing organizations with "bonus" effort—effort that their less passionate colleagues may not put toward their jobs.

ARE PASSIONATE WORKERS PREFERRED BY EMPLOYERS?

Employers have a clear incentive to hire employees who will work hard. But passion is not the only personal investment in work that might keep workers motivated and on track. Employees might work hard because they are committed to their colleagues or the organization they work for, even if they don't like their particular line of work. Others may strive for promotion or advancement and are therefore invested in excelling at their jobs. Organizational dedication and promotion are both personal motivations for high work effort that do not require passion for the substantive elements of one's field. Employers might even prefer organizational devotees and career climbers over passionate workers. Many white-collar workers take a "high performance, low loyalty" approach to their jobs: they are deeply dedicated to their work, but if there is a chance for a job that is a better fit for them or is in better alignment with their interests, they have little loyalty to the organization that employs them.[31] If passion is attached to one's substantive career field and not necessarily to the specific position one occupies or the organization one works for, then passionate workers whose passion is not well served by their specific jobs might leave to take jobs elsewhere.[32] Organizational devotees and career climbers, in contrast, may be more committed to their specific organizations and thus may be less of a flight risk than passion-seekers.

So do employers actually prefer passionate employees to employees with other reasons to work hard in their jobs? The Passion Principle Experiment (PPE) provided an opportunity to explore this question.

PPE respondents were presented with descriptions of three fictitious workers with different personal motivations for hard work. Employee A was motivated by salary, Employee B was motivated by interest in a promotion, and Employee C was motivated by passion for the work.

- **Employee A** is primarily motivated by the salary of his job. The primary purpose of working in this job is to support his life and hobbies outside of work. Although employee A receives great reviews from his boss, he often wishes time would pass more quickly at work. He greatly appreciates weekends and vacations and is looking forward to retirement in the future. Although he likes the colleagues he works with, he would probably not go into the same occupation if he lived his life over again.

- **Employee B** enjoys his work but does not expect to be in his current job five years from now. Instead, he plans to move on to a higher-level job in the company with more status and more responsibility. He has several goals for the advancement of his career. Sometimes his work seems like a waste of time, but he knows that he must do sufficiently well in his current position in order to get a promotion. For him, a promotion means recognition of good work and a sign of his success.

- **Employee C**'s job is one of the most important parts of his life. He is very pleased that he is in this line of work. Because what he does for a living is a vital part of his identity, it is one of the first things he tells people about himself. Employee C feels good about his work because he loves it. He finds the content of his work interesting and engaging.[33]

Respondents were asked which employee of the three they preferred on a variety of measures. Figure 5.2 presents the proportion of respondents who preferred each of the three fictitious employees across four considerations: which person they would most like to supervise, which person they think would be the hardest worker, which one they would most like to hire, and which they think would be the most reliable employee. Is the promotion-oriented employee (employee B) preferred over the passionate one (employee C)? Not often. Among the PPE respondents, the passionate employee was preferred 5 to 1 over the promotion-motivated employee. Consistent with the general cultural devaluation of money-seeking workers, passionate employees were preferred more than 15 to 1 over the salary-motivated employee. The majority of respondents said employee C, the passionate employee, would be the hardest worker (69%) and the most reliable employee (80%) of the three. The great majority also said they would prefer to hire the passionate employee (79%) and supervise the passionate employee (77%), compared to the other two.

This pattern was not simply a matter of the preferences of respondents without any personal experience hiring workers. When I restricted the sample to just those respondents who had hiring authority in their own jobs (36% of the sample; N = 637), the results were virtually identical (the right-hand bar in each pair in Figure 5.2): hiring managers said they would prefer to hire the passionate employee (employee C) 5 to 1 over the promotion-motivated employee (employee B) and nearly 23 to 1 over the salary-motivated employee (employee A). Hiring managers also preferred the passionate employee over the others in their assessment of who would be the most reliable employee and the hardest worker (78% and 67%, respectively, preferred passionate employees over the others).[34]

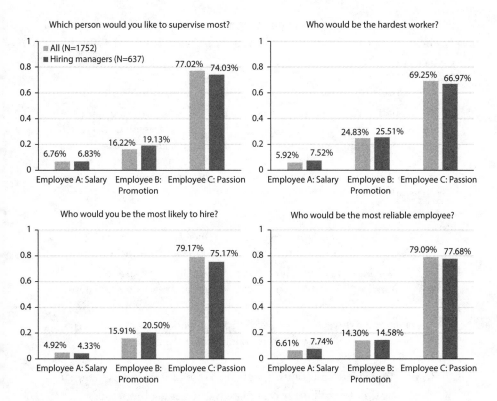

Figure 5.2 Proportion of college-educated workers who preferred employee A, B, and C on four considerations, for all respondents (light bars) and for the subsample of respondents with hiring authority (dark bars) (PPE data).

These vignettes uncover the relative valuation of abstract categories of employees by these college-educated workers. Yet the employees depicted in these vignettes are artificial archetypes with limited applicability to concrete organizations or actual workers. Are passionate employees preferred over workers motivated by other factors in more realistic scenarios?

PREFERRING PASSIONATE APPLICANTS

The PPE included an experiment to test respondents' reactions to a randomly assigned realistic job application portfolio. The description of the exercise instructed respondents to assume they were evaluating a real applicant for an actual job. Respondents were given the following instructions.

Instructions

As part of this study, we are interested in how workers assess the appropriateness of applicants for different jobs. You will be presented with a job advertisement and then randomly assigned an applicant to review. We will show you the *cover letter* and *résumé* of the applicant. Please carefully review the application materials. You will be asked about your opinion of the candidate after viewing the application.

Important notes:

(1) *We are interested in your perspective as a member of the workforce*; please provide your best professional assessment of the applicant.

(2) You will have only one opportunity to review the job advertisement and the applicant. You will not be able to go back and review these materials later. Please read these documents carefully before clicking "NEXT."

(3) Later in the survey, you will be asked 1–3 attention check questions of medium difficulty based on these application materials.

Respondents were randomly assigned to one of four different versions of an application portfolio for one of two different job openings (a 4x2 design). The first job was a youth program manager position in a fictitious community nonprofit I called CommunityThrive. The second job was a staff accountant position in a fictitious IT firm I called TelMark IT. Compared to the youth program manager position, this accounting job was designed to seem less likely to require passion as a job skill.[35] (See Appendix C.2 for the job ads.) Both companies were located in Columbus, Ohio. Respondents were shown a Monster.com-style advertisement for one of these positions, along with a résumé and cover letter from the applicant, "Riley Williamson."[36]

I created two versions of Riley Williamson's résumé, one for each job, that listed education and internship experiences appropriate for each position (see Appendixes C.5 and C.6). The cover letters, however, varied within each job. They expressed one of four different rationales for Riley's interest in the job: (1) the salary is commensurate with Riley's expectations; (2) Riley is excited about the city where the job is located; (3) Riley is committed to the organization where the job is located; or (4) Riley is passionate about the job content. The wording in the cover letters for each job was identical except for the following sentences.

Youth Program Manager Job at "Community Thrive"

- **Passion Condition:** "I am also passionate about child development; facilitating kids' learning is exciting and interesting to me and I really enjoy the work."
- **Company Condition:** "I also like this organization—I would appreciate being affiliated with such a well-respected non-profit."
- **Location Condition:** "I also like the city where the job is located."
- **Salary Condition:** "This position also meets my salary expectations."

Accounting Job at "TelMark IT Solutions"

- **Passion Condition:** "I also have a passion for accounting—managing financial accounts is exciting and interesting to me and I really enjoy the work."
- **Company Condition:** "I also like the organization—I would appreciate being affiliated with such a well-respected IT company."
- **Location Condition:** "I also like the city where the job is located."
- **Salary Condition:** "This position also meets my salary expectations."

Each respondent was assigned to review an application with one of these eight job-letter pairings. The only thing that varied within each job was the single sentence in Riley's cover letter indicating why Riley was interested in the job. (See Appendixes C.3 and C.4 for the cover letter templates for each job.)

The goal of this experiment was to see which applicant was given the highest average rating for each job and to understand why those applicants were most highly rated. Because this experimental design holds everything else about the applicant constant across the treatment conditions, including things like education level, work experience, and grade point average, I can precisely determine the effects of the different motivations expressed in the cover letter on the likelihood that respondents would want to hire their assigned applicant.

The four versions of the cover letter—expressing interest in the location, the organization, the salary, and passion for the work—represent four different types of personal motivation for engaging in work. These are proxies for different theoretical orientations in the literature on career decision-making. Neoclassical economists, who argue that workers seek to maximize their lifetime earnings, might expect that the salary-motivated applicant would be seen as the most reliable and preferable since the job's salary is commensurate with the applicant's desired compensation.[37] On the other hand, some work and occupations scholars might expect that the applicant who expressed commitment to the *organization* would best align with work devotion and ideal worker expectations, as commitment to the organization is important for worker retention and for commitment to engaging in job responsibilities for the good of the organization, not just employees' personal interest.[38] Consistent with the results in this chapter thus far, however, I expect that passionate applicants will be the most highly valued and that respondents' assessment of how hardworking the passionate applicant would be will help explain this higher valuation.

Consistent with that expectation, I found that respondents who were assigned the passionate applicant were significantly more likely to express interest in hiring that individual than those who reviewed the applicants interested in the job's organization, location, or salary. Figure 5.3 presents the proportion of respondents evaluating each version of Riley's application who agreed that they would be interested in hiring Riley for the advertised job. The top left set of bars represents results for all the respondents who saw an application for the accounting position. Here 82% of those who saw the application from passionate Riley were interested in hiring Riley, compared to only 73%, 64%, and 65%, respectively, of those who saw an application with a cover letter emphasizing Riley's commitment to the company, interest in the location, and interest in the salary. This pattern was the same among the subset of respondents who have hiring authority in their own jobs; see the top right set of bars.

These patterns were echoed among the respondents assigned to evaluate applicants to the youth program manager position. Again, a significantly higher proportion of all respondents (and hiring managers) who saw the passionate version of the application materials were interested in hiring Riley, compared to those who saw other cover letter versions. This is shown in the bottom sets of bars in Figure 5.3.

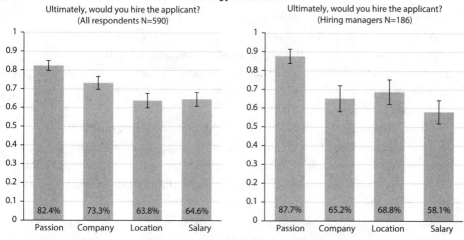

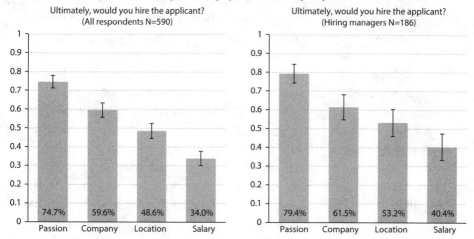

Figure 5.3 Percent of respondents interested in hiring the applicant they reviewed for the accounting job (top row) and the youth program manager job (bottom row), by cover letter emphasis (PPE data).

Again, these application materials were identical except for a single line in the cover letter that explained the applicant's motivation for applying to the position. This pattern was mirrored in the case of both the youth program manager job and the accounting job. In supplemental analyses, I found that this higher value given to passionate applicants was robust to differences in respondents' demographic characteristics, industry, education level, and the gender they believed Riley to be.

Did passionate Riley seem smarter or more skilled than the other applicant versions? Even though the résumés were identical within each job, passionate Riley was more likely to be rated as highly skilled than the other versions of Riley's application in both job conditions (see the first set of bars in Figure 5.4). For the accounting position, the passionate Riley was no more or less likely to be rated as smart than other application versions. For the youth program manager position, however, passionate Riley was more likely to be rated as smart than the versions of Riley interested in the location or salary. But passionate Riley was just as likely to be rated as smart as the organization-dedicated Riley in the context of the youth program manager position.

Beyond assessment of whether the applicant was smart or skilled, the most striking and consistent distinction between the different work motivations occurred in the assessment of how much effort respondents thought Riley would put into their job. Overall, across the two jobs, the passionate applicant was more highly valued because the raters thought they would be *hard workers*—that their particular brand of personal motivation for work would engender more engagement and work effort in ways that those motivated by interest in the organization, location, or salary might not be. Figure 5.4 shows that when Riley's cover letter expressed passion, Riley was more likely to be perceived as hardworking than when Riley's cover letter expressed other motivations for interest in the job. Respondents were also more likely to say that passionate Riley would be *willing to take on additional responsibilities without an increase in pay*. This was the case for both the accounting and the youth program manager positions.

Using the statistical modeling technique called mediation analysis, I examined whether these differential ratings of applicants as hardworking and willing to take on more responsibilities without an increase in pay

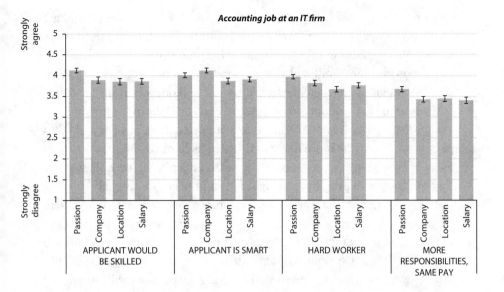

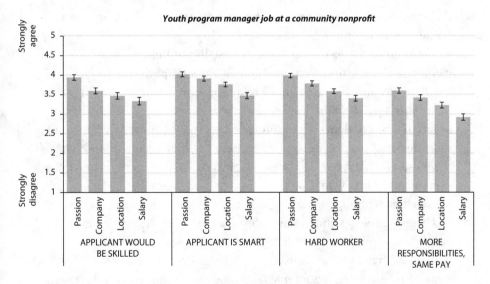

Figure 5.4 Respondents' average impressions of applicants to the accounting job (top) and the youth program manager job (bottom), by cover letter emphasis (PPE data).

helps explain respondents' greater enthusiasm for hiring the passionate applicant compared to the other three applicants.[39] Table C.7 in Appendix C presents the indirect effects of motivation type (career, salary, location, or passion) on the likelihood that respondents would want to hire Riley via assessment of Riley as hardworking. These models indicate that part of the reason that respondents expressed less enthusiasm for hiring Riley when Riley was motivated by the organization, location, or salary was that passionate Riley was more likely to be rated as hardworking and as more likely to take on greater responsibilities without a pay increase. This holds for both the youth program manager job and the accounting job.

PPE respondents showed a clear preference for passionate Riley. Were they willing to offer the passionate applicant a high salary to entice them to work for the organization? The results of the PPE experiment indicate that is not the case. Among respondents who said they would be willing to hire Riley, those who were interested in hiring the passionate Riley *did not offer significantly higher salaries* than those who were interested in hiring the versions of the applicant motivated by location, salary, or organizational commitment.[40] In other words, they believed passionate Riley would be a hard worker and stronger contributor but were not willing to compensate that work or entice Riley with greater pay.

This experiment focused on the role of passion in respondents' desire to hire fictitious but realistic applicants for a realistic-seeming job and the salary that respondents were willing to offer those applicants. The results indicated that passionate applicants were the highest rated, and part of the reason for this positive assessment was raters' presumptions that passionate applicants would be hard workers and voluntarily take on additional effort without demanding a corresponding increase in salary.

Hiring processes and salary offers are not the only ways in which employers might take advantage of a worker's passion. Jae Yun Kim and colleagues' vignette-based survey study suggested that employers may be more willing to assign additional tasks, and more unpleasant tasks, to passionate employees than they would to less passionate employees.[41] Among respondents in that study, willingness to treat workers more exploitatively was correlated with respondents' belief that passionate workers consider work its own reward.[42] The results of that study indicated that the potential exploitation of passionate workers is not just in the hiring and remuneration aspects of employment analyzed here but also in the treatment of passionate workers on a day-to-day basis.

These patterns are not isolated to experimental settings. As I showed above, among the nationally representative sample of workers in the NSCW data, those who are passionate about their work are more engaged than their colleagues and more likely to go above and beyond in their jobs (see Figure 5.1). But those same data also show that passionate employees do *not* enjoy higher salaries than otherwise similar workers (controlling for a host of demographic and job characteristics), even though passionate workers are more engaged on average and more likely to put extra effort into their work (see Table C.8 in Appendix C).

These results reveal a striking inequity in the effort-compensation equation: organizations benefit more when their employees are passionate about their jobs, but passionate employees do not earn more, on average, than their less passionate peers. Returning to the traditional Marxist language of exploitation, surplus value is the value that employees produce through their work but are not compensated for. Passionate employees may produce more surplus value than their colleagues, but this additional value may go uncompensated.[43] Say, for example, a salaried art gallery salesperson named Julie is passionate about her work. Julie spends three or four hours of her leisure time on the weekends reading art magazines and books that she purchases herself. She enjoys this reading, but it also helps her keep up on trends in the art world in ways that make a good impression on gallery customers. Yet Julie does not make more money than her coworkers who do not invest this time outside of work. The additional time she spends reading makes Julie better at working with the gallery's clients and may allow Julie to advance to her next position more quickly, but that extra time she invests on the weekends is uncompensated. It is, in other words, time that her employer benefits from but does not pay her for.[44]

Although passion is not typically conceptualized in terms of labor time, work done out of passion is still labor. The additional care and attention passionate employees put toward their work because of their personal interest may be appropriated as surplus value that employing organizations benefit from but may not compensate.

Importantly, the experimental results in this chapter suggest that employers are aware of the potential benefits of passionate workers when considering whether to hire them: respondents—including those with hiring authority—were more likely to say that passionate applicants were not only hardworking but also willing to take on more responsibility without additional compensation. This is echoed in the earlier vignette results: the majority of respondents preferred a passionate worker over one motivated by career advancement or salary, seeing the passionate employees as more hardworking and reliable than the salary- and promotion-motivated workers (see Figure 5.2). It also resonates with interviews with Silicon Valley employers that found that employers sometimes even value passion above skill because of the extra effort they believe passion will evoke from workers.[45]

EXPLOITING PASSION

The purpose of this chapter was to explore whether a possible demand-side basis of disadvantage was tied to career aspirants' and workers' passion for their work. This exploration has only scratched the surface of a complicated set of processes. Yet the results here raise a number of questions about the benefits employers receive from passionate workers—benefits they may not see the need to compensate workers for—as well as the possibility that organizations might deliberately exploit workers' personal sense of fulfillment from their work.

First, both the interview and the survey data indicated that adherents to the passion principle typically believed that pursuing passion sometimes requires sacrificing financial stability they might otherwise be able to secure with their credentials. And many career aspirants themselves prioritized passion over salary or stability when choosing their own career paths and jobs (see Chapter 3).

When I looked at workers, I saw more generally how employers benefit from passion: employees who are passionate about the substance of their work are more engaged in their jobs and more often put in effort beyond what is required by their jobs than their less passionate peers. Potential employers, for their part, seem to prefer passionate employees over workers motivated by career advancement or salary—in part because they see passionate employees as harder working.

And yet this passion-based labor may not be fully compensated. The fictitious passionate applicants in the experiment were not offered higher salaries, and passionate workers in the actual labor force do not earn higher salaries than their less passionate peers either. Other social psychological research suggests that passionate workers may be more likely than their non-passionate colleagues to encounter exploitative treatment once in their jobs.[46]

Passion is thus not just preferred by many career aspirants on the supply side; it may be unfairly taken advantage of by employers on the demand side. Returning to the concerns of the social theorists introduced above, passion is another way to solve the problem that Weber posed of the need to motivate workers and optimize their work effort. Weber argued that either compulsion or personal investment is necessary to get workers to work.[47] Passion appears to be an efficient means of such worker motivation. Certainly, all the pieces seem to be in place. Self-expression and individualism are already entrenched social and moral values. Work that aligns with one's self-expressive goals is a ready-made basis for the optimization of work output: passionate workers may work long and hard in their jobs not necessarily because they feel a moral obligation to work hard for its own sake, but because they see such work as a means to self-fulfillment and personal growth.

To be sure, workers who find their work meaningful and fulfilling may experience that work as qualitatively better on a day-to-day basis than those whose jobs are merely a means to earn a living.[48] But employers also benefit from the passion of their employees: passionate workers are more engaged and voluntarily put in more effort. This may seem like a win-win at first glance, but it points to passion as an ironic site of worker disadvantage: workers may prefer work they are passionate about, but employers may extract more labor from passionate workers without adjusted compensation. This is especially true in industries, like the technology sector, where overwork is part of a normative display of passion. Marianne Cooper, for example, found that men IT professionals "display their exhaustion in order to convey the depths of [their] commitment, stamina, and virility." Such overwork, she reports, is driven by IT professionals' *personal* investment in their work, not by external control exacted by their managers.[49]

These findings raise a number of quandaries for workers and scholars: Is it morally problematic to exploit a worker's passion? Is passion a reward in itself, or should the appropriation of this "labor of love" without additional compensation be considered exploitative? Although the day-to-day lives of individuals who love their work are likely better than those of colleagues who find the tasks of the same work unfulfilling or onerous, having passion for one's paid work does not change the employment relations of that work.[50] Just as Hochschild identified emotional labor as the transmutation of private joys into something that serves the goals and priorities of the organization in which one is employed, passion may be exploited through a similar "transmutation" process.[51] Even if felt genuinely, passion for one's paid work is still a service to the organization one works for.[52]

Beyond the transmutation of one's genuinely felt passion into a benefit for one's organization, certain fields may have *expectations* for the expression and performance of passion. In some occupations—primary education, professional sports, community organizing, for example—a worker might be expected to express passion for their work as a sign of their commitment.[53] Unlike emotional labor, where workers perform a particular emotional display, whether or not it is genuine, this expectation for passion is a forced performance of self-expressive commitment.[54] Employers may see the expression of passion as its own marker of aptitude, and employees may be judged accordingly.[55] The expression of passion for one's work may actually be a critical cultural marker used for sorting individuals into jobs and making hiring and promotion decisions within organizations.

In addition, passion may be recognized and rewarded differently depending on the applicant or employee in question. The experiment in this chapter held constant the identity of the applicant. However, in real organizations, hiring managers and supervisors may expect different intensities of passion from their applicants or employees depending on their sociodemographic characteristics. Cooper's IT workers' display of their commitment to their work was distinctly *masculine*—being a hero who pushes through deadlines with brute force and intellect. This normative way of performing passion disadvantages women IT professionals and perpetuates male dominance in Silicon Valley IT firms and beyond.[56] Similarly, racial/ethnic minorities in occupations where people of color are most severely underrepresented may be expected to enact strong passion for their work as a way to demonstrate their belonging in their field.[57] More research is needed to understand how the performance of passion (whether felt or not) might be differentially expected and exploited in ways that amplify existing ascriptive inequalities.

In sum, paid labor, even when done with passion, is still exploitative. It may just feel a little less like exploitation. It is a core irony of the passion principle that doing work for self-expressive reasons may feel to passion-seekers like a way to escape the pitfalls of the capitalist labor force but that doing so directs one's private sense of joy and excitement to the benefit of one's employer.[58] The conclusion and epilogue discuss the implications of these and other findings for sociological theory, for social science scholarship on work and labor markets, for education and workplace policy, and for public discourse about careers and career decision-making.

Conclusion

"What do you want to be when you grow up?" This question has been asked of children for generations. Yet it is a peculiar one. What the inquirer wants to know is, "What career path would you like to pursue full-time after you finish your formal education?" This, of course, presumes that "growing up" entails a linear progression from childhood to adulthood, where growing up is synonymous with, or at least runs parallel to, finishing one's training and entering the labor force. This question also presumes a core tenet of the American dream—that whatever the child wants to do can feasibly be achieved.

There's something else that is peculiar about this question. It asks not what the listener wants to *do* but what they want to *be*. To *be* something is a reflection of one's individualistic sense of self. The question, so seemingly benign and supportive of the agency of the young person to whom it is being asked, entwines one's identity with one's work—*being* with *doing*. It is but one example of how deeply culturally interconnected our sense of identity is with our contributions to the paid labor force.

This book places at its center a shared cultural model for good career decision-making, one that also entwines identity with work. Identifying the passion principle as a common but largely unexplored cultural model for good career decision-making, the book seeks to examine the broader implications of this schema: how career aspirants wanting to find work that aligns with their passion fare as they navigate the labor force with different safety nets and springboards, how the passion principle choicewashes existing patterns of occupational inequality and scaffolds meritocratic and neoliberal ideologies about the labor market, and how passion among employees might not only be preferred, but also exploited. The passion principle is a compelling cultural schema that not only informs how people think about good career decision-making in the abstract and motivates their own career paths (with divergent consequences) but also serves as a prescriptive and explanatory narrative about occupational inequalities in the labor force and one that gets enrolled in employers' assessments of good workers.

I draw on a number of sources to tell this story: interview data with 100 college students and follow-up interviews with 35 of them, interviews with 24 career counselors and coaches, a unique survey fielded to a proportionally representative sample of college-educated workers, a survey experiment, and several secondary survey data sets of representative samples of US workers. This empirical approach addresses the theoretical questions raised in this book using the data sources most appropriate to each question. My goal has been to walk around the central concept of this book to view it from several different theoretical and empirical angles.

This concluding chapter reviews and extends the arguments from the previous chapters. I start with a short summary of those arguments and draw out their structural and individual-level implications. I then discuss what these findings might mean for scholars, higher education administrators, policy makers, and individual career aspirants who are navigating complex decision-making processes. The end of this chapter and the epilogue point out the difficult existential questions these results raise about how good jobs, and even good lives, are culturally defined.

I opened the book with a seemingly straightforward question: How do career aspirants and college-educated workers conceptualize good career decision-making? This question is important theoretically because these beliefs not only inform how individual career aspirants and workers shape (or at least desire to shape) their own career paths but also how the broader public makes sense of, and even justifies, existing structures and practices of the capitalist labor force. It is not enough for social scientists to document the institutional processes that shape the economic system; in order to understand the experiences and fates of labor force aspirants and participants, we must also attend to how they make sense of the labor market and the outcomes they prioritize and work toward. In the aggregate, these meaning-making processes may also do cultural work to legitimize and enable enduring processes of sociodemographic labor force inequality.

Drawing on interview and survey data, I found that a prevailing cultural schema for defining good work and good career decision-making among college-educated career aspirants and workers is the *passion principle*: a shared cultural model that centers the pursuit of self-expressive, fulfilling work as the predominant guiding principle in career selection. Although most interview and survey respondents explained that financial stability and job security were important, these were seen by many as secondary to passion-related considerations. Over 75% of the college students I interviewed and 67% of the college-educated workers I surveyed rated the importance of passion-related factors more highly than they rated the importance of job security or salary in their abstract conceptualizations of good career decisions.

Documenting the salience of this cultural schema is an important finding in its own right. It pushes back on typical assumptions in neoclassical economics, economic sociology, and business circles that college students and college-educated workers overwhelmingly prioritize economic advancement as they think about good work and good career paths.

Career aspirants and workers were a bit more "practical" when it came to their own career decisions; they acknowledged the importance of work stability and salary for long-term financial security. Nonetheless, over two-thirds of the college graduates I interviewed sought paths that aligned with their passion after leaving college, often tolerating employment precarity or sacrificing better-paying or more stable options to pursue work they found fulfilling. Most career aspirants believed that regardless of the path they pursued, a college degree would provide an economic floor below which they would be unlikely to fall and above which they would be able to build a comfortable, middle-class life.

Furthermore, when I asked college-educated survey respondents what would be important in their own decisions about whether they would take a new job, 46% ranked passion and interest for the work as their top priority, compared to 20% and 13% who rated salary and job security, respectively, as their top priority in a new job. Further, among college-educated workers who said they had voluntarily switched paths at some point in their careers, nearly half did so to find more meaningful and fulfilling work or to "follow their dream." So while career aspirants and workers were not naive about the risks involved in a precarious labor market, and not everyone prioritized passion-seeking, the passion principle was not only a dominant cultural ideal of good career decision-making in the abstract; it served as a guiding principle for many college-educated career aspirants and workers' own decision-making.

Although this book focuses on college-going and college-educated labor force participants, the passion principle was not absent among other workers. Prioritizing meaningful and fulfilling work was just as valued among those without a four-year degree as those with one. However, likely due to the structural constraints they face finding stable, well-paid jobs, workers without a college degree tended to prioritize salary and job security above passion-related considerations when thinking about the factors important to them in a new job. Thus it is more accurate to understand educational-level differences in guiding principles for decision-making as the greater ability of workers with college degrees to access livable wages, health insurance, and other benefits rather than non-college-educated workers' deprioritization of meaning and fulfillment in their work.[1] In sum, workers across the labor force highly valued and desired jobs that offer self-expression and fulfillment, but college-educated workers' relative privilege in the labor market allows options for prioritizing these over financial security when considering their next career moves.

These patterns raised an obvious follow-up question. In the midst of employment uncertainty, increasing labor market precarity, and growing income inequality,[2] why do so many people find the passion principle a compelling guiding principle for career selection? Interview and survey data revealed that the passion principle is compelling for two main reasons. First, passion was presumed to drive hard work. Career aspirants recognized that the white-collar workforce often requires overwork and intensive dedication in order to succeed. They explained that passion provides a drive to work hard that money alone cannot provide, and they argued that genuine personal interest is the best motivation for the hard work needed for career progression. Second, and more saliently, career aspirants and college-educated workers saw passion for one's work as a keystone not only of a good job but also of a *good life*. Recognizing the potential for self-estrangement in paid work, they saw passion as potential inoculation against a "miserable life," "waking up every day hating going to work." Most career aspirants strongly criticized the demands for overwork and work devotion endemic to white-collar labor and, in turn, saw passion-seeking as a possible inoculation against the frustration, boredom, or estrangement they saw those demands entailing. The institutional structures and peer interactions in which career aspirants were embedded also generally bolstered rather than challenged their belief in passion-seeking. Career-advising professionals typically also focused on their clients' self-expressive interests when counseling them about choosing a career.

The second part of the book takes a critical lens to this cultural schema. Who actually benefits from following their passion, and whose social positions are stagnated or worsened by it? Does passion-seeking presume a stockpile of economic, social, and cultural capital (Chapter 3)? How might the belief that passion-seeking is the best way to make career decisions scaffold understandings of the labor market that deny systemic inequalities (Chapter 4)? And do employers benefit from or even exploit passion-seeking among career aspirants and workers (Chapter 5)? These three chapters raised sobering concerns about how the passion principle as an approach to career decision-making not only comes from a place of privilege, but may reinforce existing economic and social power dynamics.

Returning to the interviews with career aspirants, Chapter 3 followed a subset of the original student interviewees out of college and into the labor force. More socioeconomically privileged respondents had a better chance of securing stable employment in their passion than less privileged career aspirants. Why? More privileged respondents often had access to financial safety nets to help them weather the precarity and financial sacrifices that passion-seeking often entailed and had springboards—educational, cultural, and social capital—that helped them get the most out of college and land stable employment. The difference that such safety nets and springboards made for college graduates has been robustly documented in other research. What is new here is how especially important these resources are to help those who prioritize passion navigate the challenges and sacrifices that passion-seeking often entails, compared to simply prioritizing available, economically viable employment.

Passion-seeking and socioeconomic privilege interface in another way. In particular, passion-seeking was often more risky for career aspirants from working-class backgrounds than for their more privileged peers. Passion-seekers from less privileged families were more likely to end up in precarious employment situations (e.g., part-time baristas, Amazon warehouse pickers) far outside their academic specialization than their more privileged peers who graduated with similar degrees from the same universities. Passion-seekers, in other words, were particularly at risk of falling back into their class status of origin because of the differential resources available to them to weather the challenges and precarity of passion-seeking.

The passion principle is not just a guiding principle for individual action, however. It also does cultural work as a prescriptive and explanatory narrative. By widening the lens to shine an empirical spotlight on the web of cultural beliefs in which the passion principle is embedded, I found that passion principle believers were more likely than passion principle skeptics to presume that the labor market is fair, to individualize success and failure, and to see passion as a thoroughly idiosyncratic feature of individual persons (rather than as socially constructed). Adherents to the passion principle also were more likely to agree that women, racial/ethnic minorities, and socioeconomically disadvantaged persons can overcome gender-, race-, and class-based obstacles if they are personally invested enough in their career path and willing to work hard.

This suggests two types of cultural work that the passion principle does to reinforce labor market inequalities. First, it helps choicewash existing patterns of occupational segregation and inequality as the benign, aggregated result of individual passion-seeking. Second, it helps scaffold the meritocratic ideology and the personal responsibility trope by providing an ideal input to a presumably fairly functioning system. Holders of the meritocratic ideology typically believe that the labor market is fair and all one needs to succeed in it is hard work and dedication.[3] Those who uphold the personal responsibly trope, in turn, emphasize individuals' responsibility for their own economic fate without the help of social support infrastructures.[4] The passion principle provides an important rejoinder to these ideologies: an individualistic, identity-powered engine of hard work. Passionate workers are presumed to be motivated to work hard by their personal connection to their work, and such hard work translates into career success in the fairly functioning labor market. Thus, together, the passion principle, the meritocratic ideology, and the personal responsibility trope tell an even tidier individualized story about the labor force than each belief alone might tell. This web of beliefs may also prompt particularly strong resistance to collective solutions that address structural inequality, such as expanded social support services. It may also serve to downplay the perceived existence of structural inequality itself.

The final empirical chapter pivoted again from the passion principle as a sense-making schema to passion-based work as a possible site of demand-side exploitation. Specifically, Chapter 5 used vignette and experimental data to consider whether employers benefit from passionate workers, whether they prefer passionate workers to workers motivated by career advancement or salary, and whether they may even take unfair advantage of workers' passion for their work. Passionate workers do report that they put in effort beyond what is required of their jobs. And college-educated workers, even those with hiring authority, prefer passionate workers to those who are motivated by career advancement or salary.

In a survey experiment, I found that passionate applicants are preferred in part because they are believed to be especially hardworking. However, those who reviewed the passionate applicants' materials did not offer them higher salaries. Consistent with these experimental results, passionate workers in the college-educated labor force overall do not earn higher salaries on average than their colleagues with similar training and experience who are not as passionate, even though passionate workers are more engaged and more willing to put extra effort into their jobs. I argue that this suggests the transmutation of workers' passion for their work,[5] whereby workers' private joys, interests, and curiosities are repurposed to further the goals of the organizations in which they are employed.

This book focuses on a snapshot of career decision-making experiences: college students as they settled on a major and planned for their postgraduation paths, postcollege young adults as they took stock of their early labor market experiences and oriented themselves in their work, and US workers at a point in time in their careers. However, I suspect the passion principle plays a role in decision-making and identity formation throughout the life course. From elementary and middle school classroom dialogues about the labor force to high school teachers' and counselors' narratives about selecting a career path, the passion principle likely permeates the language primary and secondary school students hear about career selection. The passion principle likely extends far into working life as well. The recent "encore careers" movement is built around the idea of "finally" being able to follow one's passion as one approaches retirement age.[6] Wherever there are major institutional and cultural decision points related to labor force participation (postsecondary training, job searches, job changes, retirement, etc.), the passion principle may play a role. There is much more research to be done to understand how the passion principle is salient at these points in the life course, and other ways it might interface with entrenched patterns of social difference and disadvantages.

This work has important implications for social scientists. It points to the need to gain a better understanding of how self-expressive mechanisms operate in broader cultural and social processes of inequality. I have argued that passion-seeking, in prioritizing self-expression and fulfillment, not only constrains and enables individual career decision-makers, but interfaces with broader cultural beliefs like the meritocratic ideology and neoliberalism's personal responsibility trope in ways that bolster the salience of those problematic beliefs. Further, the passion principle is an example of how individual-level meaning-making about the labor market and workers' place within it may perpetuate exploitative expectations of white-collar workers in the capitalist labor force by fostering workers' complicity with those expectations. This research also points to the importance of social scientists' attention to things widely deemed preferable inside and outside the academy (e.g., telling students to pursue their passion) as possible mechanisms of disadvantage.

Broadly, the passion principle is an illuminating example of how self-expressive processes that seem agentic at the individual level can serve as subtle but potentially powerful mechanisms of inequality reproduction. Seeking passion in one's career path may increase the opportunity to engage in self-affirming activities in one's daily work life and may inoculate workers to some degree from the self-estrangement of paid labor. Yet the passion principle has potentially serious ramifications for the perpetuation of sociodemographic privilege and disadvantage in the aggregate.

THE PASSION PRINCIPLE AND THE PERPETUATION OF INEQUALITY

The previous chapters approached the passion principle from different angles, pointing out ways this schema is connected to and helps perpetuate specific processes of disadvantage. Using passion as a guide for individual career decisions can reinforce career aspirants' socioeconomic status of origin. Because of the sacrifices that passion-seeking often entails, following passion can be a path to precarious work, especially for working-class career aspirants who lack the safety nets and springboards of their more privileged peers. At the same time, those who prioritize economic advantage or employment security over their passion often see their decisions morally devalued by their peers and by popular culture at large. As a meaning-making schema, the passion principle is entwined with perspectives on the labor market that blame individuals for their own economic fate—and may help deepen resistance to the expansion of social protections like welfare and unemployment benefits. As a widely embraced attribute of the ideal worker, the passion principle may incite, and even justify, the exploitation of workers' personal commitment to their work.

Here I extend these findings from previous chapters to theorize a number of other ways the passion principle may help reproduce sociodemographic inequality. First, the prominence of the passion principle as a definition of good career decision-making may not only be intertwined with neoliberal ideals of labor force participation; it may also help entrench neoliberal policies in higher education and the labor force. US colleges and universities are increasingly aligning with a business model to serve their student "clients."[7] The passion principle, and its individualized "to each their own" notions of major and career selection, sits comfortably within this university-as-business model. It enables colleges like Wayne State to advertise themselves as a place where "passion is your career path" (Figure 6.1), despite students' uneven opportunities to secure stable, decently paying jobs that align with their passions. A student who

Figure 6.1 Highway billboard, eastern Michigan (Author photo, Fall 2017).

is passionate about sports broadcasting or hospitality is free to choose one of those as their major. But it is then their responsibility (not that of the university or other institutions) to land on their feet financially with just that certification.[8] The neoliberalization of higher education, and its emphasis on individual freedom and personal responsibility, is fully compatible with, and is bolstered by, passion-based perspectives on college major choice and career-launch decisions.

Second, adherents to the passion principle may help perpetuate the ideal worker norm in white-collar work, or the expectation that employees enact single-minded devotion to their jobs over their other life responsibilities and work longer—often far longer—than a standard forty-hour workweek.[9] The passion principle plays right into those ideal worker expectations. By fostering personal investment in one's work, the passion principle likely reinforces, rather than challenges, norms of work devotion and overwork. The interview respondents in my study generally recognized and were critical of the demands for overwork of white-collar jobs. They believed passion for one's work would make these ideal worker expectations easier to fulfill. Passion, though, is an individual-level solution to the inherently structural issues at the heart of those critiques of overwork and the ideal worker norm. Individual passion-seeking in response to these issues not only has little impact on the very ideal worker demands that career aspirants resist, but may actually help perpetuate those processes. Although the ideal worker norm may feel less oppressive to those who are passionate about their work, passionate workers may still voluntarily contribute more to their employer than they receive compensation for through salary and benefits.

Third, one's genuine passion for their paid work, and willingness to sacrifice money and time for that passion, may perpetuate demands that their colleagues or supervisees live up to these ideal worker expectations as well.[10] In some professional spaces, such as art, education, or science, the expectations for passionate dedication to one's work may be so engrained that people who treat their work as simply a way to earn a living may be seen as less competent at their jobs.[11] In addition, blue-collar and service workers may be expected to act as though they genuinely love and are personally invested in their jobs, further burdening them with a different brand of emotional labor on top of that which Hochschild originally theorized.[12] In other words, the negative consequences of the passion principle may spill over into realms dominated by non-college-educated workers, where they, in turn, are held to cultural standards of enacting a sense of passion that is much less likely to genuinely accompany their deskilled and undervalued job tasks.

Fourth, what different people are passionate about is itself an important site for the reproduction of occupational segregation. What "fits" us, excites us, and "feeds our soul" is not randomly determined. As I argued in Chapter 1, what one is passionate about is not fully idiosyncratic. Our passions are part of our self-conceptions, the complex set of beliefs we hold about ourselves.[13] Although these self-conceptions seem to us to be authentic and idiosyncratic, they are deeply shaped by our social environments—what we are exposed to and what is expected of us based on our behaviors, abilities, and interest. Our socioeconomic background, gender, and race/ethnicity also influence who we think we are and what we want to become. As such, when career aspirants follow their passion, they tend to reinforce gender, race, and class patterns of occupational segregation.

This is particularly evident in occupational gender segregation. Paradoxically, in the very decades in which women have been encouraged more than ever to stand toe to toe with men in their career pursuits, self-expressive career decision-making seems to have entrenched gender-differentiated career decision-making in a seemingly gender-neutral way. Chase, the physicist discussed in Chapter 4 who had a childhood fascination with light, may have been more encouraged in his interests by his parents and teachers than his sister would have been, but Chase's passion and career path didn't feel gendered to him. It felt individualistic and self-expressive. This may be a central reason we see stalling in the entry of women into the fields most dominated by men (e.g., physics) and men into the fields most dominated by women (e.g., nursing), even as there has been growing tolerance for gender-nonconforming behaviors and life choices over the past two decades.[14]

Such passion-based drivers of occupational segregation are extremely difficult to address with policy change or social action. Because they are inscribed in self-conceptions, these gender, race, and class influences on what people are passionate about are a degree removed from the social processes that produced them. The strategies that would most effectively address such patterns are potentially fraught; to undermine gendered, racialized, and classed exposure to occupations and task realms would require *reducing* curricular freedoms in K–12 and higher education. To make exposure to and encouragement in diverse task realms more equitable, students would need to be required to take a greater variety of subjects, like nutrition *and* physics, human development *and* ethnic studies. Such curricular rigidity goes against parents' and students' increasingly choice-based expectations of secondary education and the "choose your own adventure" model of higher education. Even with more equitable exposure, however, broadly held stereotypes of what different students are good at or capable of would likely still shape interest development in gendered, classed, and racialized ways.[15]

Finally, at the most general level, the passion principle may serve as a bulwark for postindustrial capitalism itself. Indeed, respondents gave clear-eyed critiques of the oppressive expectations of the capitalist labor force, especially its expectations for work devotion, the pervasive lack of stability, and the self-estrangement that workforce participation often entails. By framing the pursuit of self-fulfilling work as an antidote to these problems of labor force participation and by making it individuals' own responsibility to find a self-expressive place in that labor market, the passion principle may stifle such critiques of the capitalist work structure—critiques that might, under other circumstances, kindle collective demands for shorter work hours, more equitable pay, or better work-life integration.[16] The passion principle may thus help diffuse the tensions career aspirants feel between capitalist expectations for dedicated workers and cultural demands for self-expression.

In a number of ways, then, the passion principle might be a hegemonic cultural frame for career decision-making. It is not hegemonic in the sense that it is the singular ideology; employment security, salary, and work-life balance are widely culturally available guiding principles for decision-making. But it *is* hegemonic in the sense that it is a cultural perspective on a domain of life that benefits the most privileged and helps justify the existing unequal socioeconomic status quo as rational and inevitable.[17] As Chapter 4 discussed, the passion principle scaffolds meritocratic and neoliberal perspectives on the labor market that legitimize a profoundly unequal labor market. The passion principle may also facilitate the economically powerful taking advantage of the labor of passionate workers. And it may be used as a basis to devalue and delegitimate the heavily constrained choices of persons without advanced degrees or with limited opportunities to access fulfilling work.

THE PASSION PRINCIPLE'S ROLE IN EXPLOITATION

An irony at the heart of this book, then, is that the cultural schema of the passion principle, which centers self-expressive, agentic action at the individual level, can help reproduce patterns of socioeconomic disadvantage in the aggregate. But the passion principle may also be the foundation of another irony: pursuing one's passion to avoid self-estrangement in the capitalist labor force may ultimately help reproduce dynamics of exploitation—ideal worker expectations, overwork—in that very economic structure by fueling personal investment in one's paid work. The prominence of the passion principle may foreclose alternative perspectives on labor force participation like prioritizing work that supports self-expressive hobbies, work that allows one to maximize time with family and friends, and/or work that is driven by the needs of one's community rather than one's individual interests.

But what does it matter if people are passionate about their work and sacrifice money and/or time to do what they love? Is that really exploitation? Popular (and many scholarly) conceptualizations of exploitation tend to consider it in terms of discrete transactions between employers and employees such as the negotiation of wages and benefits.[18] Through this lens, does it matter if a schoolteacher or a zookeeper is paid little if they voluntarily chose those occupations and love their work? These discrete transactions are not the only way capitalist exploitation works, however. Nor is it even the primary way. Exploitation is a feature of the capitalist economic structure itself: "Capitalists are guilty of exploitation defined as the extraction of surplus value from workers. But in a more important way, it is capitalism, and not particular capitalists that deserve our blame."[19] A schoolteacher or a zookeeper may voluntarily, even joyfully, take a job in their field that pays less than a livable wage. They may be very passionate about that work and even see the low pay they receive as a sacrifice they are willing to make for their passion.[20] We must not be misled by the aspect of choice in all this. These workers are exploited because they labor in economic structures that undervalue their contributions, pay them far less than the organizational and social value they add, and offer few robust social provisions like quality health insurance. Someone's passion for their work may seem to excuse the transactional exploitation between them and their employer, but exploitation is a far deeper matter.

Under what circumstances might the pursuit of passion in paid work be less exploitative and more equitable? For one, opportunities for employment stability would need to be bolstered, as would the social welfare programs (e.g., unemployment benefits, healthcare, family leave) that make workforce participation less risky. More equitable access to education and training, lower tuition, less cross-occupation income inequality, and more support for collective bargaining would also go a long way to reduce the uneven risks of passion-seeking. As I argue above, the transmutation of one's personal interests into the tasks of their work is an exploitative process if one is not rewarded for those extra investments of energy and work. In addition, undermining stereotypes about who should be—or is—passionate about different things is important for reducing the limitations artificially put on people's exploration of possible things to be passionate about. If this sounds like a tall order, it is. As I note below, much of the inequality produced by the valorization of passion-seeking is not the outcome of passion-seeking itself but the structures in which that passion is sought.

CONSIDERATIONS FOR ACTION

The patterns documented here have implications for a variety of constituencies. They are especially relevant for university governing boards, academic administrators, and faculty. They underscore the need for colleges to do a better job of leveling the playing field for their graduates as they enter the labor force. Passion-seeking helps reproduce the socioeconomic privilege and disadvantage of college students in part because more privileged students carry less student loan debt—a problem that could be lessened with better financial aid and reduced tuition costs. In addition, passion-seeking favors those with the most extensive safety nets and springboards for navigating their job search. Although schools cannot fully make up for the divergent levels of cultural and social capital students enter college with, they could certainly improve how they educate students about the labor market and concretize connections with alumni networks and community organizations rather than trust that students can rely on their personal knowledge of these processes.

Equally important, institutions of higher education—and the secondary schools that seed them—should think critically about the messages they send to students about major selection and career choice. Passion-seeking may be the goal of many students, but it is certainly not the goal of every student. Over the past forty years, the labor force has become increasingly precarious. Though unemployment rates have ebbed and flowed, the stability of any single job and the security provided to workers has steadily trended downward.[21] There is little indication that this precarity will improve any time soon. The trends in automation, outsourcing, contract work, and the "gig" economy do not appear to be slowing, and the economic fallout of the COVID-19 pandemic has only amplified uncertainty.[22] Ensuring that career counseling and academic advising are value-neutral about students' priorities can better meet students where they are with their future goals in the labor market and can undercut the cultural devaluation of students who prioritize other factors such as financial stability, time with family, or geographic location in their career paths.

Educators who interact with students on a regular basis also need to reflect on their taken-for-granted assumptions about passion-seeking. The findings here suggest the dangers of passion-seeking as a one-size-fits-all approach to career decision-making. Students who do prioritize a passion may benefit from training in additional areas to increase their options in the labor market; for example, anthropology students might take coding courses or chemistry majors might pursue a communications minor. Also, it is important to encourage undergraduate and graduate students alike to cultivate opportunities for meaning-making and self-expression *outside* the context of the paid workforce—whether through volunteering, hiking, painting, carpentry, improvisational comedy, friendships, political engagement, or other endeavors. In the midst of intensive training, students would benefit from being reminded that there are many places beyond school and paid work to find self-expressive fulfillment.

From K–12 through postsecondary education, teachers should help students understand the importance and power of collective efforts to address workforce issues. The labor market—even for professionals—is increasingly mismatched to the needs of workers.[23] Encouraging career aspirants to seek out and engage in collective rather than individualized efforts to undermine these difficulties may not only help them advocate for their own interests; it may also help correct the decades-long decline of collective action.[24] Further, career counselors and coaches inside and outside of higher education need to pay more heed to the structural inequalities their clients are facing and encourage them to weigh a range of considerations.

At the regional and national policy levels, these results underscore the dangers of individualizing the problems of the paid workforce as workers' *personal* problems. The prominence of the passion principle as a touchstone for good career decision-making may further embolden neoliberal educational and labor force policies.[25] Passion-centric perspectives on career success and failure shift responsibility for addressing labor force problems away from legislators and workplaces and onto individual workers. Institutional programs and perspectives that encourage individual passion-seeking as a means for managing the difficulties of labor force participation also disincentivize organizations to make lasting change.

Short of overhauling cultural notions of good jobs and good career decision-making or upending capitalist labor structures, many of the ways of mitigating the negative outcomes of the passion principle parallel the sort of actions needed to reduce the vulnerabilities faced by labor force participants generally. Although seeking self-fulfillment in one's paid employment may always run the risk that such passion would be exploited, there are plenty of cultural and structural shifts that would make a difference. The passion principle is a risky way to approach career decision-making in part because there are fewer and fewer stable, well-paying jobs, and more opportunities for passionate and hard-working labor force participants to end up underpaid, uninsured, or unemployed.[26] Solutions that mitigate the risks of passion seeking would help vulnerable workers across the labor force, regardless of their priorities and career goals. These solutions include making college more affordable and need-based financial aid more generous; reducing income differentials; bolstering retirement, disability, and unemployment benefits; making access to healthcare disconnected from one's employment status; reducing bias in hiring and promotion; and expanding welfare benefits. With progress on these fronts, the passion principle might still serve as a mechanism of occupational gender, race, and class segregation and as a potential source of employer exploitation, but passion-seeking (and, indeed, all approaches to participation in the labor force) would be less risky overall.

PASSION AND CULTURAL NOTIONS OF A GOOD LIFE

The passion principle is an abstract cultural schema for understanding career decision-making. Even its most fervent adherents are mired in the complexities and constraints of the labor market and must contend with those complexities and constraints to earn a living. Nonetheless, like notions of what it means to be a good citizen or what romantic love means, these abstract schemas do important cultural work.[27] As I have illustrated, the passion principle can help shape how people prioritize competing factors in their lives, what opportunities they pursue or turn down, and how they evaluate the success and even virtuousness of others. Broadly, the passion principle provides a socially valued set of priorities along which to direct one's career path so that they can both be part of the economic system and fulfill self-expressive priorities.[28]

Because this cultural schema is partly about meanings of a good life, not just meanings of good work, my empirical investigation of the passion principle schema bumps up against much larger existential questions.[29] The book's introduction described Giddens's notion of the "reflexive project of the self"—an ever-evolving narrative about who we are as individuals that we continuously work on and reflect on over our lives.[30] Giddens argued that this self-reflexive project has become a central goal of many individuals within postindustrial, late capitalist societies. But to what end is this self-reflexive project to be directed? In the twenty-first-century United States, there are less certain answers to this question than there might have been half a century ago. Secular volunteer organizations (e.g., the YMCA, the Elks Club) that used to provide meaning and identity to community members have shriveled in size over the past several decades, and Americans are less tied to faith communities than they were in the past.[31] In a secular, highly individualistic, postindustrial society, "follow your passion" provides a direction, a *vector*, that offers an answer to the question of where we should find meaning and how we should live our lives.

Putting the passion principle under the scrutiny of sociological inquiry doesn't invalidate passion-seeking as a possible vector for these self-reflexive projects. It merely raises questions about the moral authority given to passion-seeking. Is it always the best consideration for career decision-making? What kind of space can we open up for alternatives that fulfill self-reflexive projects but decenter passion-seeking? Such space may be especially important in occupations or training programs (especially in academia) where one's identity is supposed to be bound up in one's disciplinary work. As cultural sociologists have done for decades, taking a careful look at the cultural ideologies that dominate modern meaning-making landscapes allows us to recognize, and potentially break from, the hegemony of long-valued definitions of a good life.

As a social structure, the paid workforce is neither intended nor designed to support us in our search for self-expression and meaning. It is structured to utilize our efforts for the benefit of the owners and stakeholders and stockholders of the organizations we work for. There are different kinds of paid work—including "gig" jobs, creative endeavors, work in nonprofit organizations, work that attempts to dismantle unequal social structures— but work is still work and still materially and/or reputationally enriches one's employers. Passion-seekers may make life decisions that maximize their self-expressive fulfillment in and through work, but they are nonetheless operating within a capitalist economy. We may find deep personal fulfillment in our work. But we are still workers, still participants in a capitalist labor force. What the passion principle excuses is capitalists' exploitative behavior; it does not change the fact that workers' personal commitment to their work may be exploited.

Even though the findings here suggest that the passion principle is widespread in the United States, that does not mean that it is an inevitable feature of American capitalism. The review of career advice books in the introduction showed ways of thinking about good careers that dominated prior decades' thinking—seeing ideal jobs as those within one's reach that can offer stability and economic security and finding moments of interest and curiosity, whatever one's job. But these perspectives on career approaches were popular in the context of a labor-capital accord that has largely eroded (and was only attainable for the most privileged sociodemographic groups anyway). Few today can bank on getting a job at an organization that will nurture them to rise through the ranks and will try hard to retain them through boom-and-bust profit cycles. What alternative models might be available in modern postindustrial countries?

Japanese white-collar workers work nearly as long as Americans do but often do not see jobs as a space of self-realization in the same way. Traditionally, Japanese professionals have tended to search out stable, well-paying jobs to support themselves and their families[32]—finding meaning in the economic stability they are able to provide.[33] Western European workers tend to have far shorter workweeks than US workers and enjoy much more vacation time. Many Norwegian workers, for example, strive for efficiency at work in order to invest time in family and hobbies in the evenings and on weekends.[34] And in Israel, unemployed professionals see their fate as more bound up in the structural realities of the labor market than in their own personal shortcomings.[35] The idea that our work should be such a core part of our identity may not be isolated to the US context, but its intensity may be particularly American.

Even then, the passion principle may have a cultural foothold in other societies. Particularly in national contexts (e.g., Anglophone and western European countries) where individual self-expression is ubiquitous, where higher education has expanded, and where political and economic labor force policies have shifted to neoliberal, individual responsibility models, the passion principle may be a vaunted approach to career decision-making, especially among the sociodemographically privileged.[36] There, as in the United States, the passion principle may help entrench existing labor market disadvantages and help cloak structural inequalities as choice-based acts of individualism.

The current state of global capitalism means that dealing with the potential for job insecurity and precarity is unavoidable. But individual-level solutions as the central means of responding to those arrangements is not. The fact that there is much cultural and historical variability in notions of "good" career decisions, and that collective worker movements have been successful in the past, means that we have options.

Broadly, cultural schemas like the passion principle provide us with anchor points as we navigate complex decision-making landscapes. Any cultural system where there are only a few of those anchor points, a few "best ways" for building a career or a sense of self, is inherently limiting. It also inherently demeans those whose structural circumstances do not allow them to fulfill those cultural ideals. These schemas can constrain us in powerful ways. My hope is that by putting the passion principle under the microscope, these constraints are more visible, and thus more sur-mountable, for people who wish to—or must—find other ways of orienting their careers and reflexive projects.

Epilogue

This book raises important questions for career aspirants and workers about what it means to seek self-fulfillment in paid employment. These existential questions emerge out of the empirical patterns in the previous chapters but cannot really be answered by them. Nor do these results point to a clear alternative ethos for career decision-making. I offer here several considerations for individual career decision-makers (and the families, mentors, organizations, and institutions who support them) to encourage more reflexive, holistic, and collectively oriented decision-making.

What should career aspirants who are thinking about their own future or workers considering their next career steps take from this? Perhaps the most important message I can offer is that career aspirants and workers—whether passionate about their work or not—should consider whether passion-seeking is the right approach for them. What trade-offs does it entail? Is paid work as a primary site of personal fulfillment the best option, or should paid work be used to support other meaning-making projects? How can the potential drudgery and self-estrangement of paid work, and expectations for work devotion and overwork, be managed by reducing work hours or intensity, for example, rather than going all-in for a passion-based career?

If career aspirants and workers conclude that prioritizing passion is indeed the best option, then I encourage them to keep two questions in mind. First, what will they do to minimize employers' ability to exploit their passion? Passionate workers should ask to be fairly compensated for their work effort, even if they take great joy in their work. Second, how can they contribute to collective action that pressures policy makers, business owners, and managers to ensure adequate social provisions, reduce income inequality, and provide a livable wage and access to healthcare? Social demands for better treatment of workers should not be shouldered only by those dissatisfied, disconnected, and/or alienated from their work. Career aspirants and workers, especially those passionate about their work, need to think about their embeddedness in broader labor market structures, not just their individualized career paths.

Another useful conceptual strategy is to shift from thinking about passion as a dichotomy to thinking about passion as a continuum. Rather than categorize whole fields as one's passion (or not), consider the possibility that a multitude of fields may encompass work tasks that spark curiosity, enjoyment, or fulfillment. This rhetorical shift may reduce the moral valence of finding *a* passion and open up space for nuanced interplay of more holistic sets of life and employment considerations. It may also reduce the cultural judgement that people hold of others who prioritize employment stability or work-life balance. Rather than passion-seeking, perhaps the aim should be work that combines interesting tasks with stability and decent pay, along with time and resources to find meaning outside of work.

I also wish to offer a note to passionate academics, professionals, and students. This project hit home for me in uncomfortable ways at times. My own adherence to the passion principle shaped my early career trajectory. I left a respectable, well-paying career path in engineering to follow my passion for sociology. Had I not been admitted to graduate school or secured a job afterward, that career trajectory could have put me in real financial peril. I was incredibly lucky. I had mentors who respected my work; an encouraging partner, friends, and family; and paid research and teaching assistant positions that allowed me to pay my living expenses. The privilege of my middle-class cultural capital and being white, able-bodied, and US-born surely helped me secure postdoctoral and faculty positions. There's no doubt that sociology was my passion. There's no doubt that it still is. Until I started this research, I was a believer in the passion principle and a more or less devoted evangelist of its core beliefs. As each finding of the book took shape, I had to confront my own implicit beliefs about passion-seeking. I wondered what it meant that my own identity was so wrapped up in my employment. Graduate school, a post-doc, and a pair of busy assistant professor positions left me with little time to invest in meaning-making and identity formation outside of work and family. But I also didn't try very hard. If my job disappeared, my department dissolved, or my discipline imploded, so, too, would a core part of my self-reflexive project. For me, one of the most important lessons was that I better diversify my meaning-making portfolio. Like any good investment portfolio, paid employment should not be the sole meaning-making commodity in a self-reflective project.

It is an extraordinary privilege to have access to work I am personally committed to. But it has been just that. A privilege. To not recognize the resources that are in place that allow academics and white-collar workers to do work they are passionate about while a great many people labor in jobs with very few opportunities for self-fulfillment is to belie the very structures of power and privilege that are at the heart of sociological inquiry. Similarly, to judge students for their lack of willingness to switch to majors they "really love" when faced by pressure from parents, to chide students who leave graduate school to search for more financially viable job opportunities, or to discount colleagues who make room in their lives for families and hobbies is a perspective born from the privileged positions of academics who were rewarded for and succeeded in following their passion. If nothing else, I hope that educators and mentors walk away from this book with a robust commitment to meet students where they are in their career decision-making—trusting them to know what is best for themselves and their lives and helping them connect with resources that further those goals.

Decentering passion-based career decisions is not easy, especially for those of us who inhabit institutional contexts steeped in the passion principle or those who have made life choices to strive for self-expressive, fulfilling work. Passion-seeking is a culturally validated answer to Tolstoy's question, "What shall we do and how shall we live?"[1] For many college-educated career aspirants and workers, that question is answered by seeking meaning and fulfillment in paid employment, even at the expense of time, energy, and other potentially meaningful pursuits. The passion principle, as a ubiquitous cultural schema of good career decision-making, suggests to us *how* to live, what to prioritize, but not *why*—why those are or should be our priorities. In an increasingly individualized world, we are left to answer that "why" on our own.

Let us return to the question, "What do you want to be when you grow up?" What if we centered something other than an occupation in our answer? An adjective? I want to be kind. Adventurous. Irreverent. Eccentric. Relatable. Impactful. What if we centered a set of collective actions? I want to be a community organizer. A dedicated friend. An environmental activist. One's work in the labor force might advance these senses of identity, or it might only provide funds to subsist. The point is, the answer to what one wants to *be* can and should extend far beyond one's participation in the paid workforce.

Acknowledgments

This book would not have been possible without the interview and survey respondents who gave their time to help me understand their experiences and the fantastic editorial team at the University of California Press. I thank Naomi Schneider for showing interest in this project from its early days and Summer Farah for her patient and indispensable assistance.

Countless conversations with colleagues helped the ideas in this book come to life. I am deeply grateful to Jerry Jacobs, Emilio Castilla, and Shelley Correll for spending time with me in Ann Arbor brainstorming how to make my arguments less wobbly. Jerry helped me realize just how much I was "putting my head into the wind" by critiquing passion-seeking and encouraged me to include more of myself in the manuscript. Emilio's enthusiasm for the book's multimethod approach helped buoy my confidence at a critical juncture. Shelley was a champion of this project from its infancy; she recognized the importance of interrogating the passion principle long before I fully realized where this investigation might lead. Through her example, Shelley has taught me how to be brave, and just a little irreverent, when sharing counternormative sociological insights with powerful institutions.

I appreciate Matthew Bakko, Shauna Dyer, Sidney Harris, Jeff Lockhart, and Gabby Peterson for workshopping an early version of the manuscript with me in 2019. They were the first people to read many of the ideas in this book, and their feedback fundamentally shaped its structure. I am grateful for their encouragement to make this book as much a work of public sociology as a contribution to inequality scholarship.

240   ACKNOWLEDGMENTS

The following stellar research assistants contributed to the project: Billy Rothwell, Michelle Pham, Eboni Allen, Madeline Deutsch, Brett Kellet, Sophia Hiltner, Rachel Levy, Lesley Lua, and Madison Martin. I hope they see the imprint of their efforts in this manuscript. I am indebted to many others who provided constructive feedback on drafts along the way: Elizabeth Armstrong, Amy Binder, Sarah Damaske, Isabella Furth, Jane Jones, Karin Martin, Christin Munsch, Lindsey O'Connor, Barbara Risman, Ofer Sharone, Pamela Smock, and Al Young. I also thank audiences at Rice University, University of Washington, University of Houston, UCLA, Stanford, Ohio State, Dartmouth, Harvard, Vanderbilt, and Columbia for asking insightful questions that made the work better.

Maria Charles's and Mary Blair-Loy's mentorship have been steadying ropes from my very first days at UCSD through to the final push to complete this book. Their feedback on initial drafts helped me correct course on some of my early argumentation missteps. Their penchant for asking unsettling questions about ubiquitous cultural beliefs has had an indelible impact on my own scholarly voice; I am grateful to have such exceptional role models.

I couldn't have completed this book without the support of colleagues along the way. Over lunches, hallway chats, backyard fires, and Zoom dates, Müge Göçek, Rob Jansen, Greta Krippner, Sandy Levitsky, Roi Livne, and Margo Mahan provided friendship and comradery to which the term "colleague" simply doesn't do justice. It has been a particular privilege to have Alexandra Vinson by my side at UM. From burrito Mondays in California to G&T Thursdays in Michigan, she remained a steadfast friend even when I blathered on about whatever theoretical snarls I was tackling longer than any non–blood relative should have to withstand.

My dear friends in the Rice sociology department, especially Jenifer Bratter, Sergio Chávez, Jim Elliott, Bridget Gorman, Elizabeth Long, Robin Paige, and Rob Werth, helped this project find its feet in its early days. The folks at Stanford's Clayman Institute for Gender Research (and now the VMware Women's Leadership Lab) have been the kind of intellectual family that is the stuff of academic fairy tales. And, as some of the kernels of this project emerged from my dissertation work, I thank committee members Carroll Seron, Susan Silbey, Jeanne Ferrante, and Ákos Róna-Tas for their support.

As much of this book is about the experiences of career aspirants, I would be remiss not to acknowledge the encouragement of Steve Swinford, Scott Myers, Sue Monahan, and Rachel Luft, who had a powerful impact on my own career launch when I was a student at Montana State. They convinced me that I *could* be a sociologist, whether or not that was the path I ultimately pursued. After a particularly impactful meeting with one of them, I sat on a bench and scribbled in my notebook, "You?? She thinks YOU could write a book one day??" The kindness and support of my mentors throughout my journey is why this book exists at all.

I thank my family—Meg, Mike, Molly, Eric, Ryan, Rye, Summit, and Atlas—for their support, even when the minutia of book writing was foreign to their own work experiences. From the very beginning, they pushed me to articulate the "so what" of this book beyond esoteric disciplinary concerns.

I dedicate this book to my partner, Heidi Sherick. For more than fifteen years, she has brought joy, reflectiveness, compassion, vulnerability, empathy, and silliness to my life. Over the course of this project, she has been my most constructive critic and my biggest fan. She even let me co-opt a vacation as a writing retreat and read the entire manuscript alongside me at the kitchen table. Heidi inspires me every day to be a better human and reminds me how to find meaning outside of work. She is, in a word, phenomenal.

APPENDIX A Methods

This appendix provides more detailed methodological information on the collection and analyses of the quantitative and qualitative data used in this book. The sections below describe each of the data collection efforts and their respective methodological approaches. I include information on variable construction, operationalization, and regression coefficients in the notes to the chapters in which they first appear in order to keep the information as close as possible to the narrative description of results.

CAREER ASPIRANT INTERVIEWS

I conducted in-depth interviews with 100 students enrolled at Stanford University (35 students), the University of Houston (30 students), and Montana State University (35 students) between 2012 and 2013. This combination of sites is useful: these universities are regionally diverse, differentially selective, and include a large elite private institution on the West Coast, an urban public university in the South, and a suburban flagship land grant institution in the North. All three schools have comprehensive curricular offerings across the humanities and sciences and share other features important for career decision-making, such as career counseling centers and deferred major declaration timelines. Stanford, like other elite private schools, has more resources and more extensive alumni networks than MSU and UH to help students explore and secure jobs (see Chapter 3).[1]

Consistent with national college enrollment trends,[2] the sample included slightly more women than men (56 women, 44 men). It also overrepresented racial/ethnic minority students (14% identify as Latinx, 25% as Black, 14% as Asian or Asian American, 53% as white, and 11% as another race/ethnicity). Interviewees were enrolled in a variety of college majors, with half in science, engineering, and math-related (STEM) fields. I recruited participants at MSU and UH through printed advertisements posted in campus common areas (e.g., billboards, lunch tables, residence halls). I recruited Stanford students via the university's online research study participant portal. The study was advertised as an interview-based project on "student beliefs on careers and society." Students at each school expressing interest in the study filled out a short questionnaire about their major, year in school, gender, and race/ethnicity. I used this questionnaire to diversify the sample across these dimensions to more meaningfully observe possible demographic differences and to ensure that the results did not represent perspectives of white middle-class students as the default. Specifically, I selected an interview sample that overrepresented students of color and those from non-middle-class families and split the sample roughly evenly between STEM and non-STEM majors.

Interviews lasted between 45 and 120 minutes and proceeded only after respondents agreed to the consent script approved by my university's human subjects board. I conducted them face-to-face in empty offices or conference rooms on each campus and offered each respondent fifteen dollars for their participation. The interview guide is below.

Students were first asked a series of questions about why they chose their major, what they planned to do after graduation, and the factors they were considering when making those decisions. I then asked them to articulate what they thought were "good reasons" and "bad reasons" for career decision-making and what "good work" meant to them. This question sequence was important. I expected that financial considerations would be more prominent in students' own decision-making than in their cultural schemas about career decisions broadly; students might have downplayed financial considerations when reporting their own decisions had I asked about their cultural schemas of good career decision-making first.

Further, I asked about students' decision-making in relation to both their college majors and their postgraduation career plans. The extent to which these cultural schemas organize respondents' career decision-making might differ depending on whether respondents experience the impact of those decisions immediately or in the more distant future. There is also often incongruity between the subject students major in and the career paths they end up pursuing.[3]

Interviews were audio recorded and professionally transcribed. I coded and analyzed the interview data in Atlas.ti using a dual-pass strategy.[4] In the first pass, I coded transcripts according to the central inductively derived themes in the interview guide related to respondents' cultural schemas regarding major and career decision-making, their justifications for why they chose their major, and the factors they were weighing in their postgraduation planning. In the second pass, I distilled more specific themes regarding why respondents found different schemas compelling, the perceived moral appropriateness of these guiding principles, and the perceived consequences of following different guiding principles. Unless otherwise noted, the quotations presented in the chapters are exemplars of the themes being discussed.

Respondents were asked their gender and racial/ethnic identity at the end of the interview. I determined respondents' socioeconomic status (SES) through questions that asked how "well off financially" their family was when they were in high school—for example, not so well off, very well off, or somewhere in the middle. I coded students as working class if they reported financial difficulties growing up and/or if they reported that their family "was not so well off." I coded students as middle class if they said they were somewhere between "not so well off and very well off," and I coded students as upper class if they said that their family was "very well off." I checked students' self-assessment of their SES against standard sociological markers of SES such as students' descriptions of their parents' jobs and education levels, descriptions of financial hardship, and family vacations.

As a white queer woman without disabilities who was a postdoctoral fellow and then an assistant professor during data collection, my positionality may have influenced students' responses. If the passion principle is a dominant (white, privileged) narrative in students' institutional contexts, interviewees may have overemphasized self-expression and downplayed money and job security considerations in their narratives. As I described in Chapter 1, I sought to mitigate social desirability pressures in the interviews in several ways. Such social desirability may speak to the salience of this schema: respondents who would be eager to cast their career choices in terms of passion in an interview would likely do so with classmates and professors. However, respondents may have been more honest with me than they might have been in career planning conversations with familiar people in their lives. In contrast to conversations with their friends and classmates (who might judge them), their professors and advisers (who might have a stake in their decisions), or their family members (who might be financially and emotionally invested in their choices), these interviews provided a context with comparatively low stakes for honest commentary on their beliefs about career decision-making. The supplemental analyses with survey data of college students below echoed the high value put on passion-seeking among interviewees and the general consistency of results across sociodemographic contexts.

INTERVIEW GUIDE: STUDENTS AT STANFORD, MSU, AND UH

First, I would like to ask you some questions about your major:

- How did you end up in your major?
- What was most important to you in your major?
- *If they said that they liked it, enjoyed it, and/or had a passion for the topic:*
  - Why do you say you like it/have passion for it? What about it do you like/ have passion for?
  - Why is it important to you that you like it/have passion for it?
  - What about financial considerations? Job security? Skill?
- What are "good" reasons for choosing a major, do you think? "Bad" reasons?
- What does "good work" mean to you?

Next, I would like to ask you some questions about your career, what you plan to do after graduation. Specifically, I am interested in the process through which you came to decide on a career path (or, if you don't know yet, what you are weighing as you make your decisions).

- What do you plan to do after graduation? What factors influenced your decision?
- What is most important out of those factors in your choice of a path after graduation?
- *If they said they like it, enjoy it, and/or have a passion for the career path:*
  - Why do you say you like it/have passion for it? What about it do you like/ have passion for?
  - Why is it important to you that you like it/have passion for it?
  - What about financial considerations? Employment stability?
- What are bad reasons for choosing a career, do you think?
- What are good reasons for choosing a career, do you think?
- How do your friends talk about choosing a major or career? How do they talk about that choice?
- How do your parents talk to you about your choice of a major or career? What is important in their eyes?
- Do you feel pressure one way or another about what major you choose or what you'll do in the future?

Finally, I have some basic demographic questions:

- What gender do you identify as?
- Do you identify with one or more races/ethnicities?

- What is your sexual identity?
- What is your political orientation?
- Would you say that when you were in high school, was your family was pretty well-off financially, or not so well-off? Or somewhere in the middle? Explain.
- Where did you grow up and go to high school?

Is there anything else that we haven't talked about in relation to these topics that you think is important for me to know or understand?

CAREER ASPIRANT FOLLOW-UP INTERVIEWS

Using the email addresses provided in the previous round of interviews, I attempted to contact each of the original 100 interviewees in the second half of 2018. Approximately a third of the original sample had nonworking emails, and I could not locate them through LinkedIn or other social networking websites. Of the respondents for whom I had working contact information, half (35 of 62 individuals) replied to my email invitation, agreeing to participate in a follow-up interview (56% acceptance rate). Two former respondents replied by declining to participate; the others did not respond.

Compared to the original interview sample, the follow-up interview sample slightly overrepresented women and had greater representation of racial/ethnic minority respondents (21 of the 35 were nonwhite). The follow-up sample included roughly equal proportions of students from the three schools and mirrored the class breakdown of the original sample. Among the respondents in the follow-up interview sample, 14 were STEM majors and 19 were non-STEM majors. Two left college before graduating. Selection into the follow-up interviews (e.g., willingness and time to participate and availability of contact information) may have skewed the sample to those who were, or perceive themselves to be, more "successful" in their career launch. However, a number of respondents openly described experiences of failure, frustration, or disappointment in their postcollege journeys, and I did not perceive hesitation when respondents discussed times their planned career trajectories went off course.

I conducted the follow-up interviews via online video conferencing platforms (typically Skype or BlueJeans), and respondents received a $25 gift card for their participation. I read participants a consent script, and we proceeded only after they gave their consent. The interviews lasted 65 minutes on average and covered respondents' trajectories at the end of their time in college and after leaving college and their aspirations for their future career paths.

As with the original interviews, I used a dual-pass coding strategy in Atlas.ti, first gathering broad themes about postcollege paths and then capturing more nuanced meaning-making about their experiences in college and the labor market and their beliefs about the labor force more broadly. I also analyzed these interviews alongside the first round of interviews, assessing longitudinal patterns among the respondents as well as cross-sectional variation across follow-up interview participants.

INTERVIEW GUIDE: FOLLOW-UP INTERVIEWS

First, I would like to ask you some questions about what transpired since we talked:

- You were a _____ in college, and you were a _____ major.
  - Did you end up graduating from [University]?
  - What major(s) did you graduate with?
  - What is your current occupational status?
  - Can you walk me through what happened to you career-wise after college?
  - Any other big life events?

Questions about current occupational location:

- What factors led you to be on this particular occupational path, do you think? How did you end up here?
  - What factors were most important in your decision-making about your path? Why are those important?
- *If said they liked it, enjoyed it, and/or had a passion for the topic:*
  - Why do you say you like it/have passion for it?
  - Why is it important to you that you like it/have passion for it?
  - What about financial and job security considerations?
- Do you think your career path is a good fit for you? How do you know?

As you think about your career prospects down the line:

- If you were to consider a different job, what factors would be most important in your decision?
- What path do you hope your career takes? What considerations are most important to you?
- Do you have any thoughts about changing career paths entirely? What are those thoughts?
- How do your parents/family talk to you about your career path?
- Did you feel pressure one way or another about your career path?
- Approx. how many hours/week do you currently work?

- Was this *how you thought things would unfold* for you after graduation?
  - Was there anything unanticipated in what happened (obstacles, unforeseen opportunities)?
- Did you receive any *guidance or assistance* from family members after college?
  - E.g., Help you move, transition, pay rent, connect you with jobs, talk to you about resumes, introduce you to their social networks?
- Did you contribute to your family financially or otherwise after college?

Housekeeping/context questions about college:

- Did you work while you attended school? Doing what? How many hours/week?
- Did you work with career counselors or coaches?
- Did you pursue an internship? What was it? Paid/unpaid?
- Approximately how much debt do you currently have from student loans?

When I conducted these interviews the first time around, passion was the most common reason given for choices of majors and career plans after graduation.

- How do you feel about passion as a motivator for career decision-making?
- Did that understanding change at all after leaving college?

Finally, I have some basic demographic questions:

- Where are you currently living?
- Approximately what is your income (hourly, weekly, annually)?
- Do you have any other sources of financial support?
- What is your political orientation?

Anything else that we haven't talked about in relation to these topics that you think is important for me to know or understand?

INTERVIEWS WITH CAREER COUNSELORS AND COACHES

The professions of career counseling and coaching claim jurisdiction over advice-giving to clients about career decision-making.[5] The cultural frames counselors and coaches use when giving such advice may have an enormous influence on their clients' decision-making. To understand how their perspectives and approaches might amplify or provide alternatives to the passion principle, I analyzed in-depth interviews with 24 career-advising professionals. Seven were career counselors serving students at Stanford, MSU, and UH; seven were career counselors working for other academic institutions; and ten were private career coaches who worked for professional clients in the Detroit and Houston areas outside of formal university contexts. A research assistant conducted 4 of the interviews with Detroit-area private career coaches. I conducted the remaining 20 interviews. Using contact information from each university's career counseling office websites, I emailed each career counselor at MSU, UH, and Stanford in 2018. Due to a number of high-profile college admissions scandals at that time, several career counselors at MSU and Stanford were hesitant to participate in an interview about their counseling practices with an unaffiliated researcher. I therefore sought out supplemental interviews with career-advising professionals at institutions where I was currently or formerly a faculty member or where I had personal connections (University of Michigan, Rice University, and Houston Community College).

I used web searches and career counselor directories to locate private career-advising professionals in the Houston and Detroit areas. These career coaches worked with both current and recently graduated college students as well as professionals who have been in the workplace for longer periods.

Interviews with career-advising professionals were conducted in person or over online video conferencing software after respondents consented to an interview. Interviews lasted 50 minutes on average and covered their general philosophy of advising, their approaches for orienting new clients, and their strategies for helping clients negotiate conflicting goals or expectations. As before, I used a dual-pass strategy to code and analyze the data.

INTERVIEW GUIDE: CAREER-ADVISING PROFESSIONALS

- To begin, please tell me about your work. How did you get into career advising?
- How do you define the role of career counseling/career coaching? What would you say is the value that this work provides that is different from other places that someone might seek out career advice from?
- What type of questions or needs do your clients start their advising with? How long do you tend to work with clients?
- What is your general strategy with new clients?
- Do you use any particular tools in your advising work (e.g., the Strong Interest Inventory)? What do you use the tools for?
- What would you say are good reasons for making career decisions? Bad reasons?
- How does your clients' understandings of good and bad reasons for career decision-making tend to align with or diverge from yours?
- I am going to provide you with some hypothetical situations, which you may or may not have encountered in your work. How would you respond to the following situations?

- A client who was struggling to decide between a well-paying job and a job that they were passionate about.
- A client who had great interest and passion for an occupation but was not particularly good at that occupation.
- A client who was very interested in a field that was likely to yield little money but the client needed to support their family.
- Is there anything else that you think is important for me to know in order to understand your work as a career-advising professional or your philosophy on career decision-making?

Interview concluded with demographic questions.

PASSION PRINCIPLE SURVEY

Early on in the project, it became clear that it was vital to understand the passion principle not only from the perspective of career aspirants, but among college-educated workers more broadly. No existing survey data have sufficient questions to provide the nuanced measures I needed for these analyses. As such, I opted to field my own survey. I fielded the Passion Principle Survey (PPS) in October 2020 to a sample of 1,750 US college-educated workers via the survey platform Qualtrics.[6] The sample is proportionally representative of the US college-educated workforce by gender, race/ethnicity, age cohort, and a 14-category occupation code (see list of occupations in Appendix C, Figure C.1). Previous research has found Qualtrics' national sampling procedure generally reflective of the US population along a variety of demographic and attitudinal factors: even without the quota sampling I used, Qualtrics produces samples that are within 7% on average of corresponding values in the US population on factors ranging from income to marital status.[7]

The PPS survey was advertised as a "University of Michigan Survey of Employed College Graduates" and included over two dozen questions about workers' attitudes about career decision-making and the labor force, allowing for statistical analyses of patterns related to the passion principle, choicewashing, and other processes while accounting for variation by respondents' demographics and job characteristics. To increase the quality and reliability of the resulting data, the survey included four attention filters.[8]

Although not a strictly representative sample, the PPS data usefully allowed me to assess the passion principle with precisely worded questions explicitly designed for this purpose. I pretested operationalization and measurement reliability of focal measures through a survey of college-educated workers fielded through the piece-rate worksite MTurk (N = 502).

PPS Measures and Operationalization

I describe the operationalization of the passion principle scale and the focal dependent measures in chapter endnotes when they first appear. Unless otherwise noted, the figures in this book using the PPS data present predicted means for people with low and high adherence to the passion principle (i.e., passion principle skeptics and passion principle believers; see Chapter 2, note 37), holding constant variation by gender identity (woman, man),[9] race/ethnicity (Black, Latinx, Asian, Native American and Asian Pacific Islander, white), age (by decile: 20s, 30s, 40s, 50s, 60s, 70 and above), highest degree (bachelor's, master's, or PhD/professional degree), immigrant status (whether born in the United States), class background (working class, middle class, upper class), employment sector (7-category measure) and occupation (14 categories; see Appendix C, Figure C.1, for list). Presenting these predicted means in the bar charts rather than raw means allows me to visually represent differences in the focal variables by adherence to the passion principle while holding constant possible variation along these other demographic dimensions. I produced predicted means through the margins command in Stata via ordinary least squares (OLS) regression models controlling for demographic and job characteristics listed above. Where appropriate, I also report the unstandardized coefficient estimates (B-values) and statistical significance (p-values) from these regression models. To simplify the presentation of empirical results, these coefficient estimates are given in chapter notes.

PPS in 2018 versus 2020

The 2020 PPS is the second iteration of a nearly identical survey I fielded in 2018. The 2018 survey asked the same questions discussed in Chapters 1–4 and also included the survey experiment described below. The 2018 survey also used the same proportionally representative sampling strategy as the 2020 survey. The COVID-19 pandemic hit the United States just as I was finishing this book. In a matter of weeks, the economic gains made in the decade since the Great Recession evaporated. Millions of people were unemployed, and millions more had their work and family lives disrupted. As a sociologist interested in the cultural mechanisms of inequality reproduction, I train my gaze on cultural beliefs and practices I suspect are quite durable to social, political, and economic change. While I presumed that the cultural schema of the passion principle would be generally robust to these uncertainties, the economic crisis and other disruptions may have altered career aspirants' and college-educated workers' calculus about what they prioritize in career decisions in their own lives and what advice they would give to others. As such, I decided to refield the PPS in October 2020.[10]

Comparing results from the 2018 and 2020 survey waves, the patterns are remarkably similar. Figure A.1 presents means on focal measures from the two waves of the survey. Although I find slight differences consistent with the

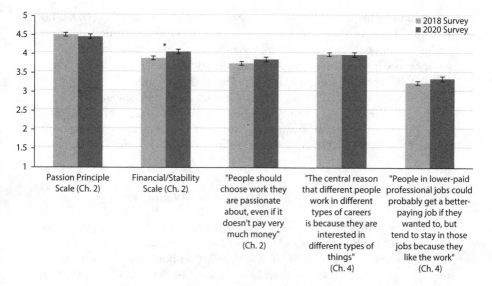

Figure A.1 Means on focal measures from the 2018 and 2020 waves of the PPS survey (2018 N = 1,752; 2020 N = 1,750). Bars represent 95% confidence intervals.

increased financial and employment strain of 2020—i.e., the mean on the financial/stability scale is slightly higher in 2020 than 2018 (4.06 vs. 3.89), while the proportion of respondents who prioritized passion over economic concerns in their abstract conceptualization of good career decision-making was slightly lower (67% in 2020 vs. 72% in 2018)—the results are strikingly consistent. Figure A.1 shows there is no significant difference in average adherence to the passion principle among college-educated workers between 2018 and 2020 (left-most pair of bars), or on focal measures from the analyses in Chapters 2 and 4.

The consistency of the patterns of results from the 2018 and 2020 surveys indicates that, even in the midst of a tumultuous economy and labor market, college-educated workers still generally valued the passion principle and saw it as a central consideration in their own decision-making. This comparison of the 2020 data with 2018 trends also provides reassurance that the PPS results discussed throughout the book are not a relic of the economic and social upheaval surrounding the COVID-19 pandemic and are likely to remain salient with a return to more typical economic circumstances.

PASSION PRINCIPLE EXPERIMENT

The 2018 PPS included an experiment incorporated at the end of the survey that explored the "demand side" of the passion principle. Respondents were randomly assigned to review one of four fictitious job applications to either an accounting job at an IT firm or a youth program manager job at a community nonprofit (4x2 design). The applicants' cover letters varied by a single sentence, with one cover letter expressing passion for the work and the other three expressing interest in the city, the organization, or the salary. This design allowed me to determine whether passionate applicants were rated higher than other applicants on average and whether those preferences are because passionate applicants were presumed to be especially hard workers. I pretested all experimental materials using MTurk (N = 502). See Appendixes C.2 through C.8 for experimental materials.

NATIONAL SURVEY OF THE CHANGING WORKFORCE

The 2008 NSCW is a nationally representative survey of adult, noninstitutionalized workers in the civilian labor force fielded by the Families and Work Institute. NSCW respondents were 18 years of age or older at the time of the survey and resided in the lower 48 states. Respondents were selected via a region-stratified unclustered random probability sample, generated by random digit dialing. The original sample has approximately 3,500 respondents. Unless otherwise noted, I draw on the 1,002 respondents in NSCW with a four-year college degree. For these analyses, I used only respondents who are employed by someone else, as self-employed respondents have more control over their work. I handled missing data on the independent measures using multiple imputation (chained command in Stata with 20 imputations); imputed variables had no more than 6% missingness. Operationalization of dependent variables and focal independent variables used in the NSCW data analyses are included in chapter notes where they first appear.

Unless otherwise noted, figures in the book using NSCW data present predicted means controlling for a variety of demographic controls: whether they are the parent of a child under 18 (1 = yes, 0 = no), have eldercare responsibilities (1 = yes, 0 = no), are an immigrant (1 = yes, 0 = no), and are married or partnered (1 = yes, 0 = no). Models control for gender (man, woman), race/ethnicity (African American, white, other nonwhite), age, years worked, average hours worked per week, and education level (high school degree or less, some college, college degree or higher). They also include controls for the following job characteristics: occupational category (professional or technical, sales, administrative, service, production and operations, or managerial), employment sector (public, nonprofit, private), establishment size, and the natural log of yearly salary.

I used ordered logistic regressions to test for demographic variation in the importance to respondents of meaningful work, salary, and job security in the event they were deciding to take a new job (Chapter 1) and OLS regressions with MI to test for salary differences by respondents' level of passion for their work

(Chapter 5). All regression models include the controls above, were weighted using the weight provided in NSCW, and were adjusted for the complex sampling design using the SVY command in Stata.

MERIT PRINCIPLES SURVEY

The 2016 MPS is a nationally representative survey of US federal employees. MPS was completed by 14,473 workers employed in 25 federal agencies (OPM 2015). The US Office of Personnel Management (OPM) administers the MPS every other year. The 2016 MPS was administered electronically to a representative sample of permanent, nonseasonal employees in federal agencies representing all major departments and independent agencies and had a 38.7% response rate.

Unless otherwise noted, figures using MPS data present predicted means controlling for a variety of demographic measures: education level (1 = less than associate's degree, 2 = associate's or bachelor's degree, 3 = graduate degree), whether respondent is under the age of 40 (1 = yes, 0 = no), the length of time they have been a federal civil service employee (center-coded values in the following ranges: 0–3 years, 4 or more years), tenure at their current agency (0–3 years, 4–11 years, 12–19 years, 20–31 years, 32 or more years), supervisory status (1 = non-supervisor, 2 = team leader, 3 = supervisor, 4 = manager, 5 = executive), whether respondent is currently eligible to retire (0 = no, 1 = yes), whether they are employed at the headquarters of their agency rather than a field site (1 = yes, 0 = no), and their salary level (center-coded in the following ranges: less than $75,000 to $150,000 or more). I also controlled for whether they are a dues-paying member of a union (1 = yes, 0 = no). Operationalization of dependent variables and focal independent variables used in the MPS data analyses are included in chapter notes where they first appear.

GENERAL SOCIAL SURVEY DATA

The GSS is a representative survey of US adults conducted every other year by NORC at the University of Chicago. The GSS contains modules that are repeated at regular intervals. In the 1989, 1998, 2006, and 2016 survey waves, GSS asked a set of questions that tapped the importance to respondents of interesting work and a high salary. Specifically, respondents were asked, "On the following list there are various aspects of jobs. Please circle one number to show how important you personally consider it in a job": "An interesting job" and "salary" (1 = not important at all to 5 = very important; variable INTJOB). Figure 2.2 in Chapter 2 presents the weighted means on this variable for each of the four survey waves, differentiated by three education levels: whether the respondent has a high school degree or less, some postsecondary education but less than a college degree, or a college degree or higher.

FUNDING AND LAND ACKNOWLEDGMENT

Financial support for data collection and analysis was generously provided by the Michelle R. Clayman Institute for Gender Research at Stanford University, the Department of Sociology at Rice University, and the Department of Sociology and the Population Studies Center at the University of Michigan. Any opinions, findings, conclusions, or recommendations expressed in this book are mine alone and do not necessarily reflect the views of these institutions.

The academic institutions where I have studied and worked while conducting this research, like most universities in the United States, stand on grounds obtained through colonizing practices that have for thousands of years been part of the traditional lands of the Crow, Blackfeet, Kumeyaay, Akokisa, Chippewa, Ottawa, and Potawatomi peoples. I honor those lands and am grateful to have lived and worked on them.

Supplemental Analysis of
2020 College Student Survey

The career aspirant interview sample used in this book is relatively large and includes students who were enrolled in three demographically and regionally diverse universities. However, it cannot speak to the perspectives of students at other types of institutions and is not well equipped to assess nuanced demographic similarities or differences across students.

In order to assess the relevance of the passion principle across a more institutionally diverse sample, I conducted a supplemental survey of college students via the MTurk virtual work platform in June 2020 (N = 522). Although MTurk is not representative of the US college student population, researchers frequently use it to triangulate general descriptive patterns identified through other analytic procedures.[1] Prior research has found that MTurk surveys are roughly reflective of the US population along a variety of demographic and attitudinal dimensions and produce samples that are within 9% on average of corresponding values in the US population.[2]

The survey asked college students a number of questions about their priorities in their academic major decisions, postgraduation planning, demographics, institution type, and academic major. The survey results reported below are intended to provide support for the findings presented in the main text. Similar descriptive patterns produced via a much different empirical approach at a different time point helps support the claim that the patterns of adherence to the passion principle found in the student interview data are not merely an artifact of that empirical approach. In addition, this survey was conducted in the midst of the economic and social fallout from the COVID-19 pandemic. Given the uncertain educational and economic circumstances that survey respondents faced, these survey results are likely a more conservative estimate of the prevalence of the passion principle among students before and after this period.

DATA AND METHODS

Respondents were invited to participate in the survey via MTurk. Those who met the screening criteria (current undergraduate students at US colleges) were directed to a survey fielded through Qualtrics. As is common practice with online samples, the survey included five speed and attention checks.

The proportion of students by racial/ethnic and gender categories in this sample is roughly consistent with US census data on current four-year college students: Percent Latinx (survey: 12.1%; US: 16.4%); percent Black (survey: 10%; US: 13.8%); percent Asian (survey: 11.1%; US: 10.2%); percent white (survey: 73.9%; US: 71.6%,); percent women (survey: 52.2%; US: 55.3%). The survey sample also reflects broad enrollment patterns by institution type: 71.9% of the survey sample were enrolled in a public 4-year institution (vs. 77.2% of students in the US) and 19.8% were enrolled in private, nonprofit colleges (vs. 21.3% of students in the United States).

In the figures below, I present several questions capturing respondents' adherence to the passion principle as it relates to their beliefs about career decision-making in the abstract and the factors they prioritize in their own majors and postcollege career paths. Students were asked the same set of questions that make up the passion principle adherence scale in the PPS (see Figure 1.1 in Chapter 1). A second set of questions assessed respondents' prioritization of passion-related considerations in their own career decisions. One question asked the extent to which they agreed that "pursuing my personal interests or passion was the most important factor to me in choosing my college major" (1 = strongly disagree to 5 = strongly agree). Figure B.1 presents the average on this measure for all respondents and means separately by demographic categories, holding variation by all other controls constant. I produced predicted means via an OLS regression model in Stata and margins commands for each focal demographic category (holding all other measures at their mean).

To better understand respondents' relative prioritization of factors in their postcollege career paths, the survey included a forced-rank question that asked respondents to rank a set of factors from most to least important in their decisions about their career path after graduation (5 = highest priority to 1 = lowest priority). Figure B.2 presents the average priority rankings for each factor.

Finally, the survey asked respondents whether they had changed majors over the course of their time in college (31.8% had). The survey asked those who had

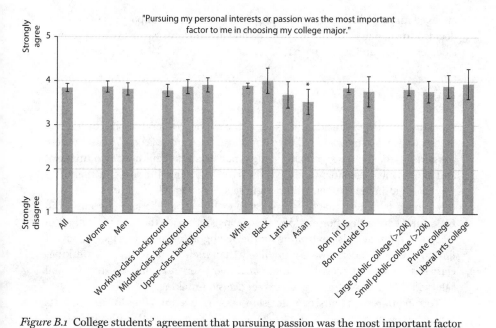

Figure B.1 College students' agreement that pursuing passion was the most important factor when choosing their college major (N = 522).

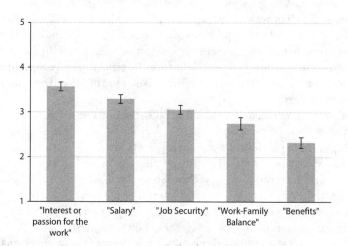

Figure B.2 Average ranking of the importance of five factors in college students' postgraduation career planning (N = 522). Higher values indicate higher average rankings (5 = highest rated to 1 = lowest rated).

changed majors which of the following factors was "most important in why you decided to change your major." They could choose from reasons related to passion, job opportunities, salary potential, benefits, and work-life balance.

RESULTS

As with the college-educated workers in the survey, 76% rated passion-related factors between somewhat and very important on average. And 67% rated these passion-related factors significantly higher on average than they rated financial and employment considerations. This mirrors the general finding in the interview data: although students didn't ignore salary and job security constraints, they tended to believe that passion-related factors should be more important in major and career decision-making. Also consistent with the interview data, in OLS regression models controlling for the demographic measures listed above, I find that Asian students were more likely than their white peers, and working-class students more likely than their wealthier peers, to value job security and salary in their assessment of good career decision-making.

Turning to respondents' own decision-making, overall, 70.1% of respondents somewhat or strongly agreed that passion and interest were the most important consideration in their career decision-making. To assess demographic differences in the prioritization of passion in major choice, Figure B.1 above presents predicted means on this question for each demographic group, holding constant variation along all other measures. Here Asian students were significantly less likely than white students to prioritize passion in their major choices. However, the survey revealed no other racial/ethnic differences. And, as with the interview data, there were also no significant differences by gender, class background, US-born status, or institution type in students' likelihood of prioritizing passion in their major choices.

Another question asked students to rank a set of factors as most to least important in their postgraduation career decisions. Figure B.2 above presents the average ranking of each factor, from highest to lowest average priority. As the figure indicates, passion-related considerations were ranked as the highest priority on average, followed by salary, then job security. In addition, respondents were more than twice as likely to rate "interest or passion" as their top priority than salary or job security. OLS regression models showed no significant gender, racial/ethnic, or institution type differences in these ratings.

A final set of questions asked the subset of students who reported changing their major at some point in college why they had done so. Here changing one's major to a subject one was "more interested in or passionate about" was the most frequent reason students gave for this change: 42% changed majors to find a subject they were more passionate about, while only 22% and 17% changed majors to seek greater job opportunities or salary potential, respectively. This suggests that many students were willing to make changes to their academic trajectories in order to move to something that interested them more, and such switches were more common than changing to subjects that would offer better opportunities for employment security and higher salaries. Eleven percent said they changed their major to a subject they believed they could be more successful in academically, and 8% changed to a subject they thought would provide more work-life balance.

These survey results are not representative of all college students, nor are they directly comparable to the interview sample. Nonetheless, they show similar overarching patterns: college students tended to value passion-related considerations in their assessments of good career decision-making in the abstract and in their own decision-making about majors and future career priorities. Like the interview data, this prioritization of passion-seeking was generally consistent across demographic groups and institution types in the sample. Future research with large, representative, longitudinal samples is needed to further explore these processes.

APPENDIX C **Supporting Data**

Appendix C presents supplemental figures, tables, and other information for Chapter 1 (Appendix C.1) and Chapter 5 (Appendixes C.3–C.8).

APPENDIX C.1: ADHERENCE TO PASSION PRINCIPLE BY FIELD

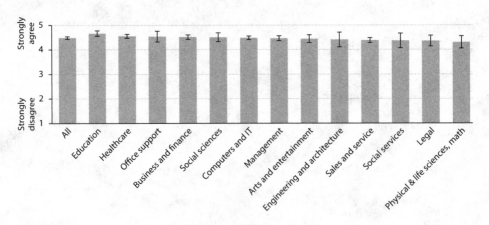

Fig. C.1 Adherence to passion principle among college-educated workers, by field (PPS data).

APPENDIX C.2: JOB ADVERTISEMENTS

YOUTH PROGRAM MANAGER JOB SUMMARY

About the Organization: CommunityThrive
CommunityThrive
500 S. State St.
Columbus, Ohio

For over 30 years, CommunityThrive has supported the children and families of the greater Columbus, Ohio, area. Our mission is to ensure that all children have the opportunity to succeed at school, at home, and in life. To achieve this, we provide mentoring, education, and support to over 7,000 children and parents in the area. CommunityThrive has developed critical community partnerships that result in high quality services, maximization of scarce resources, and powerful impact on outcomes for children.

What Is Expected of a Youth Program Manager:

- Design 7–10 youth programs each year for children ranging from 5 to 12 years old.
- Oversee the operation of existing summer camps series "CommunityKIDS," including:
  - Hiring and supervising teen camp counselors
  - Managing registration procedures
  - Arranging alternative activities during inclement weather
- Assist with grantwriting and community fundraising
- Cultivate partnerships with local businesses and foster existing partnerships

Youth Program Manager Qualifications:

- Bachelor's degree in child development or related field, or equivalent work experience
- Experience with community programming preferred
- Experience with youth-focused organizations preferred

Compensation:
Salary range: $32,000–$55,000

STAFF ACCOUNTANT JOB SUMMARY

About the Company: TelMark IT Solutions

TelMark IT Solutions

500 S. State St., Suite 703

Columbus, Ohio

For over 25 years, TelMark IT Solutions has been a regional provider of advanced organization and decision management solutions. Our customer-centric tools and services enable TelMark's clients to add value while providing nimble, scalable solutions for specific business objectives. TelMark's network is distributed across three world-class data centers in the Columbus, OH, area and provide unmatched security and flexibility.

What Is Expected of a Staff Accountant:

- Prepare monthly journal entries, including customer rebate accruals
- Identify possible solutions to budgetary problems and take actions to resolve them
- Good communication skills—ability to work cross functionally with other Finance teams
- Experience resolving balance sheet items
- Assist in implementing accounting practices in accordance with corporate accounting policies, internal controls, and financial information systems

Staff Accountant Qualifications:

- Bachelor's degree in related field, or equivalent work experience
- Experience with SAP or large ERP preferred
- Proficient with MS Excel

Compensation:

Salary range: $32,000–$55,000

APPENDIX C.3: COVER LETTER FOR YOUTH PROGRAM MANAGER POSITION

Riley Williamson
1638 N. Avers Ave.
Chicago, IL 60647

September 21, 2017

Human Resources
CommunityThrive
500 S. State St.
Columbus, OH

To Whom It May Concern,

I am applying for the Youth Program Manager position at CommunityThrive, posted on Monster.com earlier this month.

I am especially interested in this position because it would advance my career. I am also passionate about child development; facilitating kids' learning is exciting and interesting to me and I really enjoy the work.

As someone with a strong academic background and child development experience gained inside and outside the classroom, I believe I would be a great fit at CommunityThrive.

Sincerely,
Riley Williamson

APPENDIX C.4: COVER LETTER FOR ACCOUNTING POSITION

Riley Williamson
1638 N. Avers Ave.
Chicago, IL 60647

September 21, 2017

Human Resources
TelMark IT Solutions
500 S. State St, Suite 703
Columbus, OH

To Whom It May Concern,

I am applying for the Staff Accountant position at TelMark IT Solutions, posted on Monster.com earlier this month.

I am especially interested in the position because it would advance my career. I also have a passion for accounting—managing financial accounts is exciting and interesting to me and I really enjoy the work.

As someone with a strong academic background and accounting experience gained inside and outside the classroom, I believe I would be a great fit for your company.

Sincerely,
Riley Williamson

APPENDIX C.5: RÉSUMÉ FOR APPLICATIONS TO
YOUTH PROGRAM MANAGER POSITION

Riley Williamson
1638 N. Avers Ave., Chicago, IL 60647, riley.k.williamson@gmail.com

Objective
Recent graduate seeking position in child development and youth programming or similar.

Education
INDIANA UNIVERSITY—BLOOMINGTON
2017—Bachelor of Science in Psychology
GPA: 3.3/4.0

Skills & Abilities
CERTIFICATION & TRAINING
- First Aid and CPR Trained (June 2017)
- Experience with all Microsoft Office Applications (Excel, Word, PowerPoint, Outlook)
- Experience with Asana (project management software)

COMMUNICATION
- Excellent communication skills, and ability to present complex information in an easy-to-understand format

Relevant Experience
INTERNSHIP, BOYS & GIRLS CLUB (CHICAGO, IL)
- 8-week summer internship

- Shadowed senior program administrators and assisted with grantwriting (proofreading, formatting)
- Assisted with interviews to screen middle-school mentors for elementary school children.
- Planned and implemented a week-long sports summer camp for 3rd and 4th graders.

VICE-PRESIDENT, IU CHAPTER OF ASSOCIATION OF PSYCHOLOGY UNDERGRADUATES
- Elected to office for the 2015–2016 academic year
- Responsible for organizing outside speakers for monthly chapter meetings
- Coordinated annual chapter fund-raiser

APPENDIX C.6: RÉSUMÉ FOR APPLICATIONS TO ACCOUNTING POSITION

Riley Williamson
1638 N. Avers Ave., Chicago, IL 60647, riley.k.williamson@gmail.com

Objective
Recent graduate seeking staff accounting position or similar.

Education
INDIANA UNIVERSITY—BLOOMINGTON
2017—Bachelor of Science in Accounting
GPA: 3.3/4.0

Skills & Abilities
CERTIFICATION
- Certified Public Accountant (passed exam in June 2017)

SOFTWARE
- Experience with all Microsoft Office Applications (Excel, Word, PowerPoint, Outlook)
- Training and experience with Oracle and SAP
- Experience with QuickBooks Pro and QuickBooks Online

COMMUNICATION
- Excellent communication skills, and ability to present complex information in an easy-to-understand format

Relevant Experience
INTERNSHIP, STIEGEL DUNBAR & COMPANY (CHICAGO, IL)
- 8-week summer internship
- Shadowed senior accountants and assisted with monthly journal entries and resolving balance sheets.
- Assisted with researching and implementing budget resolutions

VICE-PRESIDENT, STUDENT CHAPTER OF INSTITUTE OF MANAGEMENT ACCOUNTANTS
- Elected to office for the 2015–2016 academic year
- Responsible for organizing outside speakers for monthly chapter meetings
- Coordinated annual chapter fundraiser

Table C.7 Indirect effects from structural equation models predicting college-educated workers' likelihood of recommending hiring an applicant, by cover letter condition, mediated by assessment of applicant as a "hard worker" and "willing to take on additional responsibilities without an increase in pay" (PPE data)

	Youth Program Manager Job		Accounting Job	
	INDIRECT EFFECT		INDIRECT EFFECT	
	Coefficient	*SE*	*Coefficient*	*SE*
Mediation Measure: Riley Is Hardworking				
Likes Organization → Hard Worker→ Interested in Hiring Riley	−.097***	*.024*	−.036 +	*.021*
Likes Salary → Hard Worker → Interested in Hiring Riley	−.048**	*.022*	−.049*	*.020*
Likes Location → Hard Worker → Interested in Hiring Riley	−.164***	*.028*	−.071**	*.021*
Mediation Measure: Riley Would Take on Additional Responsibilities without an Increase in Pay				
Likes Organization → Take on Additional Responsibilities → Interested in Hiring Riley	−.028 +	*.018*	−.030*	*.012*
Likes Salary → Take on Additional Responsibilities → Interested in Hiring Riley	−.109***	*.023*	−.032**	*.013*
Likes Location → Take on Additional Responsibilities → Interested in Hiring Riley	−.059**	*.018*	−.027*	*.012*

NOTE: Each respondent reviewed one application either for the youth program manager job or the accounting job. Significant indirect effects indicate that the impact of viewing that version of the cover letter (compared to viewing the passion-based version) on respondents' interest in hiring Riley is partly explained by respondents' assessment of Riley as hardworking (top rows) and the assessment of Riley's willingness to take on additional responsibilities (bottom row). See question wording and operationalization in Chapter 5 notes.

*** p < .001, ** p < .01, * p < .05 + p < .10.

Table C.8 OLS regression model predicting respondent salary (logged value), with passion for work and controls (all workers; NSCW data)

	Logged Salary		
	COEFF.	SE	
Respondent is passionate about their work	**0.039**	*0.038*	
Female	−0.134	*0.035*	***
Education	0.253	*0.018*	***
Children under 18	0.035	*0.038*	
Eldercare indicator	0.012	*0.002*	***
Married/partnered	−0.057	*0.037*	
Black	0.116	*0.039*	**
Other race	−0.202	*0.065*	**
Hours worked	−0.067	*0.059*	
Age	0.012	*0.002*	***
Government sector	0.006	*0.002*	***
Public sector	−0.086	*0.041*	*
Nonprofit sector	−0.055	*0.056*	
Professional or technical occupation	0.064	*0.041*	
Establishment size	0.054	*0.016*	**
Constant	1.413	*0.108*	***

NOTE: "Passionate about work" is a scale measure that is an average of two variables: "The work I do in my job is meaningful to me" and "I feel I can really be myself at work" (1 = strongly disagree to 5 = strongly agree).

*** p < .001, ** p < .01, * p < .05.

Notes

INTRODUCTION

1. "'You've Got to Find What You Love,' Jobs Says," *Stanford News*, June 14, 2005, http://news.stanford.edu/news/2005/june15/jobs-061505.html.

2. E.g., Carmine Gallo, "Why Steve Jobs' Commencement Speech Still Inspires 10 Years Later," *Forbes*, June 12, 2015, www.forbes.com/sites/carminegallo/2015/06/12/why-steve-jobs-commencement-speech-still-inspires-10-years-later/#bcd33a348d83; John Naughton, "Steve Jobs: Stanford Commencement Address, June 2005," *Guardian*, October 8, 2011, www.theguardian.com/technology/2011/oct/09/steve-jobs-stanford-commencement-address.

3. Tokumitsu 2015.

4. All respondents' names used in this book are pseudonyms.

5. This irony is made more glaring by the fact that about half of the workers in typical Silicon Valley firms are replaced every two years (Pugh 2015; Reichheld 2001).

6. Blair-Loy 2003; Perlow 2012; Williams, Blair-Loy, and Berdahl 2013.

7. Blair-Loy 2003.

8. Correll et al. 2014; Kalleberg 2012; Pugh 2015; Williams 2000.

9. Bellah et al. 1985; Inglehart and Welzel 2005.

10. Charles 2011; Charles 2017; Frank and Meyer 2001; Inglehart 1997; Inglehart and Welzel 2005.

11. Inglehart and Welzel 2005.

12. Blau and Duncan 1967; Griffin and Kalleberg 1981; Silva 2013.

13. Swidler 2001; Young 2000.

14. McRobbie 2016; Umney and Kretsos 2015.

15. Becker 1964; Blau and Duncan 1967; Gemici and Wiswall 2014; Rosenfeld 1992.

16. Plumeri 2015.

17. Hannon 2010.

18. Vallerand 2008.

19. Although I describe the experiences of *feeling passionate* similarly, my use of "passion" is distinct from the typical use of this term in psychology in a couple of ways. First, psychologists like Vallerand and colleagues (2003, 2012) often conceptualize passions as leisure activities one does *outside* of school and work (e.g., guitar playing, sports). In contrast, I use "passion" specifically in reference to respondents' sense of connection to career paths. Second, psychological literature on passion (esp. harmonious passion [Vallerand 2008]) typically emphasizes its autonomous, individualistic dimensions. In contrast, this book emphasizes that *what people are passionate about* is deeply influenced by, and may influence in turn, gender, race, and class structures. This emphasis on the patterning of people's passions along sociodemographic lines undergirds my sociological arguments about the passion principle's potential role in perpetuating occupational inequalities. Finally, my use of "passion" relates to one's sense of connection to occupational career paths rather than to the specific conditions of their jobs and organizations (Zigarmi et al. 2009).

20. Gecas 1982; Markus and Wurf 1987.

21. Cech 2013; Eccles and Wigfield 2002; Markus and Nurius 1986.

22. Rather than focus on the *content* of passion—who becomes passionate about what (as some of my previous work has done [Cech 2013, 2016])—this book attends to the cultural belief that passion-seeking is a good basis for career decisions.

23. In the nineteenth century, especially in western Europe, only the bourgeoisie could pursue "inactive passions," where "occupants [were] relatively rich in both economic capital and cultural capital." These "inactive men" refused industrial pursuits and the trappings of bourgeois life and instead became artists or playwrights. The idea of engaging in a pursuit (whether artistic or not) for "passion" rather than industrial ends was highly unusual and available only to those with means to support themselves with or without formal employment (Bourdieu and Koch 1987).

24. Correll et al. 2014; Davies and Frink 2014; Mills 1956; Whyte 1956.

25. To assess the norms of career advice books over the past half century, a research assistant and I surveyed those published from 1950 to 2017. Over that time, the number of these books published per year increased tenfold, from an average of 3 per year in the 1950s to an average of 29 per year between 2000 and 2010 (Library of Congress classification numbers HF5381–HF5386). The books

quoted here are exemplars taken from three time periods: postwar period to 1970 (Gates and Miller), 1970 to 1990 (Uris), and 1990 on (Kaplan).

26. Gates and Miller 1958, p. 20.

27. Gates and Miller 1958, p. 16.

28. Gates and Miller 1958, p. 56.

29. Gates and Miller 1958, p. 16.

30. Gates and Miller 1958, p. 55.

31. Uris 1974, pp. 127–28.

32. Uris 1974, pp. 11–12.

33. The Ngrams in Chapter 2 vividly depict the exponential rise in the term "follow your passion" in books published starting in the late 1980s.

34. Kaplan 2013, pp. 1–2.

35. Kaplan 2013, p. 81.

36. Kaplan 2013, p. 204. Emphasis original.

37. Rao and Tobias Neely 2019; Sweet and Meiksins 2017.

38. Davies and Frink 2014; Mills 1956; Sharone 2013; Whyte 1956. As a particularly striking example of such company loyalty, in 1930, at the heart of the Great Depression, the Kellogg Company shifted from an 8-hour a day, 40-hour workweek to a 6-hour a day, 30-hour workweek. Concerned with the possible effect a major layoff might have on its workers, the management saw giving more shifts to fewer people as a way to "give work and paychecks to the heads of 300 more families" (Hunnicutt 1996, p. 13). Other companies followed suit, and this idea of sharing jobs across more people won national support from leaders of both business and labor in depression-era America (Davies and Frink 2014).

39. Sweet and Meiksins 2017. Many large technology companies (e.g., Google, Facebook) have invested in features like hair salons and dry cleaners on their campuses. These benefits are not, as they might seem, proxies for dedication to employees; they are recruitment tools. Accommodation of workers' personal needs is not the same as long-term loyalty and investment in workers' careers.

40. Rao and Tobias Neely 2019.

41. Kalleberg 2009; Sweet and Meiksins 2017.

42. Hacker 2019.

43. Pugh 2015; Wilson 2019.

44. Centeno and Cohen 2012; Hacker 2019.

45. Hacker 2019; Silva 2013.

46. Bellah et al. 1985; Frank and Meyer 2001.

47. Charles and Bradley 2009.

48. Bellah et al. 1985; Hochschild 2012.

49. Giddens 1991.

50. Here and in Chapter 4, I describe cultural beliefs as "scaffolding" one another. By this, I mean that they help support and stabilize one another in the cultural landscape.

51. Blair-Loy 2003.

52. Sewell 1992.

53. Spillman and Strand 2013. Here I use the conceptualization of cultural schemas developed by Mary Blair-Loy (2003) as shared cultural perspectives that encompass moral and emotional commitments as well as cognitive maps. This is in contrast to the idea of "cognitive schemas" sometimes used in cultural sociology, which focus much more narrowly on the "cognitive associations" that may underlie cultural beliefs (Hunzaker and Valentino 2019).

54. Hays 1994.

55. Swidler 1986; Vaisey 2009.

56. Kalleberg 2009.

57. Structurally oriented sociological research is often critiqued for dismissing the agency of individual actors (Hays 1994). An important corrective is to give specific attention to actors' meaning-making processes, which interact with the structural and institutional contexts in which they are embedded (Spillman and Strand 2013).

58. Vaisey 2009.

59. Silva and Snellman 2018.

60. Giddens 1991; Inglehart and Oyserman 2004; Inglehart and Welzel 2005.

61. Frenette and Ocejo 2018; Ocejo 2017; Umney and Kretsos 2015.

62. Collamer 2013; Moen 2016.

63. Collamer 2013.

64. The average college student graduating with a 4-year degree in 2018 had $28,650 in student loan debt. See Zack Friedman, "Student Loan Debt Statistics in 2019: A $1.5 Trillion Crisis," *Forbes*, February 25, 2019, www.forbes.com/sites /zackfriedman/2019/02/25/student-loan-debt-statistics-2019/#738817d9133f.

65. Sweet and Meiksins 2017.

66. Cech 2013; Charles 2011; Charles and Bradley 2009.

67. Young 2000.

68. Ocejo 2017; Rao and Tobias Neely 2019.

69. See Appendix A for details on operationalization of respondents' socioeconomic status (SES).

70. Brown and Lent 2013.

71. Sáenz and Sparks 2020.

72. This is consistent with prior research on racial/ethnic and class differences in career field choices (Beasley 2012; Cech 2013).

73. Frank and Meyer 2001; Inglehart and Oyserman 2004.

74. Charles and Grusky 2004; Cotter, Hermsen, and Vanneman 2011.

75. Baker, Klasik, and Reardon 2018.

76. Cech and Blair-Loy 2010; Hacker 2019; Kluegel and Smith 1986.

77. Duggan 2003; Hacker 2019.
78. Kalleberg 2012.
79. Marcuse 1968.
80. Weber [1919] 1981, p. 147.

CHAPTER 1. WHAT IS THE PASSION PRINCIPLE?

1. This movement was given energy and relevance by a growing neoliberal emphasis on individuals' responsibility to chart their own paths to success (McGee 2005).

2. Rao and Tobias Neely 2019.

3. Davies and Frink 2014; Kalleberg 2009.

4. This book necessarily excludes or touches only briefly on many potentially important considerations related to the cultural schema of the passion principle. Chapter 2 discusses family, curricular, peer, and career adviser influences, but many other contextual factors are likely in play.

5. Wright 2002.

6. Marx [1872] 1972; Marx [1887] 1972.

7. Weber [1919] 1981; Weber [1930] 1992.

8. Although the idea of a "calling" is popularly used to refer to a career pursuit that one feels called to as a matter of individualistic self-fulfillment, this was not Weber's intent (Bellah et al. 1985). For Weber, a calling to work meant that work "subsumes self into a community of disciplined practice and sound judgement whose activity has meaning and value in itself" (Bellah et al. 1985, p. 66; Weber [1930] 1992). The notion of a calling that emerges from the Protestant ethic is tied to one's moral duty to use one's "God-given talents and skills" for the good of humanity. "Neoclassical" notions of a calling are more secular but still retain the idea (1) that one is putting one's unique gifts and talents to good use and (2) that such effort is for a bigger cause than oneself (Bunderson and Thompson 2009). *Passion*, as I define it here, diverges from this notion of calling in that conceptualizations of passion in the passion principle do not have to be based in a natural skill or talent (anyone can be passionate about anything, and skill can be learned with enough passion) and do not require contributions of one's work to the collective good of one's community. Personal, self-expressive investment in one's career field has equal billing under the banner of passion, regardless of whether one's passion is public health or online video entertainment.

9. Bellah et al. 1985; Weber [1930] 1992.

10. Becker 1964; Gemici and Wiswall 2014; Turner and Bowen 1999.

11. Gemici and Wiswall 2014; Jacobs 1995; Turner and Bowen 1999.

12. Pew 2012; Rosenfeld 1992.

13. Blau and Duncan 1967; Griffin and Kalleberg 1981; Schoon 2008.

14. Davies and Guppy 1997; Ma 2009; Mullen 2014.

15. Binder, Davis, and Bloom 2016; Rivera 2015.

16. Lamont 2020.

17. Armstrong and Hamilton 2013.

18. Wilson 2019, p. 4.

19. Becker 1985; Eccles 2011; Frome et al. 2006.

20. Cech 2016; Pedulla and Thébaud 2015.

21. Gerson 2010; Lamont 2020.

22. Cech and Blair-Loy 2019; Jacobs 1989; Jacobs and Gerson 2005. Research on parents'—especially mothers'—experiences in the full-time workforce demonstrates that the difficulties of balancing caregiving responsibilities with full-time professional careers can push women to pursue other career paths or leave the labor force entirely (Blair-Loy 2003; Blair-Loy and Cech 2017; Jacobs and Gerson 2005).

23. Beasley 2012; Cech et al. 2018; Fryberg and Markus 2007; Mullen 2010; Smith et al. 2014.

24. Cech, Smith, and Metz 2019.

25. Cech 2013; Charles and Bradley 2009; Cotter, Hermsen, and Vanneman 2011; England 2010.

26. Ehrhart and Makransky 2007; Spokane 1985; Tinsley 2000. Research in counseling, coaching, and applied psychology similarly centers "interests" and "fit" in their theories of career decision-making (Baggini 2018; Brown and Lent 2013; Holland 1959).

27. Armstrong and Hamilton 2013; Castilla, Lan and Rissing 2013a; Castilla, Lan, and Rissing 2013b; Granovetter 1973.

28. Bourdieu 1984; Castilla and Rissing 2019; Jacobs, Karen, and McClelland 1991; Rivera 2015.

29. MacLeod 1987; Mullen 2010; Mullen 2014; Silva 2013.

30. Bertrand and Mullainathan 2004; Castilla 2008; Correll, Benard, and Paik 2007; Tilcsik 2011.

31. For more information, see the definition and discussion of cultural schemas in the introduction.

32. Cech 2013.

33. Gecas 1982; Markus and Nurius 1986; Markus and Wurf 1987.

34. Charles 2011; Fouad 2007; Jacobs, Karen and McClelland 1991; Lueptow, Garovich-Szabo, and Lueptow 2001; Markus and Kitayama 2003.

35. Beasley 2012; Bourdieu 1984; Cech 2013.

36. Interest in an occupation or field cannot develop without both access to a realm of knowledge or practice and structured encouragement of that interest (Eccles and Wigfield 2002; Silvia 2006).

37. This echoes the "high performing, low loyalty" perspective of many college-educated workers who are highly devoted to their work tasks but not to their particular employer (Pugh 2015).

38. Passion for one's work is certainly correlated with job and organization satisfaction, but they are conceptually distinct (Bunderson and Thompson 2009; Zigarmi et al. 2009). Much of the work satisfaction literature does not disentangle workers' attachment to the specific conditions of their employment from their commitment to their career fields more generally. This distinction is important, as workers—especially those with advanced training—have a much harder time switching career fields than switching employers. My focus on passion dovetails with recent calls in work and occupations literature to bring occupations and professions back in to understandings of workforce inequality (Ocejo 2017; Weeden and Grusky 2005).

39. Swidler 2001.

40. This is consistent with "to each their own" notions of individualism in the United States, where people are allowed their "own bit of space" to be themselves (Bellah et al. 1985, p. 76).

41. A career counselor at the University of Michigan (see Chapter 2 for details on the career counselor interviews) spoke similarly about her observations of students who were anxious because they hadn't identified a passion: "It can feel like debilitating if they can't figure out like what the 'it' is for them" (white woman, early thirties).

42. As I argue elsewhere (Cech 2016), family-related considerations such as flexibility and breadwinning were rare among this sample of college students.

43. Goyette and Xie 1999.

44. See, e.g., Feffer 2014; Hannon 2010; Lebowitz 2015.

45. Duckworth 2016; McGee 2005.

46. Brown and Lent 2013.

47. I conducted the PPS after completing the interviews with students. The inductive analysis of these interview data allowed me to identify themes that I then operationalized in survey questions.

48. All figures in this chapter present predicted means rather than raw means for each item. These predicted means are more useful than raw means because they hold constant other sources of variation along demographic factors, occupation, education level, etc. Predicted means were produced as margin values out of OLS regression models that predicted each question with respondents' rating on the passion principle scale as well as controls for gender, race/ethnicity, age, nativity, class background, occupation, industry, and employer size. Error bars represent 95% confidence intervals. Non-overlapping error bars indicate that the values represented by those bars are statistically different from one another.

49. Specifically, I summed these six measures and divided by 6 to maintain a 1 (strongly disagree) to 5 (strongly agree) value range (alpha = .898). This

multivariate measure is superior to any single measure because it better captures the multidimensionality of what it means to be passionate about an occupation or productive task realm.

50. Rates in Figure 1.2 are predicted values that hold constant variation by other demographic characteristics, as well as job and education characteristics. Error bars are 95% confidence intervals. See note 48, above. NAAPI stands for the racial/ethnic category "Native American and Asian-Pacific Islander."

51. An overarching theme of this chapter is the relative commonality of the value of passion-seeking across sociodemographic groups. Because sociologists are often concerned with group-based differences, much more attention is typically paid to intergroup variation than intergroup similarity. Here, and in other chapters, I attend to sociodemographic differences when they arise in the data, but I also emphasize the striking similarity across groups where the data suggest it.

52. Values on the passion principle scale in Figure 1.3 are predicted values for each age range, holding constant variation by other demographic factors and education level. See note 47, above.

53. Coefficient for SES: B = .052, p < .01.

54. Regression coefficient: B = −.174, p < .01.

55. Chen and Lan 1998; Goyette and Xie 1999; Hanson and Gilbert 2012.

56. Regression Coefficient: B = −.187, p < .01.

57. Bertrand and Mullainathan 2004; Ma 2009; Wingfield 2007.

58. Figure C.1 in Appendix C presents predicted means on the passion principle measure across 14 occupational categories. These categories are displayed in order, from workers with the strongest average adherence to the passion principle to workers with weaker average adherence.

59. Specifically, I averaged respondents' rating of the passion-related factors for major and career selection into one scale (six measures, alpha = .898) and the job security and salary considerations measure by another scale (four measures, alpha = .799). By comparing these two scales, I was able to determine how many respondents rated passion-related factors as more important on average than they rated economic considerations (job security and salary) in their conceptualization of good career decisions.

60. Ridgeway 2011.

61. Gerson 2010; Lamont 2020. In addition, there is growing popularity of "encore careers"—whereby workers in their fifties and sixties change career paths when they near retirement and/or after their children have grown in order to find more fulfilling work (Collamer 2013; Moen 2016).

62. Cairns 2017; Kalleberg 2009.

63. Grusky, Western, and Wimer 2011.

64. Supplemental analysis by immigrant status did not reveal that students born outside the United States were more likely on average to factor in money or job security concerns than their US-born peers.

65. Recently, highly publicized results from a Higher Education Research Institute (HERI) survey of first-year college students found that over 70% reported that "being able to make more money" was very important to them in their decision to go to college. This may be as much a reflection of the precarity of the workforce for the non-college-educated than a shift toward greater financial concerns among students. Indeed, in that same survey, 84% reported that the ability to "learn more about things that interest me" was very important to them in their decision to attend college. See Ellen Bara Stolzenberg et al., *The American Freshman: National Norms Fall 2017* (Los Angeles: HERI, 2019), www.heri.ucla.edu/monographs/TheAmericanFreshman2017.pdf.

66. Rivera 2015.

67. Some women, too, noted that income security would be important for their ability to support their future families financially. See Cech 2016 for a discussion of family and breadwinner plans among this sample of students.

68. Mullen (2014) found a similar pattern among students in an elite liberal arts college: for over half of her respondents, "considerations of salary were rarely a factor, much less a priority, in their decisions" (p. 302).

69. Kalleberg 2009; Kalleberg 2012; Silva 2013. I discuss the differential vulnerabilities to these outcomes, especially among passion-seekers, in Chapter 3.

70. Armstrong and Hamilton 2013; Lamont 2020; Mullen 2010; Rivera 2015.

71. At first glance, the patterns I present in this chapter may seem to contradict findings from recent qualitative research on college students. Students who prioritized money, security, or even glamour and notoriety in career decisions were common, for instance, in Rivera's (2015) study of hiring processes of elite professional service (EPS) firms, in Armstrong and Hamilton's (2013) study of women at a large midwestern university, and in Binder and colleagues' (2016) interviews with business-oriented students at elite colleges. Much of the potential discrepancy in the prevalence of financial and status concerns across the studies can be attributed to the differences in their and my sampling strategies. Rivera's interest in how working-class students are disadvantaged in access to EPS firms selected on students who expressed interest in and applied to these firms. By the firms' own selection, the students who were even considered for recruitment were those from only the most elite universities in the country. And, as I discuss in Chapter 3, these EPS firm jobs were not the end game for most students; they were generally viewed as "elite finishing schools" on career aspirants' way to jobs in corporations, nonprofit organizations, or government agencies that were more aligned with their passion. Second, Armstrong and Hamilton's (2013) interest in how the academic and social life of campuses shapes students' life chances led them to select as a site for their ethnography a residence hall with a reputation as a "party dorm." As such, the stories of women

on the "party pathway," who emphasized socializing, heteronormative relationships, and glamour, had an outsized presence compared to a broader sample of the student population at that focal university. Although my sample of students is not statistically representative, my process of selecting students by posting flyers in academic buildings, residence halls, and student unions across campus cast a wider net and did not intentionally select on or exclude students who had particular educational or career orientations. My multicampus study design also aimed to capture students from a wider spectrum of four-year colleges. Further, the patterns in my interview data closely mirror the beliefs expressed by respondents in the proportionally representative survey data of college-educated workers (PPS data) and supplemental survey data of college students (Appendix B).

72. Among the 28 respondents who gave non-passion-related factors in their choice of major, 43% were STEM majors; 32%, social science majors; 11%, liberal arts majors; and 14%, health majors.

73. Respondents were asked, "Imagine that you were looking for a new job. Please rank the following factors in order from MOST important (#1) to least important (#5): salary, job security, work-life balance, benefits, interest or passion for the work."

74. In supplemental logistic regression models with demographic measures, I predicted the likelihood that respondents would rank passion, salary, and job security, respectively, as their top priority in a new job. As with Figure 1.3, older respondents were more likely than younger respondents to rate passion as their top priority (B = .013, p < .01), while Asian respondents were more likely than whites to rank salary and job security as their top priorities (B = .510, p < .05 and B = .565, p < .05, respectively). Also, perhaps reflecting their greater leverage for accessing more stable and better-paying professional jobs, respondents with advanced degrees were more likely to prioritize passion than respondents with only a bachelor's degree.

75. Thirty-two percent of those respondents who answered that they had switched career paths did not offer an explanation in the open-ended text box. The figures given in this paragraph are for the 68% of switchers who did provide an explanation.

76. This question asks respondents to adjudicate between meaningfulness, employment, and salary considerations at the *job* level, not the career field level. Although these are distinct arenas, factors related to respondents' considerations for switching jobs is more immediate than switching career fields, particularly because the latter may require extensive retraining.

77. Kalleberg 2009; Viscelli 2016. In addition, 19% of respondents with a high school degree or less (vs. 16% of college-educated respondents) rated salary as more important than meaningful work, and 22% of those with a high school degree or less (vs. 17% of college-educated respondents) rated job security more important than meaningful work.

78. Kalleberg 2009; Silva 2013.

79. This is mirrored in a supplemental sample of non-college-educated workers (N = 750) fielded alongside the 2020 passion principle survey. Here, those with no college or some college had significantly higher values on the financial/stability scale than the college-educated (4.17 and 4.06, respectively; coefficient for college degree in OLS regression models: −.090, p < .05) but were just as likely as those with a college degree to adhere to the passion principle (coefficient for college degree in OLS regression models: 0.06, p < .05).

80. I further examined these factors by demographic category and job characteristics with ordered logistic regression models. Importantly, neither education level nor age (nor any other demographic factors) were significant predictors of the importance of meaningful work in whether respondents would take a new job, suggesting that the emphasis on passion-related factors is not solely the purview of the college-educated. This pattern is suggested by other qualitative research as well. For example, Sharone's (2013) unemployed US white-collar workers sought fulfilling work in their job searching, and the low-income Black men in Young's (2000) study prioritized meaningful, autonomous work in their employment searches.

81. Such moves toward equality in the public sphere have not been matched in the sphere of romantic relationships and childrearing, however (Lamont 2020; Gerson 2012).

82. Lamont 2020; Gerson 2012.

83. Cech 2013.

84. It is interesting to note the general similarity in career decision-making priorities by gender. Contrary to previous eras, the men in my sample did not typically prioritize breadwinning paths, and women did not typically prioritize what they thought might be the most flexible work to balance with future childrearing plans (Cech 2016). In both the PPS and the NSCW data, further, respondents with young children did not endorse passion-seeking less strongly, nor were they less likely to value meaningful work in considerations of their next job. The norm for men and women to think beyond gendered family responsibilities when planning their careers is a positive step for gender equality (Gerson 2010). As women have enjoyed greater freedom and encouragement to pursue their professional goals, the prominence of following self-expressive paths has meant that gender-segregative processes have shifted from external and overt gender policing to seemingly gender-neutral, individual-level meaning-making processes (Cech 2013). Ironically, as a result of these processes, we may be unlikely to see much progress on gender desegregation any time soon (England 2010).

85. Fouad 2007.

86. Beasley 2012.

87. Fouad 2007.

88. Mullen 2010.

89. Ma 2009.

90. There are likely important connections between class "tastes" and class differences in who develops passion for what subjects (Bourdieu 1984; Lamont 1992; Mullen 2014).

91. Bourdieu 1984; Mullen 2014; Rivera 2015.

92. Beasley 2012; Cech 2013; Charles and Bradley 2009; Jacobs 1995. In this process of passion-seeking, seemingly individualistic career choices end up perpetuating occupational segregation. This is a process distinct from the potential perpetuation of socioeconomic inequalities discussed in Chapter 3. Here, even holding parental resources constant, individual career aspirants' seeking of fields that align with their (gendered, racialized, classed) senses of self leads to the perpetuation of occupational segregation by race, gender, and class.

93. In this chapter, I look separately at respondents' abstract conceptualization of good career decisions and the logics they use in their own career decisions. This distinction was meant to aid me in articulating patterns in the data and structuring my argument. But, of course, broad cultural schemas and plans of action are highly interconnected.

94. The passion principle may also play out across the life course, affecting not only choice of training specialization in college but also decisions about career change or skill retooling down the line. As Chapter 3 discusses, the passion principle may help perpetuate patterns of socioeconomic inequality that students entered college with because it presumes economic and cultural resources that are typical only of middle- and upper-class career aspirants and such aspirants are likely better equipped to translate their passion into gainful employment.

95. Becker 1964; Gemici and Wiswall 2014.

96. E.g., Blau and Duncan 1967; Rosenfeld 1992.

CHAPTER 2. WHY IS THE PASSION PRINCIPLE
COMPELLING?

1. Kalleberg 2012; Smith 2002; Sweet and Meiksins 2017.

2. Brady, Beckfield and Zhao 2007; DiMaggio 2001; Sweet and Meiksins 2017.

3. Elcioglu 2010; Kalleberg 2012; Kenworthy 2004; Osnowitz 2010; Ravenelle 2019.

4. Hacker 2019; Harvey 2005.

5. Correll et al. 2014; Kalleberg 2012; Pugh 2015.

6. Sharone 2013.

7. Arum and Roksa 2011; Charles and Bradley 2009; Sweet and Meiksins 2017.

8. McCall 2013; Sáenz and Sparks 2020; Silva 2013.

9. Pugh 2015.

10. Rao and Tobias Neely 2019.

11. Henly and Lambert 2014; Lambert, Fugiel and Henly 2014.

12. Blair-Loy 2003; Correll et al. 2014; Jacobs and Gerson 2005; Perlow 2012; Williams 2000. Some technology companies and consulting firms even openly work their employees to "burnout," with the notion that the company will get several productive, overworked years from them before having to replace them with new recruits (Hsieh 2010). Additionally, workers are largely left on their own to manage personal issues like childcare and eldercare responsibilities (Padavic and Reskin 2002).

13. Pugh 2015.

14. Rao and Tobias Neely 2019.

15. E.g., Gemici and Wiswall 2014.

16. Pugh 2015; Spillman 2017; Willis 1981; Zelizer 2017.

17. Bellah et al. 1985; Durkheim [1953] 2009.

18. Frank and Meyer 2001.

19. Inglehart 1997; Inglehart and Welzel 2005.

20. Bellah et al. 1985, p. 76.

21. Charles 2011; Charles 2017; Inglehart and Welzel 2005.

22. Frank and Meyer 2001; Giddens 1991.

23. Owens, Robinson and Smith-Lovin 2010; Schlenker and Trudeau 1990; Swann 1983; Swann 1987. Greater opportunities for self-expressive action is correlated with increased satisfaction, decreased depression, and greater intrinsic motivation (Swann 1983; Swann 1987; Vallerand 2008; Vallerand 2012).

24. Bourdieu and Passeron 1990; Charles and Bradley 2009; Inglehart and Oyserman 2004.

25. Padavic and Reskin 2002.

26. As colleges sought to cater to a growing number of students in the 1970s and 1980s, particularly women, institutions began to expand the number of majors they offered and provided greater flexibility for selecting and changing one's major (Charles and Bradley 2009).

27. Cech 2016; Gerson 2010; Lamont 2020.

28. Cech 2016; Lamont 2020.

29. McGee 2005; Sharone 2013.

30. Duggan 2003; Silva 2013.

31. According to Marx's definition, self-estrangement is "the alienation of man's essence, man's loss of objectivity and his loss of realness as self-discovery, manifestation of his nature, objectification and realization" (Marx 1932 [1844]). In the context of work, self-estrangement is the feeling of personal isolation or exclusion from one's work process and work outcome and of feeling like one loses one's sense of self at work.

32. Shapin 2009; Weber [1919] 1981. The passion principle's emphasis on self-expression and self-improvement has precedent in Confucian and Greek philosophical traditions (Baggini 2018; McGee 2005; Shapin 2009). However, having work that dovetails with projects of self-improvement was usually only the purview of the most privileged men who could rely on inherence and/or on others' labor to support themselves.

33. Spillman 2017.

34. Google Books Ngram Viewer, https://books.google.com/ngrams. Similar patterns emerged for search times like "do what you love" and "meaningful work."

35. This consistency in the value of passion-seeking is echoed in more recent data as well. The passion principle survey (PPS) I use in this book was conducted in October 2020, in the midst of the economic and social turmoil of the COVID-19 (coronavirus) pandemic. As I explain in Appendix A, this was a re-fielding of a survey I had originally conducted two years prior. In 2018, at the height of a strong (albeit highly unequal) economy, I found that the passion principle was highly salient across college-educated workers. Given the economic turmoil that the country endured in the wake of the pandemic, I wondered whether this pattern was robust to different sets of cultural and social circumstances. Evincing the stability of the salience of this cultural schema, adherence to the passion principle among college-educated workers was not statically different between 2020 and 2018. See Figure A.1 in Appendix A.

36. Passion Principle Scale mean: 4.46, alpha = .898. See Chapter 1 for description of scale creation and Figure 1.1 for means on individual scale measures.

37. The "passion principle believers" category represents respondents who answered "very important" to all 6 of the passion principle measures noted above (29% of the sample fit this characteristic). The "passion principle skeptics" category represents respondents who gave an average of 2, or "somewhat unimportant" across the six questions are coded as "passion principle skeptics." Values in columns represent predicted means, holding constant variation by demographics, job characteristics, and education level.

38. Passion principle skeptics were not notably distinct from passion principle believers, nor was skepticism of passion-seeking isolated to particular socio-demographic groups. Passion principle skeptics were more likely than passion principle believers to be Asian, to be in their 30s, and to be IT workers. There were no other differences by gender, race/ethnicity, education level, or other demographic category in adherence to the passion principle.

39. Eccles and Wigfield 2002; Gerhart and Fang 2015.

40. One counterargument is that the passion principle is just a more socially acceptable cover story for those who were really just invested in being professionally successful in their jobs for the sake of money and prestige. While this could have been the case for a few respondents, the results in Chapter 3 show

numerous examples of career aspirants moving away from prestigious career paths in medicine, engineering, accounting, etcetera, to pursue passion-based paths with far less occupational prestige or employment stability. See also the discussion of the passion principle as a justificatory narrative in Chapter 1.

41. Correll et al. 2014; Davies and Frink 2014; Rao and Tobias Neely 2019; Spillman 2017.

42. Research in social psychology suggests that disliking the content of one's work can indeed have negative career and wellness consequences (Carr 1997; Cennamo and Gardner 2008; Hardie 2014).

43. Additionally, respondents were not talking about conditions or arrangements of particular organizations, but rather one's career field in general. Choosing the right career field was seen as more important than the specific jobs or employing organizations, because one could switch employers much more easily than career fields.

44. To be sure, students' assessment of the potential drudgery they might encounter if they worked outside of their passion leaves little possibility for them to develop interest and personal investment in their jobs over time. Their gloomy assessment of what the labor force is like for those who do not follow their passion likely is part of the draw of passion-seeking.

45. Ocejo 2017, p. 134.

46. There was no expectation that one had to remain passionate about the same thing over the course of their working lives. Rather, passion-seeking simply meant prioritizing one's passion (whatever that passion might be at the time) in one's career decisions.

47. Duffy et al. 2013; Sabat et al. 2019; Tokumitsu 2015; Zigarmi et al. 2009.

48. In regression models predicting several health measures, the coefficients for "my work is meaningful to me" were as follows: sleep interruptions (meaningful work coefficient: $B = -.134$, $p < .01$); depressive symptoms (meaningful work coefficient: $B = -.289$, $p < .001$), and stress (meaningful work coefficient: $B = -.113$, $p < .001$). Models included controls for gender, race/ethnicity, education level, age, tenure, class background, hours worked, sector, industry, immigrant status, and whether they have health insurance.

49. I chose the name "Joe" and use male pronouns in the vignette because, in the instance that respondents feminized passion-seeking, I wanted to use the less obvious case of a man considering whether to follow his passion. Because there is no clear racial/ethnic or class markers in this vignette, I suspect that most respondents read Joe as a white middle-class man.

50. Joe's story is not outlandish; many of the formerly-white-collar-employed bartenders, butchers, barbers, and distillers Ocejo (2017) studied had similar stories. A bartender in Ocejo's study named Rob, for example, left a full-time job in tech support with good pay and benefits to bartend, saying "I can really try and strive to make six figures, sit behind a desk, and feel removed, or I do

something where I make less, but feels fulfilled and more connected to what I do." Rob did not regret his choice.

51. Importantly, this question was answered in the context of COVID-19, when many restaurants had to dramatically shift how they operated to uphold physical distancing regulations. Indeed, a fifth of respondents mentioned the employment uncertainty of the context of COVID in their open-ended responses. However, even in this context, two thirds of college-educated workers advised Joe to take the risk and leave his IT job.

52. One respondent explained that the vignette was very similar to her husband's story: "ironically, my husband was in this almost very exact position. He stayed in his IT job way past when he should have, but just didn't want to leave the salary behind . . . [He] ultimately got a job teaching which had always been his lifelong dream but never pursued it because of the low paying salary . . . .my husband is happier than he's ever been. I wish my husband had quit his job seven years before he was fired to follow his dreams. I would recommend to anyone unhappy in their job to quit and do something they really want to do, even if it wasn't a sure thing."

53. College-educated workers certainly encounter a myriad of contextual factors that may challenge or reinforce their adherence to the passion principle. I attend here to the contextual factors that most clearly emerged in the student interview data and the career advising professionals who have formal jurisdiction over career advice within the context of higher education.

54. Silva and Snellman 2018.

55. Nelson 2012; Pugh 2018.

56. Armstrong and Hamilton 2013, p. 184.

57. Armstrong and Hamilton 2013.

58. Traditionally, young men were pressured to pursue breadwinner careers and young women were expected to align their career priorities with their caregiving plans (Cech 2016). Yet, there is evidence that these gender dynamics in parental pressure are shifting. For example, Lamont's (2020) study of college-educated young adults in the San Francisco area found that women experienced pressure from families to find lucrative careers more frequently than men, while men were encouraged to find enjoyable careers they could work hard at and still find "fulfilling."

59. Respondents were asked "Think back to when you were deciding on a career path in college. Please indicate the extent to which you agree that the statements applied to you at the time . . . I felt pressure from parents/guardians to:" "choose a career field that would make a lot of money," "choose a career field that would lead to a prestigious career," and "choose a career field that would provide many employment opportunities" (1 = strongly disagree to 5 = strongly agree). In OLS regression models controlling for other demographics, respondents from upper and upper-middle class families were more likely than those from less well-off families to report pressures to choose a well-paying field (B =

.358, p < .001), a field with employment opportunities (B = .411, p < .001) and more likely to feel pressure to choose a prestigious field (B = .287, p < .001).

60. In the above question, respondents were also asked to indicate their agreement with the following statement in relation to their choice of career field in college: "My ability to pay off student loans or other debt influenced my career decision-making" and "My ability to help financially support my parents or family members influenced my career decision-making" (1 = strongly disagree to 5 = strongly agree). In OLS regression models controlling for other demographics, I found that respondents from working-class families were more likely than their peers from more privileged backgrounds to say that loans and debt influenced their decisions (B = .239, p < .05) and that they were impacted by their ability to help financially support their parents (B = .219, p < .01). They were also less likely than their peers from wealthier families to agree that "My parents/guardians encouraged me to follow my personal interests, regardless of the pay or prestige of the field" (B = −.199, p < .01).

61. OLS regression coefficients for racial/ethnic status were as follows: Asian respondents were more likely than peers to have felt pressure from their parents to choose fields with opportunities for high salaries (B = .468, p < .001) and less likely to have felt encouraged to follow their interests when selecting a career path (B = .396, p < .001). Black respondents were also more likely than their peers to have been encouraged to choose high-paying fields (B = .535, p < .001). Asian respondents (B = .538, p < .001) and those born outside the US (B = .330, p < .01), were more likely than their white and US-born peers to say that supporting their families impacted their career decisions, net of controls.

62. Hanson and Gilbert 2012.

63. There were also some gender differences in parental pressure among older PPS cohorts. Among respondents over 40, women were less likely to be encouraged to pursue employment opportunities by parents (B = −.420, p < .001), less likely to be expected to help support their families (B = −.667, p < .001), and less likely to be encouraged to follow their interests (B = −.261, p < .001). However, these differences did not hold among younger cohorts (under 40 years old), suggesting this may be relics of gendered parental advice given to women and men college students.

64. Career aspirants' resistance to parental pressures to prioritize economic and employment concerns conflicts with assumptions in the social mobility literature that children generally adopt the labor market stances of their parents. These results point to college-educated children's pushback on their parents' labor market priorities as a potential complication to the more straightforward intergenerational transmission of socioeconomic privilege often presumed in intergenerational mobility research.

65. OLS regression coefficient for parental encouragement to "follow my personal interests, regardless of the pay or prestige of the field" predicting the

passion principle scale: B = .035; p < .01. The model also controlled for gender, race/ethnicity, age, whether respondents were born in the US, education level, and job characteristics.

66. Charles and Bradley 2009.

67. Kaplan 2016.

68. Binder, Davis and Bloom 2016; Rivera 2015.

69. Rivera 2015.

70. Rivera 2015.

71. As shown in the supplemental survey results from college students in Appendix B, there was little statistical variation in the prevalence of the passion principle across school types.

72. Since the 1980s, US colleges have seen a decline in the number of humanities degrees conferred and an expansion of more vocational and applied majors, especially in health services (AAA&S 2017). Such changes do not necessarily contradict the salience of the passion principle. There are now more paths than ever (e.g., sports administration, criminology) for students to tailor to their passion. Accordingly, I did not encounter large cadres of students who expressed passion for these declining degrees (e.g., classics) but then decided to pursue more applied fields instead. Far more common was career aspirants switching majors or career paths *toward* fields they were passionate about than the proportion who switched out of their passion in search of fields with greater employment opportunities (see Chapter 3). Additionally, as illustrated in Appendix B among a supplemental survey sample of college students, 43% of students who switched majors said they did so to move to a subject that was closer to their interests, compared to 22% who changed majors to pursue greater job opportunities.

73. Stanford Career Education and Student Affairs website, https://beam .stanford.edu.

74. In the PPS data, 42% of respondents reported seeking out advice from career advisers or career counselors. Younger cohorts were less likely than older cohorts to have seen a career counselor, and Black and Latinx respondents were more likely to have seen a career counselor than their white peers.

75. Lola Fadulu, "Why Aren't College Students Using Career Services," *Atlantic*, January 20, 2018, www.theatlantic.com/education/archive/2018/01 /why-arent-college-students-using-career-services/551051.

76. Brown and Lent 2013.

77. Strong Interest Inventory, www.cpp.com/products/strong/index.aspx; Gallup StrengthsFinder tool, http://strengths.gallup.com/private/Resources /CSFTechnicalReport031005.pdf. According to the Strong Interest Inventory website, the SII is intended to guide individuals "their search for a rich and fulfilling career."

78. Brown and Lent 2013.

79. Coefficients for experience with career counselors in OLS regression model predicting passion principle adherence: B = .741, p < .010, net of demographic, occupation, and job controls.

80. At the end of the follow up interviews, I explained that one of the central themes from the first interviews was the prominence of passion-based considerations in students' career decision-making. I then asked them what they thought about that pattern. Although two of the 35 interviewees used that as an opportunity to offer critiques of the passion principle itself, even this direct line of questioning did not elicit widespread critiques of this career decision-making schema.

81. Kosowski 2010.

82. Rao and Tobias Neely 2019. Indeed, expectations for overwork among white-collar workers have exploded over the past several decades. In a recent study of professionals, managers and executives, those who interacted with work through smartphones (the vast majority of professionals) were connected to work over 72 hours per week, including 13.5 hours each weekday (Deal 2015).

83. See, e.g., Schulz 2015.

CHAPTER 3. THE PRIVILEGE OF PASSION?

Epigraph: Dirty Heads is an American reggae-ska alternative rock band. Their 2017 song "Vacation" was written by Dustin Bushnell, Justin Jeberg, and Jared Watson.

1. The original interviews were with students in their first through senior year in college, so some had more experience in the labor force than others by the time I reinterviewed them. Respondents' paths tended to stabilize—whether in part-time jobs, in graduate programs, or in full-time jobs—within about eighteen months after they left college (see also Wilson 2019). As such, the period between the first and second interviews might not have been long enough to see all phases of uncertainty, but it likely encompasses some of the greatest challenges that college-educated respondents experienced attempting to launch their careers.

2. Going into the follow-up interviews, my working hypothesis was that I would find a "passionate until reality hits" story. I expected a marked shift toward more pragmatic decision-making criteria after graduation. I suspected that career aspirants in the follow-up interviews would shift their priorities to consider economic and security concerns much more centrally—snatching up opportunities for secure work they came across that offered solid opportunities or good pay. As this chapter shows, respondents were certainly more pragmatic about salary and security considerations then they were in college, but there was notable tolerance for employment precarity, for sacrificing economically viable opportunities, and for switching gears to a different field in pursuit of work that better aligned with their passion.

3. Castilla 2008; Petersen and Saporta 2004.

4. Armstrong and Hamilton 2013; Rivera 2015; Umney and Kretsos 2015; Wilson 2019.

5. This is consistent with the PPS results from college-educated workers, who were more likely to rank passion or interest for work as the most important factor in whether they would choose a new job than employment security, salary, or benefits (see Figure 1.6).

6. As I noted in Chapter 1, there was ample room in the cultural schema of the passion principle for people to "discover" a new passion or fall out of love with an earlier passion as they became more familiar with the topic. Of course, what respondents perceived as a shift in their own passion could very well have been driven by structural obstacles that blocked their path (e.g., poor grades in a prerequisite course). Here I am attentive to respondents' understandings of their own experiences and motivations rather than adjudicating what parts of their passion might be structurally derived.

7. Thomas, a graduate of the music program at MSU, noted how common this deprioritization of salary was among his classmates: "I think everybody kinda in that [music] degree just kind of sticks their fingers in their ears and pretends like it's not an issue, but it's a really serious issue. You need to realistically think about your debt that you're coming out with, which hit me pretty hard" (white working-class man).

8. Kalleberg 2009; Kalleberg 2012.

9. These categorizations are based on current economic status (for those employed) or potential economic opportunities conferred by the graduate training they are pursuing. I cannot project where their career paths might go from here. However, the quantitative NSCW data of US college-educated workers suggests that the class distinction in access to the top-right quadrant isn't isolated to this interview population.

10. I certainly could have arrayed respondents along a number of other axes, such as support for one's outside-work activities, the characteristics of their organizations, etc. Here, I juxtapose the two factors most culturally and practically in tension in this chapter. Also, I map all interview respondents onto these axes regardless of whether they prioritized passion in their job searches. Since the desire to follow passion was fairly evenly distributed among respondents as students, I focus here on their destinations several years after college.

11. Because of the small sample size, the follow-up interviews are ill equipped to examine possible intersectional class processes with race and gender categories. I discuss the potential gendering and racialization of these processes at the end of this chapter.

12. Respondents' class background is divided into three categories (working, middle, and upper class) in this figure for ease of interpretation. I provide more

nuanced breakdown of middle-class backgrounds (the largest class group) into upper middle class, middle class, and lower middle class in the text of the chapter.

13. See the operationalization of passion-based work in NSCW noted in Chapter 5. Class background was determined by a question that asked NSCW respondents whether they grew up in a family that was "worse off," "better off," or "the same as" "the average American family." In regression models controlling for respondents' demographic characteristics, employment sector, occupation, hours worked, education level, and whether they were first-generation college graduates, workers from "worse off" families (which I coded as working-class) were less likely than those from "better off" families (which I coded as upper-class) to report stable, passion-based work ($B = -.071$, $p < .05$). Further, respondents from "worse off" families were more likely than those from "better off" families to be in precarious employment outside of their passion (22% vs. 14%, respectively; coefficient estimate for "worse off" background indicator in regression model: $B = .073$, $p < .05$). Here precarious work is characterized as work that fits one or more of the following criteria: respondent is underemployed, lacks health insurance through their workplace, has frequent unplanned hour reductions if work is slow, work is seasonal, and/or job pays less than $20,000 annually.

14. Padavic and Reskin 2002.

15. Addo, Houle, and Simon 2016.

16. Armstrong and Hamilton 2013; Mullen 2010; Rivera 2015.

17. Rivera 2015.

18. Armstrong and Hamilton 2013.

19. Research on creative industry workers such as jazz musicians also reveals the importance of family resources and cultural capital for allowing artists to prioritize (often economically risky) paths that give them the most freedom to pursue gigs that align with their passion (McRobbie 2016; Umney and Kretsos 2015; Wilson 2019).

20. For broader discussion of the so-called boomerang generation, or the trend of young adults moving back in with their parents after college graduation, see Britton 2013 and Stone et al. 2014.

21. Rivera 2015, pp. 64–65.

22. Bourdieu 1984; Bourdieu 2001.

23. For example, Armstrong and Hamilton (2013) demonstrated that cultural and social capital helped women who graduated in majors like hospitality and sports broadcasting get jobs, and Hamilton (2014) described the ways that the parents of privileged college students intervened in their education to set them up for success.

24. Rivera (2015) found that cultural capital is critical for students from elite schools like Stanford to actually get offers from the EPS firms that recruit them.

Having the right "pedigree" included the right hobbies, extracurricular activities, and a personal ease that is cultivated in upper-class circles.

25. Bourdieu 1984.

26. See Castilla et al.'s (2013a, 2013b) review of the influence of social networks on employment processes.

27. This alumni network was cultivated formally by the career counseling office at Stanford and informally through alumni-only social media groups.

28. Rivera (2015) and Castilla and Rissing (2019) document similar processes whereby students at elite institutions use their networks for getting jobs and accessing advanced degree programs.

29. Non-degree-granting graduate certificate programs are "stop-gap opportunities" offered to graduates who aren't ready to commit to graduate school or who want to "update [their] skills" (e.g., http://scpd.stanford.edu/programs /graduate-certificates). These programs are usually shorter than master's programs and focus on specific topics in education, healthcare, or computer programming and are not accredited. Although these programs have a net financial benefit (raising men's earnings by about 25% and women's earnings by about 13%), they can be expensive (Georgetown University Center on Education and the Workforce 2015). Certification program enrollees typically pay per graduate credit hour. Because they are non-degree-granting programs, enrollees are typically not eligible for federal financial aid.

30. While terminal master's programs typically are eligible for federal student loans, they less frequently provide stipends or access to paid employment (e.g., as teaching or research assistants) than PhD programs.

31. Safety nets and springboards often accompanied one another. Respondents with strong safety nets often also had the advantage of one or more springboards. I distinguish them here conceptually, but safety nets and springboards are part of the bouquet of benefits socioeconomically privileged parents offer their children to help them be successful in the labor market (also see Armstrong and Hamilton 2013; Hamilton 2016).

32. This internalization of the difficulty of obtaining a job as a personal failing is consistent with many of the unemployed professionals Sharone (2013) interviewed in the United States and the recent college graduates from working-class backgrounds Silva (2013) interviewed.

33. Also see Sharone 2015; Silva 2013.

34. Armstrong and Hamilton 2013; Castilla, Lan, and Rissing 2013a; Castilla, Lan, and Rissing 2013b; Granovetter 1973; Rivera 2015.

35. Baker, Klasik, and Reardon 2018.

36. Addo, Houle, and Simon 2016; Oliver 2000.

37. BLS 2018.

38. Bertrand and Mullainathan 2004; Devah Pager 2003; Rivera 2012.

39. Hacker 2019.

40. We can't know whether the working-class students who prioritized passion might have been able to shore up the differences between them and their more privileged peers had they followed the options available to them that led to the greatest financial security. The point is, they shouldn't be asked to divert their energies from their passion while their more privileged peers take advantage of access to safety nets and springboards.

41. Arum and Roksa 2011; Federal Reserve Bank of New York 2019.

42. Hamilton 2016.

CHAPTER 4. THE PASSION PRINCIPLE AS PRESCRIPTIVE AND EXPLANATORY NARRATIVE?

1. Wilson 2005.

2. Brickmakers in Baja California face difficult conditions and constrained life choices. Although many of the brickmakers Wilson (2005) interviewed took pleasure in not having a boss, setting their own hours, and working only when they needed to financially, the work was often punishing. They mentioned scalding summer sun, icy mud in winter, and the "punishment of the mosquitoes that makes one want to weep" (p. 142). Many were unable to find other work, since other jobs in the area usually required primary school education and over 80% of brickmakers in Wilson's study had not completed primary school. Brickmaking may be creative, agency-driven work that can evoke pride in a job well done, but it is "fueled by necessity, an alternative to underemployment or unemployment among the reserve army of the landless" (p. 157).

3. Castilla 2017; Kluegel and Smith 1986.

4. Centeno and Cohen 2012; Hacker 2019; Pugh 2015.

5. Hacker 2019.

6. I use "scaffold" metaphorically here to refer to the way that cultural schemas may provide a supporting cultural framework that helps stabilize and secure other cultural beliefs.

7. Blair-Loy 2003.

8. Blair-Loy 2003; Blair-Loy 2010. Schemas can also be transposed to novel social settings, where they are used to make sense of new sets of social interactions (Enriquez and Saguy 2015; Sewell 1992).

9. McCall 2013; Swidler 1986; Swidler 2001.

10. Frye 2017.

11. Sewell 1992.

12. Cech and Blair-Loy 2010; Cech, Blair-Loy, and Rogers 2018.

13. Duggan 2003; Hacker 2019; Kluegel and Smith 1986; McCall 2013.

14. Castilla and Bernard 2010; Cech 2017; Hochschild 2016; McCall 2013.

15. Centeno and Cohen 2012; Duggan 2003; Hacker 2019; Kalleberg 2009.

16. My term "choicewashing" is an homage to whitewashing, or the absence of acknowledgment of oppression and racism in accounts of historical events or social processes (Brown et al. 2005).

17. Castilla 2017; Cech and Blair-Loy 2010; Kluegel and Smith 1986; Olson and Hafer 2001; Taylor and Merino 2011.

18. Arrow, Bowles, and Durlauf 2000; Bell 1973; Young 1994.

19. Kluegel and Smith 1986.

20. McCall 2013.

21. Brickman et al. 1981; Castilla 2017; Castilla and Bernard 2010; Meyer 2001. The meritocratic ideology is also a moral judgment. It legitimates the unequal distribution of rewards as the outcome of morally acceptable processes (Della Fave 1991; Kelman 2001; Major and Schmader 2001). As long as individuals accept the mechanisms that produce unequal outcomes, the outcomes themselves are considered legitimate (Zelditch 2001).

22. These career aspirants were seeking work in an economy that had generally recovered from the recession that shaped many of their understandings of work when they were in high school (Grusky, Western, and Wimer 2011). As such, I suspect that the steady reduction in unemployment rates over their time in college may have increased a sense that the labor market is fair.

23. In the interview sample as well as in the United States in general, women and people of color were more likely than white men to recognize structural barriers in the labor force and less likely to adhere to the meritocratic ideology (Davis and Robinson 1991; Hunt 1996; Jackman and Muha 1984; Kane 1992; Kane 1998; Kane and Kyyrö 2001).

24. Bertrand and Mullainathan 2004; Cech and Rothwell 2020; Correll, Benard, and Paik 2007; Rivera 2012.

25. I measured adherence to the passion principle with a scale that combines respondents' answers to three questions regarding their attitudes toward choosing a college major and three questions regarding attitudes toward choosing a career field. See Chapter 1 for scale construction and means on individual measures.

26. Figure 4.1 presents predicted means on these labor force fairness measures among passion principle believers and passion principle skeptics, holding constant variation by demographic characteristics, education, sector, industry, and whether respondents are passionate about their own job. For the "passion principle believers" bar in the predicted probabilities model, the passion principle value was set at 5, or where respondents answered "very important" to all 6 of the passion principle measures noted above (29% of the sample met this criteria). For the "passion principle skeptics" bar, the passion principle value in the models was set to 2, or "somewhat unimportant." All other measures were set at the mean.

27. Predicted means were produced as margins from OLS regressions predicting each outcome measure with the passion principle scale and demographic and

job-related controls. In multivariate regression models, I used the passion principle scale measure to predict college-educated workers' agreement with the listed statements (1 = strongly disagree vs. 5 = strongly agree). The regression coefficient for the passion principle scale (net of controls) predicting each of the outcome measures in Figure 4.1 were as follows: (A) opportunities for advancement are available to those who look for them: B = .199, $p < .001$; (B) professional success is the result of hard work and dedication: B = .185, $p < .001$; (C) individuals are personally responsible for their success: B = .104, $p < .05$; (D) those in need have to learn to take care of themselves and not depend on others: B = .081, $p < .05$; (E) people work in different careers because of different interests: B = .202, $p < .001$; (F) anyone can succeed no matter their gender: B = .103, $p < .05$; (G) anyone can succeed no matter their race/ethnicity: B = .098, $p < .05$; (H) anyone can succeed no matter their economic background: B = .089, $p < .05$; (I) lack of opportunities can be overcome with hard work and dedication: B = .128, $p < .001$; and (J) people stay in jobs with low pay because they like the work: B = .136, $p < .001$.

28. These results are based on cross-sectional data, so I cannot establish the temporal ordering of respondents' adherence to the passion principle and the meritocratic ideology. They are likely co-constitutive over time. I use the passion principle to predict the belief that the labor force is fair (rather than the other way around) because I want to see whether there is a connection net of other descriptive variables and net of whether they are passionate about their own jobs.

29. Harvey 2005.

30. Polanyi, cited in Centeno and Cohen 2012.

31. Harvey 2003, pp. 65–66.

32. For example, Congressman Paul Ryan of Wisconsin, speaking about the austerity of his budget plan in 2015, said, "We don't want to turn the safety net into a hammock that lulls able-bodied people to lives of dependency and complacency, that drains them of their will and their incentive to make the most of their lives" (Hacker 2019, p. 26).

33. Hacker 2019; Silva 2013.

34. Silva 2013.

35. Sharone 2013.

36. Pugh 2015.

37. The American unemployed workers' self-blame for their situation was starkly contrasted with the Israeli unemployed workers Sharone (2013) interviewed; although they were sometimes demoralized by unemployment, the job search process was not the threat to their core sense of identity that it was for American unemployed workers. Instead, the Israeli unemployed were more likely to blame the economic system for their difficulties.

38. Newman 1999. This aligns with the System Justification and Just World literatures in social psychology that suggests that many people, even some

individuals who are disadvantaged, are generally unwilling to attribute negative outcomes to systemic disadvantages. System justification, the "social and psychological need to imbue the status quo with legitimacy and to see it as good, fair, natural, desirable, and even inevitable" (Jost and Banaji 1994, p. 2), is the process whereby individuals develop strategies to protect their belief that social arrangements are legitimized, even at the expense of one's personal interests (Jost, Banaji, and Nosek 2004).

39. I discuss in Chapter 2 how the passion principle rests on American cultural understandings of individualism. Neoliberalism is also anchored in the ideology of individualism (Harvey 2005). Here neoliberalism promotes the idea that it is individuals' responsibility to take charge of their own lives and succeed by their own course of action.

40. Cech 2013; Markus and Nurius 1986; Markus and Wurf 1987.

41. Some career aspirants were more aware of the social constructedness of their interests than others. For example, Lindsey, a management consulting engineer from Stanford, explained how her reflexivity about her positionality shaped her career interests:

> I really wanna make sure what I'm doing has people impact not just impact. . . . I'm a woman and I'm biracial. I'm half Black, half white. So in a lot of ways just naturally, I personally face different types of . . . I wouldn't say oppression. I've been pretty privileged in life. But, just unfairness or hardship because of who I am. And so, that has made me have a perspective of like, 'How do you help people?' And yeah, so I think it came from a more personal place. (Upper-class Black and white woman)

Lindsey recognized her drive to have "people impact" as a structurally based outcome of her racial and gender identity as well as her idiosyncratic interests.

42. In this instance, respondents' recall bias did not necessarily distort their actions of passion-seeking. It does not matter whether they accurately recall the development of their passion, just that they have a vivid sense of personal connection to that subject.

43. Beasley 2012; Cech 2013; Charles and Bradley 2009.

44. Many career aspirants I interviewed tended to downplay or dismiss the enduring power of structural disadvantages. Sara, for example, explained her belief that homelessness is a situation that can be overcome with sufficient effort by drawing on an example of her colleague's father:

> I'm of the opinion that in a free market economy it's—if you have the opportunity and you're making money, then that's great. . . . I just think at the end of the day, different things motivate different people, and they measure their happiness different than I do. . . . I actually have one of my accounting peers, her dad is homeless. She tries to help him out now that she's established in the accounting field. Her dad always rejects her handouts because he said, "I don't want to work. I don't want to do anything, and there are already social programs that exist to get me by." He has no drive or incentive to push him to pursue more. I know that's not indicative of the

entire homelessness population . . . [but] there are people who got themselves into that position. (Middle-class Asian and white woman)

45. Davis and Robinson 1991; Hunt 1996; Jackman and Muha 1984; Kane 1992; Kane 1998; Kane and Kyyrö 2001.

46. Specifically, in supplemental analyses with interaction terms between passion principle adherence and demographic measures (one at a time, in separate models), I did not find significant passion principle X demographic factor interaction effects. This suggests that the impact of high levels of adherence to the passion principle on respondents' adherence to these choicewashing beliefs were not divergent by gender or race/ethnicity.

47. This is also consistent with experimental research that suggests that people are often willing to attribute a desire to work hard in jobs where there are higher levels of exploitation to workers' passion for that work (Kim et al. 2019).

48. Cech 2017.

49. In other words, the interplay between adherence to the passion principle and dismissal of structural inequalities in the data is not simply a manifestation of white men respondents' privileged lack of recognition of structural bias.

50. Armstrong and Hamilton 2013; Beasley 2012; Correll 2004; Ridgeway 2011; Rivera 2015.

51. Pink 2015.

52. Centeno and Cohen 2012, p. 331.

53. Duggan 2003; Hacker 2019; McCall 2013.

54. Centeno and Cohen 2012; Hacker 2019; Harvey 2005; McCall 2013.

55. McCall 2013.

56. Burstein 1985; Cech 2017. While most Americans support the idea of equality in the abstract, there is a "principle-policy gap," meaning that many do not support group-based policies like affirmative action. The most tolerated policy solutions are those that advance opportunities for everyone (McCall 2013; Tuch and Hughes 2011).

CHAPTER 5. EXPLOITING PASSION?

1. Wolf et al. 2016.

2. Rao and Tobias Neely 2019.

3. Marx [1887] 1972; Weber [1930] 1992; Wright 2002.

4. Weber [1930] 1992; Wright 2002.

5. Blair-Loy 2003; Rao and Tobias Neely 2019.

6. Weber [1930] 1992.

7. Gershon 2017.

8. These identity-based forms of social control greatly benefit organizations because workers become self-motiving and self-surveilling (Cooper 2000).

9. Marx [1872] 1972; Marx [1887] 1972; Wright 2002.

10. Zwolinski 2012.

11. Mills 1956.

12. Benditt 2015; Pettijohn and Boris 2013.

13. Rao and Tobias Neely 2019; Wolf et al. 2016.

14. Hochschild 2012.

15. Similarly, 71% of respondents in the PPS agreed that "people should choose work they are passionate about even if it doesn't pay very much money" (43% somewhat agreed, and 27% strongly agreed). Only 9% of the sample somewhat or strongly disagreed.

16. Bunderson and Thompson 2009.

17. Burke and Fiksenbaum 2008; Duffy et al. 2013; Wrzesniewski et al. 1997.

18. Kim et al. 2019.

19. Williams, Blair-Loy, and Berdahl 2013.

20. Further, only 32% of PPS respondents agreed that "someone motivated by money will work harder at their job than someone motivated by their personal interest in the work" (45% disagreed). See Figure 2.3 in Chapter 2.

21. Zigarmi et al. 2009.

22. There is likely a positive feedback loop between being passionate about one's substantive work and engagement in one's day-to-day job tasks. But engagement in one's job tasks, if driven by enjoyment of one's colleagues or commitment to the organization, may never spark one's passion for the substantive area of work.

23. I coded MPS workers as "passionate" if they "somewhat agree" or "strongly agree" with all six of the following statements: "I do my work with passion" (82% agreed), "I care deeply about my work" (92% agreed), "I feel personally connected to my work" (83% agreed), "I find my work fulfilling" (77% agreed), "My work gives me a good opportunity to do things I am passionate about" (64% agreed), and "My work is a good fit for who I am" (77% agreed). In the MPS sample, 54.2% fit this criteria of a passionate worker.

24. In multivariate OLS models (controlling for gender, race, supervisory level, tenure, salary, and education), being passionate about work predicted respondents' agreement that "I try to learn ways to do my work better" (B = .722, p < .001), "I look for potential problems, obstacles, or risks related to work" (B = .350, p < .001), "I look for ways I can help others with their work" (B = .383, p < .001), and "I try to help my colleagues see their value and importance at work" (B = .489, p < .001).

25. Workers in the NSCW data were coded as "passionate" if they strongly agreed with both the following measures: "The work I do in my job is meaningful to me" and "I feel I can really be myself at work" (1 = strongly disagree to 5 = strongly agree). In the NSCW college-educated sample, 49.4% fit this standard.

26. In OLS regression models (controlling for respondents' gender, race/ethnicity, caregiver status, hours worked, age, sector, education, employment size), I

find that passionate workers are more likely to agree that "I feel personally responsible for my work" (B = .126, p < .001), "I feel I am really a part of the group of people I work with" (B = .494, p < .001), and "I often think good thoughts about my job while doing something else" (B = .544, p < .001).

27. Hewlett 2007.

28. Fleming and Sturdy 2011; Rich, Lepine, and Crawford 2010.

29. Specifically, MPS respondents who were passionate about their jobs were significantly less likely to intend to leave their occupation or line of work in the next year (logistic regression coefficient B = −0.604, p < .001) or leave the federal government entirely (B = −.446, p < .001), net of demographic and job controls. NSCW respondents who were passionate were less likely than their peers to say they would try to find a new job in the next year (B = −.295; p < .001), net of demographic and job controls.

30. Cardon et al. 2009; Ho, Wong, and Lee 2011.

31. Pugh 2015.

32. This is acknowledged in some management literature that has pivoted to emphasizing ways to motivate workers to love working for the company rather than loving the company per se (Fleming and Sturdy 2011).

33. These vignettes were adapted from Wrzesniewski and colleagues' (1997) research.

34. Hiring managers have a slightly better impression of the promotion-motivated employee than do respondents without hiring authority. Net of variation by respondents' demographics and job characteristics, hiring managers are slightly more likely than those without hiring authority to prefer to work with, supervise, and hire employee B.

35. Rao and Tobias Neely 2019.

36. As of 2017, "Riley" was the most gender-balanced name in the United States: roughly 50% of people named Riley are men. To make sure the results were not name-specific, I also tested the design with the name "David Williamson." In order to ensure that respondents had adequately read the application materials, I included two attention checks (e.g., "what school did Riley graduate from?") at the end of the survey experiment. Respondents who did not pass this attention check were excluded from the analyses below (final sample size for this experiment was N = 1,301).

37. Becker 1964; Gemici and Wiswall 2014.

38. Blair-Loy 2003; Rao and Tobias Neely 2019. Commitment to an organization and passion for the work are conceptually distinct, but they likely reinforce one another in practice (Rao and Tobias Neely 2019). Passion-seeking may lead career aspirants to choose organizations they are also more committed to because they allow for the practice of that passion, and one's commitment to one's organization may amplify one's passion.

39. Mediation analyses were conducted with structural equation models (SEM) in Stata 15. See Table C.7 in Appendix C for direct and indirect coefficient estimates.

40. Specifically, the average salary (and *standard error*) for those who wanted to hire Riley for the accounting position, by cover letter type, was as follows: Passionate: $37,409 *($491)*, Company: $37,393 *($643)*, Location: $37,746 *($707)*, and Salary: $37,336 *($681)*. The average salary (and *standard error*) for those who wanted to hire Riley for the youth program manager position, by cover letter type, was Passionate: $38,021 *($366)*, Company: $38,159 *($451)*, Location: $37,181 *($519)*, and Salary: $37,721 *($803)*. The wording of the salary question in the survey was as follows: "Please type in the box below (in increments of $1,000) what starting salary you would offer this applicant. As a reminder, the salary range for this position is $32,000–$55,000 per year. The average starting salary for this position: $40,000. Only 10% of those hired for this position receive a salary over $53,000." The only significant differences in salary by condition was in the youth program manager case: those who evaluated the "location" condition offered Riley significantly lower salaries than the other three conditions.

41. Kim et al. 2019.

42. Kim and colleagues' (2019) study has many benefits, including its robust design and its focus on both uncompensated and unpleasant tasks. However, it is a vignette-based study, wherein respondents rated carefully worded narratives rather than assess actual or realistic candidates. In addition, most of the data were collected in a digital piece-rate work platform called MTurk. Although MTurk is a useful platform in many ways, it is not reflective of the workforce. As such, the results of that study, while insightful, need validation using more robust samples and with more realistic assessment opportunities.

43. Some companies are willing to take extreme measures to stack their workforce with passionate employees. The online shoe store Zappos.com, for instance, offered $2,000 for new employees to leave if they do not want to continue working at Zappos after the four-week training period. Those willing to forego the $2,000 leaving bonus, Zappos wagered, are especially dedicated and will be reliably committed down the line. Underscoring Zappos's desire to be part of its workers' meaning-making, it lists "Be passionate and determined" as one of its core values (Hsieh 2010).

44. As an example of this in the blue-collar sector, Ocejo (2017) tells a story of Joaquin (pseudonym), a passionate bartender in an upscale Brooklyn bar: "Joaquin wakes up at noon, gets out of bed, and spends a couple of hours trolling around food and drink websites and blogs to stay ahead of the latest trends. Today, he is most interested in learning about new ingredients the chefs are using, for inspiration" (p. 1). Like Julie, Joaquin invests hours of his own time preparing for his job because of his passion for his craft.

45. Gershon 2017.

46. Kim et al. 2019.

47. Weber [1930] 1992; Wright 2002.

48. Blair-Loy and Cech 2017; Burke and Fiksenbaum 2008; Duffy et al. 2013; Ocejo 2017; Wrzesniewski et al. 1997.

49. Cooper 2000, p. 383.

50. Kim et al. 2019.

51. Hochschild 2012.

52. Bunderson and Thompson 2009; Fleming and Sturdy 2011; Hochschild 2012.

53. Kim et al. 2019.

54. Wolf et al. 2016.

55. Rao and Tobias Neely 2019.

56. Cooper 2000.

57. Rao and Tobias Neely 2019; Rivera 2015.

58. A common mantra of passion principle adherence, "You won't work a day in your life if you love what you do," could be considered a modern and particularly pernicious manifestation of Marxist notions of "false consciousness," a cultural ideology that conceals the exploitation of postindustrial capitalist economy (Marx [1887] 1972). Here one's personal commitment and sense of self-fulfillment from their engagement in the paid workforce conceals the ways that passion-driven labor is exploited.

CONCLUSION

1. See, e.g., Sharone 2013; Young 2000.

2. DiMaggio 2001; Kalleberg 2009; Kalleberg 2012.

3. Kluegel and Smith 1986.

4. Hacker 2019.

5. Hochschild 2012.

6. Collamer 2013; Moen 2016.

7. Armstrong and Hamilton 2013; Lynch 2015; O'Connor et al. 2017.

8. Armstrong and Hamilton 2013.

9. Correll et al. 2014; Jacobs and Gerson 2005; Rao and Tobias Neely 2019; Williams 2000; Williams, Blair-Loy and Berdahl 2013.

10. Rao and Tobias Neely 2019.

11. Blair-Loy and Cech 2017; Bunderson and Thompson 2009; Gershon 2017.

12. A notable exception to this expectation is the work requirements for welfare recipients (Duggan 2003, Hays 1994). In this case, the demand for self-sufficiency by any means necessary has little affordance for individuals' interests. This demand may exclude welfare recipients from moral claims to be allowed to pursue their passion.

13. Cech 2013; Markus and Kitayama 2003.
14. England 2010; England, Levine, and Mishel 2020; Risman 2018.
15. Correll 2004.
16. See, e.g., Schulz 2015.
17. Gramsci 1971.
18. Zwolinski 2012.
19. Zwolinski 2012, p. 158.
20. Bunderson and Thompson 2009; McRobbie 2016; Umney and Kretsos 2015.
21. Kalleberg 2009; Kalleberg 2012.
22. Osnowitz 2010.
23. Correll et al. 2014.
24. Rosenfeld 2019; Sweet and Meiksins 2017.
25. Duggan 2003.
26. Hacker 2019.
27. Alexander and Smith 2003; Swidler 2001.
28. Giddens 1991.
29. It is neither my intention nor my desire to weigh in on what a "good life" is. After all, Weber said a century ago that social science inquiry couldn't shed light on that anyhow.
30. Giddens 1991.
31. Putnam 2000.
32. Hidaka 2010; Matthews 1996.
33. However, this may be changing. Young Japanese career aspirants, especially those from more privileged families, are increasingly prioritizing fulfillment rather than economic viability in their career decisions (Matthews and White 2004).
34. Schulz 2015.
35. Sharone 2013.
36. Charles and Grusky 2004; Charles and Bradley 2009; Inglehart and Oyserman 2004.

EPILOGUE

1. Weber [1919] 1981.

APPENDIX A. METHODS

1. See also Binder, Davis, and Bloom 2016; Rivera 2015.
2. DiPrete and Buchmann 2013.
3. DiPrete and Buchmann 2013.

4. Lofland et al. 2006; Saldaña 2009.

5. Brown and Lent 2013.

6. Qualtrics uses professionally curated respondent pools that include hundreds of thousands of potential respondents nationwide. Qualtrics is used for both academic and commercial applications and typically produces more representative, high-quality samples than comparable survey platforms like Survey-Monkey or Amazon Mechanical Turk (Heen, Lieberman, and Miethe 2014).

7. Heen et al. (2014) compared the online sampling approaches of Qualtrics, SurveyMonkey, and Amazon Mechanical Turk and found that Qualtrics provided the most accurate representation of respondents by gender, age, race/ethnicity, and education level.

8. The attention filters directed respondents to choose a specific answer (e.g., "This is an attention filter. Please select 'somewhat agree'") or to answer a question with a logically appropriate selection (e.g., "Which is a color?" blue, sad, happy, excited). Those who failed one or more of the attention filters were excluded from the quota sample. These attention filters substantially increase the quality of online survey responses (Oppenheimer, Meyvis, and Davidenko 2009).

9. Although survey respondents were given the option to identify as gender nonbinary in the survey, no respondent did so. Thus the gender identity comparison is between women and men.

10. By then, an economic recovery, although deeply uneven, was beginning to take hold: unemployment had dropped to 8%, and most businesses had reopened.

APPENDIX B. SUPPLEMENTAL ANALYSIS OF 2020 COLLEGE STUDENT SURVEY

1. E.g., Kim et al. 2019.

2. Heen, Liberman, and Mieth 2014.

References

AAA&S. 2017. "Bachelor's Degrees in the Humanities." [Database.] American Academy of Arts & Sciences, Washington, DC.

Addo, Fenaba R., Jason N. Houle, and Daniel Simon. 2016. "Young, Black, and (Still) in the Red: Parental Wealth, Race, and Student Loan Debt." *Race and Social Problems* 8(1):64–76.

Alexander, Jefferey, and J. Smith. 2003. *The Meanings of Social Life: A Cultural Sociology*. New York: Oxford University Press.

Armstrong, Elizabeth A., and Laura T. Hamilton. 2013. *Paying for the Party: How College Maintains Inequality*. Cambridge, MA: Harvard University Press.

Arrow, Kenneth, Samuel Bowles, and Steven Durlauf. 2000. "Introduction." Pp. ix–xv in *Meritocracy and Economic Inequality*, edited by Kennith Arrow, Samuel Bowles, and Steven Durlauf. Princeton, NJ: Princeton University Press.

Arum, Richard, and Josipa Roksa. 2011. *Academically Adrift: Limited Learning on College Campuses*. Chicago: University of Chicago Press.

Baggini, Julian. 2018. *How the World Thinks: A Global History of Philosophy*. London: Granta Books.

Baker, Rachel, Daniel Klasik, and Sean F. Reardon. 2018. "Race and Stratification in College Enrollment over Time." *AERA Open* 4(1):2332858417751896.

Beasley, Maya A. 2012. *Opting Out: Losing the Potential of America's Young Black Elite*. Chicago: University of Chicago Press.

Becker, Gary S. 1964. *Human Capital: A Theoretical and Empirical Analysis.* Chicago: University of Chicago Press.

———. 1985. "Human Capital, Effort, and the Sexual Division of Labor." *Journal of Labor Economics* 3(1):S33–S58.

Bell, Daniel. 1973. *The Coming of Post-Industrial Society.* New York: Basic Books.

Bellah, Robert N., Richard Madsen, William M. Sullivan, Ann Swidler, and Steven M. Tipton. 1985. *Habits of the Heart: Individualism and Commitment in American Life.* New York: Harper & Row.

Benditt, Lauren. 2015. "Race, Gender, and Public-Sector Work: Prioritizing Occupational Values as a Labor Market Privilege." *Research in Social Stratification and Mobility* 42:73–86.

Bertrand, Marianne, and Sendhil Mullainathan. 2004. "Are Emily and Greg More Employable than Lakisha and Jamal? A Field Experiment on Labor Market Discrimination." *American Economic Review* 94(4):991–1013.

Binder, Amy J., Daniel B. Davis, and Nick Bloom. 2016. "Career Funneling: How Elite Students Learn to Define and Desire 'Prestigious' Jobs." *Sociology of Education* 89(1):20–39.

Blair-Loy, Mary. 2003. *Competing Devotions: Career and Family among Women Executives.* Cambridge, MA: Harvard University Press.

———. 2010. "Moral Dimensions of the Work-Family Nexus." Pp. 439–53 in *Handbook of the Sociology of Morality*, edited by S. Hitlin and S. Vaisey. Thousand Oaks, CA: Springer.

Blair-Loy, Mary, and Erin A. Cech. 2017. "Demands and Devotion: Cultural Meanings of Work and Overload among Women Researchers and Professionals in Science and Technology Industries." *Sociological Forum* 32(1):5–27.

Blau, Peter M., and Otis Dudley Duncan. 1967. *The American Occupational Structure.* New York: Wiley & Sons.

Bolles, Richard N. 2018. *What Color Is Your Parachute? A Practical Manual for Job Hunters and Career Changers.* New York: Ten Speed Press.

Bourdieu, Pierre. 1984. *Distinction: A Social Critique of the Judgement of Taste.* Cambridge, MA: Harvard University Press.

———. 2001. *Masculine Domination.* Stanford, CA: Stanford University Press.

Bourdieu, Pierre, and Erec R. Koch. 1987. "The Invention of the Artist's Life." *Yale French Studies* (73):75–103.

Bourdieu, Pierre, and Jean-Claude Passeron. 1990. *Reproduction in Education, Society, and Culture.* Thousand Oaks, CA: Sage.

Brady, David, Jason Beckfield, and Wei Zhao. 2007. "The Consequences of Economic Globalization for Affluent Democracies." *Annual Review of Sociology* 33(1):313–34.

Brickman, Phillip, Robert Folger, Erica Goode, and Yaacov Schul. 1981. "Microjustice and Macrojustice." Pp. 173–202 in *The Justice Motive in Social Behavior: Adapting to Times of Scarcity and Change*, edited by Melvin J. Lerner and Sally C. Lerner. New York: Plenum Press.

Britton, Marcus L. 2013. "Race/Ethnicity, Attitudes, and Living with Parents during Young Adulthood." *Journal of Marriage and Family* 75(4):995–1013.

Brown, Michael K., Martin Carnoy, Elliott Currie, Troy Duster, David B. Oppenheimer, Marjorie M. Shultz, and David Wellman. 2005. *Whitewashing Race: The Myth of a Color-Blind Society*. Berkeley: University of California Press.

Brown, Steven D., and Robert W. Lent. 2013. *Career Development and Counseling: Putting Theory and Research to Work*. Hoboken, NJ: Wiley.

Bunderson, J. Stuart, and Jeffery A. Thompson. 2009. "The Call of the Wild: Zookeepers, Callings, and the Double-edged Sword of Deeply Meaningful Work." *Administrative Science Quarterly* 54(1):32–57.

Bureau of Labor Statistics (BLS). 2018. "National Occupational Employment and Wage Estimates United States." Bureau of Labor Statistics, US Department of Labor, Washington, DC.

Burke, Ronald J., and Lisa Fiksenbaum. 2008. "Work Motivations, Work Outcomes, and Health: Passion versus Addiction." *Journal of Business Ethics* 84(2):257.

Burstein, Paul. 1985. *Discrimination, Jobs, and Politics: The Struggle for Equal Employment Opportunity in the United States since the New Deal*. Chicago: University of Chicago Press.

Cairns, James Irvine. 2017. *The Myth of the Age of Entitlement: Millennials, Austerity, and Hope*. Toronto: University of Toronto Press.

Cardon, Melissa S., Joakim Wincent, Jagdip Singh, and Mateja Drnovsek. 2009. "The Nature and Experience of Entrepreneurial Passion." *Academy of Management Review* 34(3):511–32.

Carr, Deborah. 1997. "The Fulfillment of Career Dreams at Midlife: Does It Matter for Women's Mental Health?" *Journal of Health and Social Behavior* 38(4):331–44.

Castilla, Emilio J. 2008. "Gender, Race, and Meritocracy in Organizational Careers." *American Journal of Sociology* 113(6):1479–526.

———. 2017. "Meritocracy." Pp. 479–82 in *The SAGE Encyclopedia of Political Behavior*, edited by Fathali M. Moghaddam. Thousand Oaks, CA: Sage.

Castilla, Emilio J., and Stephen Bernard. 2010. "The Paradox of Meritocracy in Organizations." *Administrative Science Quarterly* 55:543–676.

Castilla, Emilio J., George J. Lan, and Ben A. Rissing. 2013a. "Social Networks and Employment: Mechanisms (Part 1)." *Sociology Compass* 7(12):999–1012.

———. 2013b. "Social Networks and Employment: Outcomes (Part 2)." *Sociology Compass* 7(12):1013–26.

Castilla, Emilio J., and Ben A. Rissing. 2019. "Best in Class: The Returns on Application Endorsements in Higher Education." *Administrative Science Quarterly* 64(1):230–70.

Cech, Erin A. 2013. "The Self-Expressive Edge of Occupational Sex Segregation." *American Journal of Sociology* 119(3):747–89.

———. 2016. "Mechanism or Myth? Family Plans and the Reproduction of Occupational Gender Segregation." *Gender & Society* 30(2):265–88.

———. 2017. "Rugged Meritocratists: The Role of Overt Bias and the Meritocratic Ideology in Trump Supporters' Opposition to Social Justice Efforts." *Socius* 3:2378023117712395.

Cech, Erin A., and Mary Blair-Loy. 2010. "Perceiving Glass Ceilings? Meritocratic versus Structural Explanations of Gender Inequality among Women in Science and Technology." *Social Problems* 57(3):371–97.

———. 2019. "The Changing Career Trajectories of New Parents in STEM." *Proceedings of the National Academy of Sciences* 116(10):4182–87.

Cech, Erin A., Mary Blair-Loy, and Laura E. Rogers. 2018. "Recognizing Chilliness: How Schemas of Inequality Shape Views of Culture and Climate In Work Environments." *American Journal of Cultural Sociology* 6(1):125–60.

Cech, Erin A., Anneke Metz, Jessi L. Smith, and Karen deVries. 2018. "Epistemological Dominance and Social Inequality: Experiences of Native American Science, Engineering, and Health Students." *Science, Technology, & Human Values* 42(5):743–74.

Cech, Erin A., and William R. Rothwell. 2020. "LGBT Workplace Inequality in the Federal Workforce: Intersectional Processes, Organizational Contexts, and Turnover Considerations." *ILR Review* 73(1):25–60.

Cech, Erin A., Jessi L. Smith, and Anneke Metz. 2019. "Cultural Processes of Ethnoracial Disadvantage among Native American College Students." *Social Forces* 98(1):355–80.

Cennamo, Lucy, and Dianne Gardner. 2008. "Generational Differences in Work Values, Outcomes and Person-Organisation Values Fit." *Journal of Managerial Psychology* 23(8):891–906.

Centeno, Miguel A., and Joseph N. Cohen. 2012. "The Arc of Neoliberalism." *Annual Review of Sociology* 38(1):317–40.

Charles, Maria. 2011. "A World of Difference: International Trends in Women's Economic Status." *Annual Review of Sociology* 37:355–71.

———. 2017. "Venus, Mars, and Math." *Socius* 3:2378023117697179.

Charles, Maria, and Karen Bradley. 2009. "Indulging Our Gendered Selves? Sex Segregation by Field of Study in 44 Countries." *American Journal of Sociology* 114(4):924–76.

Charles, Maria, and David B. Grusky. 2004. *Occupational Ghettos: The Worldwide Segregation of Men and Women.* Stanford, CA: Stanford University Press.

Chen, H., and W. Lan. 1998. "Adolescents' Perceptions of Their Parents' Academic Expectations: Comparison of American, Chinese-American, and Chinese High School Students." *Adolescence* 33(130):385–90.

Collamer, Nancy. 2013. *Second-Act Careers: 50+ Ways to Profit from Your Passions during Semi-Retirement.* Berkeley, CA: Ten Speed Press.

Cooper, Marianne. 2000. "Being the 'Go-To Guy': Fatherhood, Masculinity, and the Organization of Work in Silicon Valley." *Qualitative Sociology* 23(4):379–405.

Correll, Shelley J. 2004. "Constraints into Preferences: Gender, Status, and Emerging Career Aspirations." *American Sociological Review* 69(1):93–113.

Correll, Shelley J., Erin L. Kelly, Lindsey Trimble O'Connor, and Joan C. Williams. 2014. "Redesigning, Redefining Work." *Work and Occupations* 41(1):3–17.

Correll, Shelley J., Stephen Benard, and In Paik. 2007. "Getting a Job: Is There a Motherhood Penalty?" *American Journal of Sociology* 112(5):1297–339.

Cotter, David, Joan M. Hermsen, and Reeve Vanneman. 2011. "The End of the Gender Revolution? Gender Role Attitudes from 1977 to 2008." *American Journal of Sociology* 117(1):259–89.

Davies, Andrea Rees, and Brenda D. Frink. 2014. "The Origins of the Ideal Worker: The Separation of Work and Home in the United States from the Market Revolution to 1950." *Work and Occupations* 41(1):18–39.

Davies, Scott, and Neil Guppy. 1997. "Fields of Study, College Selectivity, and Student Inequalities in Higher Education." *Social Forces* 75(4):1417–38.

Davis, Nancy J., and Robert V. Robinson. 1991. "Men's and Women's Consciousness of Gender Inequality: Austria, West Germany, Great Britain, and the US." *American Sociological Review* 56(1):72–84.

Deal, Jennifer J. 2015. "Always On, Never Done? Don't Blame the Smartphone." Center for Creative Leadership, New York. http://cclinnovation.org/wp-content/uploads/2020/02/alwayson.pdf.

Della Fave, L. Richard. 1991. "Ritual and the Legitimation of Inequality." *Sociological Perspectives* 34(1):21–38.

DiMaggio, Paul. 2001. *The Twenty-First-Century Firm: Changing Economic Organization in International Perspective.* Princeton, NJ: Princeton University Press.

Duckworth, Angela. 2016. *Grit: The Power of Passion and Perseverance.* New York: Simon and Schuster.

Duffy, Ryan D., Blake A. Allan, Kelsey L. Autin, and Elizabeth M. Bott. 2013. "Calling and Life Satisfaction: It's Not about Having It, It's about Living It." *Journal of Counseling Psychology* 60(1):42–52.

Duggan, Lisa. 2003. *The Twilight of Equality? Neoliberalism, Cultural Politics, and the Attack on Democracy.* Boston, MA: Beacon Press.

Durkheim, Emile. [1953] 2009. *Sociology and Philosophy.* New York: Taylor & Francis.

Eccles, Jacquelynne. 2011. "Gendered Educational and Occupational Choices: Applying the Eccles et al. Model of Achievement-Related Choices." *International Journal of Behavioral Development* 35(3):195–201.

Eccles, Jacquelynne S., and Allan Wigfield. 2002. "Motivational Beliefs, Values, and Goals." *Annual Review of Psychology* 53(1):109–32.

Ehrhart, Karen Holcombe, and Guido Makransky. 2007. "Testing Vocational Interests and Personality as Predictors of Person-Vocation and Person-Job Fit." *Journal of Career Assessment* 15(2):206–26.

Elcioglu, Emine Fidan. 2010. "Producing Precarity: The Temporary Staffing Agency in the Labor Market." *Qualitative Sociology* 33:117–36.

England, Paula. 2010. "The Gender Revolution: Uneven and Stalled." *Gender and Society* 24(2):149–66.

England, Paula, Andrew Levine, and Emma Mishel. 2020. "Progress toward Gender Equality in the United States Has Slowed or Stalled." *Proceedings of the National Academy of Sciences* 117(13):6990–97.

Enriquez, Laura E., and Abigail C. Saguy. 2015. "Coming out of the Shadows: Harnessing a Cultural Schema to Advance the Undocumented Immigrant Youth Movement." *American Journal of Cultural Sociology* 4:107–30.

Federal Reserve Bank of New York. 2019. "The Labor Market for Recent College Graduates." Economic Research [online resource]. www.newyorkfed.org /research/college-labor-market/index.html.

Feffer, Mark. 2014. "3 Great Opportunities for Encore Careers." *Forbes*, December 16.

Fleming, Peter, and Andrew Sturdy. 2011. "'Being Yourself' in the Electronic Sweatshop: New Forms of Normative Control." *Human Relations* 64(2):177–200.

Fouad, Nadya A. 2007. "Work and Vocational Psychology: Theory, Research, and Applications." *Annual Review of Psychology* 58(1):543–64.

Frank, David John, and John W. Meyer. 2001. "The Profusion of Individual Roles and Identities in the Postwar Period." *Sociological Theory* 20(1):86–105.

Frenette, Alexandre, and Richard E. Ocejo. 2018. "Sustaining Enchantment: How Cultural Workers Manage Precariousness and Routine." Pp. 35–60 in *Race, Identity and Work*, edited by Ethel L. Mickey and Adia Harvey Wingfield. Bingley, UK: Emerald Publishing Ltd.

Frome, Pamela M., Corinne J. Alfeld, Jacquelynne S. Eccles, and Bonnie L. Barber. 2006. "Why Don't They Want a Male-Dominated Job? An Investiga-

tion of Young Women Who Changed Their Occupational Aspirations."
Educational Research 12(4):359–72.

Fryberg, Stephanie A., and Hazel Rose Markus. 2007. "Cultural models of
education in American Indian, Asian American and European American
contexts." *Social Psychology of Education* 10(2):213–46.

Frye, Margaret. 2017. "Cultural Meanings and the Aggregation of Actions: The
Case of Sex and Schooling in Malawi." *American Sociological Review*
82(5):945–76.

Gates, James E., and Harold Miller. 1958. *Personal Adjustment to Business.*
Englewood Cliffs, NJ: Prentice-Hall.

Gecas, Viktor. 1982. "The Self-Concept." *Annual Review of Sociology* 8:1–33.

Gemici, Ahu, and Matthew Wiswall. 2014. "Evolution of Gender Differences in
Post-Secondary Human Capital Investments: College Majors." *International
Economic Review* 55(1):23–56.

Georgetown University Center on Education and the Workforce. 2015. "Learning
While Earning: The New Normal." Georgetown University, Washington, DC.

Gerhart, Barry, and Meiyu Fang. 2015. "Pay, Intrinsic Motivation, Extrinsic
Motivation, Performance, and Creativity in the Workplace: Revisiting
Long-Held Beliefs." *Annual Review of Organizational Psychology and
Organizational Behavior* 2(1):489–521.

Gershon, Ilana. 2017. *Down and Out in the New Economy: How People Find (or
Don't Find) Work Today.* Chicago: University of Chicago Press.

Gerson, Kathleen. 2010. *The Unfinished Revolution: How a New Generation Is
Reshaping Family, Work, and Gender in America.* New York: Oxford
University Press.

Giddens, Anthony. 1991. *Modernity and Self-Identity: Self and Society in the
Late Modern Age.* Cambridge: Polity.

Goyette, Kimberly, and Yu Xie. 1999. "Educational Expectations of Asian
American Youths: Determinants and Ethnic Differences." *Sociology of
Education* 72(1):22–36.

Gramsci, Antonio. 1971. *Selections from the Prison Notebooks.* Edited by
Quintin Hoare and Geoffrey Nowell Smith. London: Lawrence & Wishart.

Granovetter, Mark S. 1973. "The Strength of Weak Ties." *American Journal of
Sociology* 78(6):1360–80.

Griffin, Larry J., and Arne L. Kalleberg. 1981. "Stratification and Meritocracy
in the United States: Class and Occupational Recruitment Patterns." *British
Journal of Sociology* 32(1):1–38.

Grusky, David B., Bruce Western, and Christopher Wimer. 2011. *The Great
Recession.* New York: Russell Sage Foundation.

Hacker, Jacob S. 2019. *The Great Risk Shift: The New Economic Insecurity and
the Decline of the American Dream.* New York: Oxford University Press.

Hamilton, Laura. 2016. *Parenting to a Degree: How Family Matters for College and Beyond.* Chicago: University of Chicago Press.

Hannon, Kerry. 2010. *What's Next? Follow Your Passion and Find Your Dream Job.* San Francisco, CA: Chronicle Books.

Hanson, Sandra L., and Emily Gilbert. 2012. "Family, Gender and Science Experiences: The Perspective of Young Asian Americans." *Race, Gender & Class* 19(3–4):326–47.

Hardie, Jessica Halliday. 2014. "The Consequences of Unrealized Occupational Goals in the Transition to Adulthood." *Social Science Research* 48:196–211.

Harvey, David. 2005. *A Brief History of Neoliberalism.* New York: Oxford University Press.

Hays, Sharon. 1994. "Structure and Agency and the Sticky Problem of Culture." *Sociological Theory* 12(1):57–72.

Henly, Julia R., and Susan J. Lambert. 2014. "Unpredictable Work Timing in Retail Jobs." *ILR Review* 67(3):986–1016.

Hewlett, Sylvia A. 2007. *Off-Ramps and On-Ramps: Keeping Talented Women on the Road to Success.* Cambridge, MA: Harvard Business Press.

Hidaka, Tomoko. 2010. *Salaryman Masculinity: Continuity and Change in Hegemonic Masculinity in Japan.* Leiden: Brill.

Ho, Violet T., Sze-Sze Wong, and Chay Hoon Lee. 2011. "A Tale of Passion: Linking Job Passion and Cognitive Engagement to Employee Work Performance." *Journal of Management Studies* 48(1):26–47.

Hochschild, Arlie Russell. 2012. *The Managed Heart: Commercialization of Human Feeling.* Berkeley: University of California Press.

———. 2016. *Strangers in Their Own Land: Anger and Mourning on the American Right.* New York: New Press.

Holland, J. L. 1959. "A Theory of Vocational Choice." *Journal of Counseling Psychology* 6(1):35–45.

Hsieh, Tony. 2010. *Delivering Happiness: A Path to Profits, Passion, and Purpose.* New York: Grand Central Publishing.

Hunnicutt, Benjamin Kline. 1996. *Kellogg's Six-Hour Day.* Philadelphia, PA: Temple University Press.

Hunt, Matthew O. 1996. "The Individual, Society, or Both? A Comparison of Black, Latino, and White Beliefs about the Causes of Poverty." *Social Forces* 75(1):293–322.

Hunzaker, M. B. Fallin, and Lauren Valentino. 2019. "Mapping Cultural Schemas: From Theory to Method." *American Sociological Review* 84(5):950–81.

Inglehart, Ronald. 1997. *Modernization and Postmodernization: Cultural, Economic, and Political Change in 43 Societies.* Princeton, NJ: Princeton University Press.

Inglehart, Ronald, and Daphna Oyserman. 2004. "Individualism, Autonomy, Self-Expression: The Human Development Syndrome." *International Studies in Sociology and Social Anthropology* 93:74–96.

Inglehart, Ronald, and Christian Welzel. 2005. *Modernization, Cultural Change, and Democracy: The Human Development Sequence.* Cambridge: Cambridge University Press.

Jackman, Mary R., and Michael J. Muha. 1984. "Education and Intergroup Attitudes: Moral Enlightenment, Superficial Democratic Commitment, or Ideological Refinement?" *American Sociological Review* 49(6):751–69.

Jacobs, Jerry A. 1989. *Revolving Doors: Sex Segregation and Women's Careers.* Stanford, CA: Stanford University Press.

———. 1995. "Gender and Academic Specialties: Trends among Recipients of College Degrees in the 1980s." *Sociology of Education* 68(2):81–98.

Jacobs, Jerry A., and Kathleen Gerson. 2005. *The Time Divide: Work, Family, and Gender Inequality.* Cambridge, MA: Harvard University Press.

Jacobs, Jerry A., David Karen, and Katherine McClelland. 1991. "The Dynamics of Young Men's Career Aspirations." *Sociological Forum* 6(4):609–39.

Jost, John T., and Mahzarin R. Banaji. 1994. "The Role of Stereotyping in System-Justification and the Production of False Consciousness." *British Journal of Social Psychology* 33(1):1–27.

Jost, John T., Mahzarin R. Banaji, and Brian A. Nosek. 2004. "A Decade of System Justification Theory: Accumulated Evidence of Conscious and Unconscious Bolstering of the Status Quo." *Political Psychology* 25(6):881–919.

Kalleberg, Arne L. 2009. "Precarious Work, Insecure Workers: Employment Relations in Transition." *American Sociological Review* 74(1):1–22.

———. 2012. *Good Jobs, Bad Jobs: The Rise of Polarized and Precarious Employment Systems in the United States, 1970s–2000s.* New York: Russell Sage Foundation.

Kane, Emily W. 1992. "Race, Gender, and Attitudes toward Gender Stratification." *Social Psychology Quarterly* 55(3):311–20.

———. 1998. "Men's and Women's Beliefs about Gender Inequality: Family Ties, Dependence, and Agreement." *Sociological Forum* 13(4):611–37.

Kane, Emily W., and Else K. Kyyrö. 2001. "For Whom Does Education Enlighten? Race, Gender, Education, and Beliefs about Social Inequality." *Gender and Society* 15(5):710–33.

Kaplan, Greg. 2016. *Earning Admission: Real Strategies for Getting into Highly Selective Colleges.* n.p.: CreateSpace Independent Publishing.

Kaplan, Robert Steven. 2013. *What You're Really Meant to Do: A Road Map for Reaching Your Unique Potential.* Boston, MA: Harvard Business Review Press.

Kelman, Herbert C. 2001. "Reflections on Social and Psychological Processes of Legitimization and Deligitimization." Pp. 54–76 in *The Psychology of*

Legitimacy: Emerging Perspectives on Ideology, Justice, and Intergroup Relations, edited by John T. Jost and Brenda Major. Cambridge: Cambridge University Press.

Kenworthy, Lane. 2004. *Egalitarian Capitalism: Jobs, Incomes, and Growth in Affluent Countries*. New York: Russell Sage Foundation.

Kim, Jae Yun, Troy H. Campbell, Steven Shepherd, and Aaron C. Kay. 2019. "Understanding Contemporary Forms of Exploitation: Attributions of Passion Serve to Legitimize the Poor Treatment of Workers." *Journal of Personality and Social Psychology* 118(1):121–48.

Kluegel, James R., and Eliot R. Smith. 1986. *Beliefs about Inequality: Americans' Views of What Is and What Ought to Be*. New York: Aldine de Gruyter.

Kosowski, Lukasz. 2010. *Noema and Thinkability: An Essay on Husserl's Theory of Intentionality*. Berlin: De Gruyter.

Lambert, Susan J., Peter J. Fugiel, and Julia R. Henly. 2014. "Precarious Work Schedules among Early-Career Employees in the US: A National Snapshot." University of Chicago, Employment, Instability, Family Well-Being, and Social Policy Network.

Lamont, Ellen. 2020. *The Mating Game: How Gender Still Shapes How We Date*. Oakland: University of California Press.

Lamont, Michèle. 1992. *Money, Morals, and Manners: The Culture of the French and the American Middle Class*. Chicago: University of Chicago Press.

Lebowitz, Shana. 2015. "7 Simple Ways to Find Work You're Really Passionate About." *Business Insider*, June 1.

Lueptow, Lloyd B., Lori Garovich-Szabo, and Margaret B. Lueptow. 2001. "Sex Change and the Persistence of Sex Typing: 1974–1997." *Social Forces* 80(1):1–35.

Lynch, Kathleen. 2015. "Control by Numbers: New Managerialism and Ranking in Higher Education." *Critical Studies in Education* 56(2):190–207.

Ma, Yingyi. 2009. "Family Socioeconomic Status, Parental Involvement, and College Major Choices—Gender, Race/Ethnic, and Nativity Patterns." *Sociological Perspectives* 52(2):211–34.

MacLeod, Jay. 1987. *Ain't No Makin' It: Leveled Aspirations in a Low-Income Neighborhood*. New York: Westview Press.

Major, Brenda, and Toni Schmader. 2001. "Legitimacy and the Construal of Social Disadvantage." Pp. 176–204 in *The Psychology of Legitimacy: Emerging Perspectives on Ideology, Justice, and Intergroup Relations*, edited by John T. Jost and Brenda Major. Cambridge: Cambridge University Press.

Marcuse, Herbert. 1968. *One-Dimensional Man: Studies in the Ideology of Advanced Industrial Society*. New York: Beacon Press.

Markus, H., and P. Nurius. 1986. "Possible Selves." *American Psychologist* 41(9):954–69.

Markus, Hazel, and Shinobu Kitayama. 2003. "Culture, Self, and the Reality of the Social." *Psychological Inquiry* 14(3&4):277–83.

Markus, Hazel, and Elissa Wurf. 1987. "The Dynamic Self-Concept: Social Psychological Perspective." *Annual Review of Psychology* 38:299–337.

Marx, Karl. [1844] 1932. *Economic and Philosophical Manuscripts of 1844*. Moscow: Progress Publishers.

———. [1872] 1972. "Manifesto of the Communist Party." Pp. 469–500 in *The Marx-Engels Reader*, edited by Robert C. Tucker. New York: Norton.

———. [1887] 1972. "Capital, Volume 1." Pp. 294–438 in *The Marx-Engels Reader*, edited by Robert C. Tucker. New York: Norton.

Matthews, Gordon. 1996. *What Makes a Life Worth Living? How Japanese and Americans Make Sense of Their Worlds*. Berkeley: University of California Press.

Matthews, Gordon, and Bruce White. 2004. *Japan's Changing Generations*. New York: Routledge.

McCall, Leslie. 2013. *The Undeserving Rich: American Beliefs about Inequality, Opportunity, and Redistribution*. Cambridge, MA: Cambridge University Press.

McGee, Micki. 2005. *Self-Help, Inc.: Makeover Culture in American Life*. New York: Oxford University Press.

McRobbie, Angela. 2016. *Be Creative: Making a Living in the New Culture Industry*. Cambridge: Polity Press.

Meyer, John W. 2001. "The Evolution of Modern Stratification Systems." Pp. 730–37 in *Social Stratification in Sociological Perspective: Class, Race, and Gender*, edited by David B. Grusky. Boulder, CO: Westview Press.

Mills, C. Wright. 1956. *White Collar*. New York: Oxford University Press.

Moen, Phyllis. 2016. *Encore Adulthood: Boomers at the Edge of Risk, Renewal, and Purpose*. New York: Oxford University Press.

Mullen, Ann L. 2010. *Degrees of Inequality: Culture, Class and Gender in American Higher Education*. Baltimore, MD: Johns Hopkins University Press.

———. 2014. "Gender, Social Background, and the Choice of College Major in a Liberal Arts Context." *Gender & Society* 28(2):289–312.

Nelson, Margaret K. 2012. *Parenting out of Control: Anxious Parents in Uncertain Times*. New York: New York University Press.

Newman, Katherine S. 1999. *Falling from Grace: Downward Mobility in the Age of Affluence*. Berkeley: University of California Press.

Ocejo, Richard E. 2017. *Masters of Craft: Old Jobs in the New Urban Economy*. Princeton, NJ: Princeton University Press.

O'Connor, Pat, Estrella Montez López, Clare O'Hagan, Andrea Wolffram, Manuela Aye, Valentina Chizzola, Ornella Mich, Georgi Apostolov, Irina Topuzova, Gulsun Sağlamer, Mine G. Tan, and Hulya Çağlayan. 2017.

"Micro-Political Practices in Higher Education: A Challenge to Excellence as a Rationalising Myth?" *Critical Studies in Education* 61(2):1–17.

Oliver, Melvin L. 2000. *Securing the Future: Investing in Children from Birth to College.* New York: Russell Sage Foundation.

Olson, James M., and Carolyn L. Hafer. 2001. "Tolerance of Personal Deprivation." Pp. 157–75 in *The Psychology of Legitimacy: Emerging Perspectives on Ideology, Justice, and Intergroup Relations,* edited by John T. Jost and Brenda Major. Cambridge: Cambridge University Press.

Osnowitz, Debra. 2010. *Freelancing Expertise: Contract Professionals in the New Economy.* Ithaca, NY: Cornell University Press.

Owens, Timothy J., Dawn T. Robinson, and Lynn Smith-Lovin. 2010. "Three Faces of Identity." *Annual Review of Sociology* 36(1):477–99.

Padavic, Irene, and Barbara Reskin. 2002. *Women and Men at Work.* Thousand Oaks, CA: Pine Forge Press.

Pager, Devah. 2003. "The Mark of a Criminal Record." *American Journal of Sociology* 108(5):937–75.

Pedulla, David S., and Sarah Thébaud. 2015. "Can We Finish the Revolution? Gender, Work-Family Ideals, and Institutional Constraint." *American Sociological Review* 80(1):116–39.

Perlow, Leslie A. 2012. *Sleeping with Your Smartphone: How to Break the 24-7 Habit and Change the Way You Work.* Cambridge, MA: Harvard Business Review.

Petersen, Trond, and Ishak Saporta. 2004. "The Opportunity Structure for Discrimination." *American Journal of Sociology* 109(4):852–901.

Pettijohn, Sarah L., and Elizabeth T. Boris. 2013. "Nonprofit-Government Contracts and Grants: Findings from the 2013 National Survey." Urban Institute, Washington, DC.

Pew. 2012. "Pursuing the American Dream: Economic Mobility across Generations." Pew Charitable Trusts, New York.

Pink, Daniel H. 2015. "What Happened to Your Parachute?" *Fast Company* [online], August 31.

Plumeri, Joe. 2015. *The Power of Being Yourself: A Game Plan for Success—by Putting Passion into Your Life and Work.* Philadelphia, PA: Da Capo Press.

Pugh, Allison J. 2015. *The Tumbleweed Society: Working and Caring in an Age of Insecurity.* New York: Oxford University Press.

———. 2018. "Parenting in an Insecure Age: Class, Gender and the Flexible Child." *Sociologica* 12(3):14.

Putnam, Robert D. 2000. *Bowling Alone: The Collapse and Revival of American Community.* New York: Simon & Schuster.

Rao, Aliya Hamid, and Megan Tobias Neely. 2019. "What's Love Got to Do with It? Passion and Inequality in White-Collar Work." *Sociology Compass* 13:e12744.

Ravenelle, Alexandrea. 2019. *Hustle and Gig: Struggling and Surviving in the Gig Economy.* Berkeley: University of California Press.

Reichheld, Frederick. 2001. *Loyalty Rules: How Today's Leaders Build Lasting Relationships.* Cambridge, MA: Harvard Business School Publishing.

Rich, Bruce Louis, Jeffrey A. Lepine, and Eean R. Crawford. 2010. "Job Engagement: Antecedents and Effects on Job Performance." *Academy of Management Journal* 53(3):617–35.

Ridgeway, Cecilia L. 2011. *Framed by Gender: How Gender Inequality Persists in the Modern World.* New York: Oxford University Press.

Risman, Barbara J. 2018. *Where the Millenials Will Take Us: A New Generation Wrestles with the Gender Structure.* New York: Oxford University Press.

Rivera, Lauren A. 2012. "Hiring as Cultural Matching." *American Sociological Review* 77(6):999–1022.

———. 2015. *Pedigree: How Elite Students Get Elite Jobs.* Princeton, NJ: Princeton University Press.

Rosenfeld, Jake. 2019. "US Labor Studies in the Twenty-First Century: Understanding Laborism without Labor." *Annual Review of Sociology* 45(1):449–65.

Rosenfeld, Rachel A. 1992. "Job Mobility and Career Processes." *Annual Review of Sociology* 18(1):39–61.

Sabat, Isaac E., Alex P. Lindsey, Eden B. King, Carolyn Winslow, Kristen P. Jones, Ashley Membere, and Nicholas A. Smith. 2019. "Stigma Expression Outcomes and Boundary Conditions: A Meta-Analysis." *Journal of Business and Psychology* 35(1):171–86.

Sáenz, Rogelio, and Corey Sparks. 2020. "The Inequities of Job Loss and Recovery amid the COVID-19 Pandemic." University of New Hampshire, Carsey School of Public Policy.

Schlenker, Barry R., and James V. Trudeau. 1990. "Impact of Self-Presentations on Private Self-Beliefs: Effects of Prior Self-Beliefs and Misattribution." *Journal of Personality and Social Psychology* 58(1):22–32.

Schoon, Ingrid. 2008. "A Transgenerational Model of Status Attainment: The Potential Mediating Role of School Motivation and Education " *National Institute Economic Review* (205):72–82.

Schulz, Jeremy Markham. 2015. "Winding Down the Workday: Zoning the Evening Hours in Paris, Oslo, and San Francisco." *Qualitative Sociology* 38(3):235–59.

Sewell, William E., Jr. 1992. "A Theory of Structure: Duality, Agency, and Transformation." *American Journal of Sociology* 98:1–29.

Shapin, Steven. 2009. *The Scientific Life: A Moral History of a Late Modern Vocation.* Chicago: University of Chicago Press.

Sharone, Ofer. 2013. *Flawed System/Flawed Self: Job Searching and Unemployment Experiences.* Chicago: University of Chicago Press.

Silva, Jennifer M. 2013. *Coming Up Short: Working-Class Adulthood in an Age of Uncertainty.* New York: Oxford University Press.

Silva, Jennifer M., and Kaisa Snellman. 2018. "Salvation or Safety Net? Meanings of 'College' among Working- and Middle-Class Young Adults in Narratives of the Future." *Social Forces* 97(2):559–82.

Silvia, Paul J. 2006. *Exploring the Psychology of Interest.* New York: Oxford University Press.

Smith, Jessi L., Erin A. Cech, Anneke Metz, Meghan Huntoon, and Christina Moyer. 2014. "Giving Back or Giving Up: Native American Student Experiences in Science And Engineering." *Cultural Diversity and Ethnic Minority Psychology* 20(3):413–29.

Smith, Vicki. 2002. *Crossing the Great Divide: Worker Risk and Opportunity in the New Economy.* Ithaca, NY: Cornell University Press.

Spillman, Lyn. 2017. "Culture and Economic Life." Pp. 157–92 in *Oxford Handbook of Cultural Sociology.* New York: Oxford University Press.

Spillman, Lyn, and Michael Strand. 2013. "Interest-Oriented Action." *Annual Review of Sociology* 39(1):85–104.

Spokane, Arnold R. 1985. "A Review of Research on Person-Environment Congruence in Holland's Theory of Careers." *Journal of Vocational Behavior* 26(3):306–43.

Stone, Juliet, Ann Berrington, and Jane Falkingham. 2014. "Gender, Turning Points, and Boomerangs: Returning Home in Young Adulthood in Great Britain." *Demography* 51(1):257–76.

Swann, W. B., Jr. 1983. "Self-Verification: Bringing Social Reality into Harmony with the Self." Pp. 33–66 in *Social Psychological Perspectives on the Self,* edited by J. Suls and A. G. Greenwald. Hillsdale, NJ: Lawrence Erlbaum.

———. 1987. "Identity Negotiation: Where Two Roads Meet." *Journal of Personality and Social Psychology* 53(6):1038–51.

Sweet, Stephen, and Peter Meiksins. 2017. *Changing Contours of Work: Jobs and Opportunities in the New Economy.* Thousand Oaks, CA: Sage.

Swidler, Ann. 1986. "Culture in Action: Symbols and Strategies." *American Sociological Review* 51(2):273–86.

———. 2001. *Talk of Love: How Culture Matters.* Chicago: University of Chicago Press.

Taylor, Marylee C., and Stephen M. Merino. 2011. "Race, Religion, and Beliefs about Racial Inequality." *ANNALS of the American Academy of Political and Social Science* 634(1):60–77.

Tilcsik, András. 2011. "Pride and Prejudice: Employment Discrimination against Openly Gay Men in the United States." *American Journal of Sociology* 117(2):586–626.

Tinsley, Howard E. A. 2000. "The Congruence Myth: An Analysis of the Efficacy of the Personality-Environment Fit Model." *Journal of Vocational Behavior* 56:147–79.

Tokumitsu, Miya. 2015. *Do What You Love: And Other Lies about Success and Happiness*. New York: Reagan Arts.

Tuch, Steven A., and Michael Hughes. 2011. "Whites' Racial Policy Attitudes in the Twenty-First Century: The Continuing Significance of Racial Resentment." *ANNALS of the American Academy of Political and Social Science* 634(1):134–52.

Turner, Sarah E., and William G. Bowen. 1999. "Choice of Major: The Changing (Unchanging) Gender Gap." *Industrial and Labor Relations Review* 52(2):289–313.

Umney, Charles, and Lefteris Kretsos. 2015. "'That's the Experience': Passion, Work Precarity, and Life Transitions among London Jazz Musicians." *Work and Occupations* 42(3):313–34.

Uris, Auren. 1974. *Thank God It's Monday*. New York: Crowell.

Vaisey, Stephen. 2009. "Motivation and Justification: A Dual-Process Model of Culture in Action." *American Journal of Sociology* 114(6):1675–715.

Vallerand, Robert J. 2008. "On the Psychology of Passion: In Search of What Makes People's Lives Most Worth Living." *Canadian Psychology/Psychologie canadienne* 49(1):1–13.

———. 2012. "The Role of Passion in Sustainable Psychological Well-Being." *Psychology of Well-Being: Theory, Research and Practice* 2(1).

Vallerand, R. J., C. Blanchard, G. A. Mageau, R. Koestner, C. Ratelle, M. Leonard, M. Gagne, and J. Marsolais. 2003. "Les passions de l'ame: On Obsessive and Harmonious Passion." *Journal of Personal Social Psychology* 85(4):756–67.

Viscelli, Steve. 2016. *The Big Rig: Trucking and the Decline of the American Dream*. Oakland: University of California Press.

Weber, Max. [1919] 1981. "Science as a Vocation." Pp. 137–44 in *From Max Weber: Essays in Sociology*, edited by H. H. Gerth and C. Wright Mills. New York: Oxford University Press.

———. [1930] 1992. *The Protestant Ethic and the Spirit of Capitalism*. New York: Routledge.

Weeden, Kim A., and David B. Grusky. 2005. "The Case for a New Class Map." *American Journal of Sociology* 111(1):141–212.

Whyte, William H. 1956. *The Organization Man*. New York: Simon & Schuster.

Williams, Joan C. 2000. *Unbending Gender: Why Family and Work Conflict and What to Do about It*. Oxford: Oxford University Press.

Williams, Joan C., Mary Blair-Loy, and Jennifer L. Berdahl. 2013. "Cultural Schemas, Social Class, and the Flexibility Stigma." *Journal of Social Issues* 69(2):209–34.

Willis, Paul E. 1981. *Learning to Labor: How Working-Class Kids Get Work-ing-Class Jobs.* New York: Columbia University Press.

Wilson, Eli R. 2019. "Managing Portfolio Lives: Flexibility and Privilege amongst Upscale Restaurant Workers in Los Angeles." *Qualitative Sociology* 42(3):321–36.

Wilson, Tamar Diana. 2005. *Subsidizing Capitalism: Brickmakers on the U.S.-Mexican Border.* Albany: SUNY Press.

Wingfield, Adia Harvey. 2007. "The Modern Mammy and the Angry Black Man: African American Professionals' Experiences with Gendered Racism in the Workplace." *Race, Gender & Class* 14(1–2):196–212.

Wolf, Elizabeth Baily, Jooa Julia Lee, Sunita Sah, and Alison Wood Brooks. 2016. "Managing Perceptions of Distress at Work: Reframing Emotion as Passion." *Organizational Behavior and Human Decision Processes* 137:1–12.

Wright, Erik Olin. 2002. "The Shadow of Exploitation in Weber's Class Analy-sis." *American Sociological Review* 67(6):832–53.

Wrzesniewski, Amy, Clark McCauley, Paul Rozin, and Barry Schwartz. 1997. "Jobs, Careers, and Callings: People's Relations to Their Work." *Journal of Research in Personality* 31(1):21–33.

Young, Alford A. 2000. "On the Outside Looking In: Low-Income Black Men's Conceptions of Work Opportunity and the 'Good Job.'" Pp. 141–71 in *Coping with Poverty: The Social Contexts of Neighborhood, Work, and Family in the African American Community,* edited by Sheldon Danziger and Ann Chin Lin. Ann Arbor: University of Michigan Press.

Young, Michael. 1994. *The Rise of Meritocracy.* New Brunswick, NJ: Transac-tion Publishers.

Zelditch, Morris. 2001. "Theories of Legitimacy." in *The Psychology of Legiti-macy: Emerging Perspectives on Ideology, Justice, and Intergroup Relations,* edited by John T. Jost and Brenda Major. Cambridge: Cambridge University Press.

Zelizer, Viviana A. 2017. *The Social Meaning of Money: Pin Money, Paychecks, Poor Relief, and Other Currencies.* Princeton, NJ: Princeton University Press.

Zigarmi, Drea, Kim Nimon, Dobie Houson, David Witt, and Jim Diehl. 2009. "Beyond Engagement: Toward a Framework and Operational Definition for Employee Work Passion." *Human Resource Development Review* 8(3):300–26.

Zwolinski, Matt. 2012. "Structural Exploitation." *Social Philosophy and Policy* 29(1):154–79.

Index

advising. *See* career advisers

Apple, Inc., 1

Armstrong, Elizabeth, 36, 134, 279n71, 291n23

Asian students and workers: attitudes toward passion, 21, 44–45*table*, 48, 51, 53*fig.*, 61, 260, 280n74, 284n38; family pressures, 46, 98–99, 287n61; representation in study sample, 244, 258

assessment tools of career advisors, 104. *See also* StrengthsFinder Tool; Strong Interest Inventory

Beasley, Maya, 73

Black students and workers: attitudes toward passion, 21, 44–45*table*, 51, 53; attitudes toward structural barriers, 182, 296n41; family pressures, 287n61; inequalities, 158; recourse to career counseling, 288n74; representation in study sample, 18, 244, 258

Blair-Loy, Mary, 274n53

Bolles, Richard, 33–34, 184–85

Bourdieu, Pierre, 140

Bunderson, J. Stuart, 195

"calling," 35, 275n8

capital-labor accord, 10

career advisers: attitudes toward passion, 24, 93, 102–10, 111, 218; methodology, 249–51; proportion of use by respondents, 288n74; recommendations for, 228–29; study participation, 18, 20

case study participants, principal, 132*fig*; Aliyah, 64, 147–48, 150–51, 165; Brianna, 7, 21, 66, 88, 128–29, 131, 136–37, 168; Claire, 2–3, 21, 62, 121, 123, 136, 142– 43, 194–95, 196; Dave, 121–23, 129, 136; Devon, 25, 121–23, 169; Isaiah, 7, 96, 127, 169–70; Jasmine, 26, 128, 131, 139, 144, 145; Katelyn, 25, 124, 137; Kevin, 139–40, 145, 153–54, 155; Kiara, 26, 149–51, 160, 168; Lupita, 25, 143, 156–57; Maria, 121, 123, 130, 179; Rohan, 124–25, 130, 137–38, 165, 167– 68; Samantha, 129, 131, 135–36; Tara, 141–42, 143, 178; Theresa, 125, 130, 131, 138; Trevor, 62–63, 125, 131, 144; Xavier, 5, 21, 40, 42

choicewashing, 28, 166, 171*fig.*, 176–86, 215, 219, 294n16, 297n46. *See also* occupational segregation

class. *See* socioeconomic status

college degree, 15–16; as economic floor, 22, 61–63, 145, 156, 157, 216. *See also* passion principle: in college-educated workers;

321

Founded in 1893,
UNIVERSITY OF CALIFORNIA PRESS
publishes bold, progressive books and journals
on topics in the arts, humanities, social sciences,
and natural sciences—with a focus on social
justice issues—that inspire thought and action
among readers worldwide.

The UC PRESS FOUNDATION
raises funds to uphold the press's vital role
as an independent, nonprofit publisher, and
receives philanthropic support from a wide
range of individuals and institutions—and from
committed readers like you. To learn more, visit
ucpress.edu/supportus.